Exploring Sociabilities of Contemporary India

Exploring Sociabilities of Contemporary India

New Perspectives

edited by

SUJATA PATEL

Orient BlackSwan

EXPLORING SOCIABILITIES OF CONTEMPORARY INDIA: NEW PERSPECTIVES

ORIENT BLACKSWAN PRIVATE LIMITED

Registered Office
3-6-752 Himayatnagar, Hyderabad 500 029, Telangana, India
e-mail: centraloffice@orientblackswan.com

Other Offices
Bengaluru, Bhopal, Chennai, Guwahati,
Hyderabad, Jaipur, Kolkata, Lucknow,
Mumbai, New Delhi, Noida, Patna, Visakhapatnam

First published by Orient Blackswan Pvt. Ltd 2020

ISBN 978-93-5287-847-5

030451

Typeset in
Bembo Std 11/13
by Shine Graphics, Delhi 110 094

Printed in India at
Yash Printographics, Noida

Published by
Orient Blackswan Private Limited
3-6-752 Himayatnagar, Hyderabad 500 029, Telangana, India
e-mail: info@orientblackswan.com

Contents

Preface and Acknowledgements

The papers in this volume were presented at the four plenaries organised during the 42nd All Indian Sociological Conference by the Indian Sociological Society (ISS) at Tezpur University, Assam, held from 27 to 30 December 2016. The theme of the conference was Rethinking Sociological Traditions in India and the four plenaries were titled 'Contemporary Perspectives on Family, Marriage and Kinship', 'Class, Caste, Tribes and Exclusions', 'Faith and Religion: Contemporary Perspectives' and 'Higher Education and Its Present Crisis'.

The conference and the plenaries recognised that sociology as a subject and as a discipline of knowledge has had a long institutional history in India. Even before its first department was established in Bombay in 1919, its organisation was initiated in the colonial period. Sociologists have documented this history from its mid-nineteenth-century beginnings to its growth and expansion after Independence with the development of the university system.

With the expansion of teaching and research in the 1950s and 1960s, the discipline developed an identity through its focus on three key sociological areas: family, marriage and kinship systems; the caste system; and religious systems, more particularly Hinduism. Though ethnography was the key defining attribute of this identity, Indian sociological traditions started using a diversity of methods and perspectives to study these themes.

From the late 1970s onwards, new interests and themes of teaching, reflection and research have emerged. Sociologists started doing research on contemporary trends and on modern lives, and they have assessed the implications of development policies on various social groups (not studied till recently), processes and institutions. Massive expansion of the university system and investments in higher education across the country helped sociologists to document the diversity and uneven nature of experiences that the development processes have engendered.

Today we are in a new moment. The globalising process has the impacted social and economic lives of Indians radically; protests and subaltern churnings have challenged sociologists to relook at the past and the present in new and novel ways. These interrogations have also led some sociologists to ruminate on their disciplinary history and its constituted traditions of theories, perspectives, methods and methodologies. Sociologists are asking whether the earlier perspectives on the themes of family, marriage and kinship systems; of caste and tribal inequalities; and of religious traditions have salience in the contemporary situation. In a situation where intellectual priorities have been reorganised, should earlier perspectives and theories be reinterpreted or should these be changed and even substituted?

The plenaries in the conference were organised to reflect on these concerns and to ask questions regarding these 'classic' themes in the present context. We hoped that these considerations would build a new repertoire of issues, theories and perspectives and elaborate whether some of the old questions still have salience. Paradoxically, these concerns are being debated at a time when higher education and the university system are facing their most important crisis, which raises the question of whether these new perceptions can be institutionalised in the present context. The plenaries initiated the debate on the post-Independence sociological traditions and articulated recent perspectives that are reformulating these in fresh ways and the challenges the discipline faces in institutionalising them.

I would like to take the opportunity to thank the Organising Secretary of the conference, Professor Chandan Kumar Sharma, who, with Dr Amiya Kumar Das and Dr Sumesh Sivanand as Joint Organising Secretaries and their department colleagues, ensured that the conference not only was a success but also encouraged meaningful intellectual discussions and engagement. The conference would not have been organised without the fulsome backing and institutional assistance provided by the then Vice Chancellor, Professor Mihir Kanti Chaudhuri, the then Registrar, Dr Biren Das, and the then Dean of Humanities and Social Sciences, Professor Pradip Jyoti Mahanta, who together with the then Secretary and Treasurer of ISS, Professors Abha Chauhan and Biswajit Ghosh, the members of the ISS Managing Committee, 2016–17, and the staff of ISS ensured that conference made an intellectual contribution.

My sincere thanks to the contributors of this volume who supported this intellectual endeavour. They prepared the draft papers for presentation, revised these for submission and further revised them after receiving comments from the reviewers. Though due to personal reasons Rajesh Misra could not participate in this volume, I would like to acknowledge his help and involvement during the conference and afterwards for shaping many of its concerns.

SUJATA PATEL
September 2019

Introduction

Indian Sociology's Past-Present and Present-Futures

SUJATA PATEL

Sociology in India has had a long academic presence, going back to about 100 years when the colonial government established India's first sociology department at Bombay University in 1919. This long history suggests that it had a contemporary presence with the sociology departments that were first set up in Europe and the US. Chicago got its sociology department in 1892 and Bordeaux in 1895, while Max Weber set one up in Munich in the same year as Bombay University. In this context, the following questions need to be asked: Did this long history present sociologists in India (as against their compatriots in other social sciences) or other sociologists in the world an opportunity to reflect on the discipline's growth and evolution? Did it introduce new assessments to analyse contemporary changes in India? Did it also allow sociologists in India to define their social, cultural and professional identity?

About two decade back, writing on the history of the discipline, Patricia Uberoi argued that some sociologists in India have shown a partiality towards a reflexive stance and that they have questioned and probed their disciplinary proclivities. She was intrigued enough by this phenomenon to make a survey of the themes addressed by the question: 'Why do Indian sociologists among all social scientists introspect so much publicly and so regularly about the nature of their discipline?' (Uberoi 2000: 18). Introspection of the discipline, she argued, was related to doubts among sociologists in India—whether their positions can grasp the complexities structuring contemporary India, whether they have the appropriate intellectual tools to comprehend the fast-changing processes occurring in India and whether their theories are relevant to India's specific context.

One of the key themes that has organised the idea of relevance of the discipline is the debate on 'academic colonialism', that is, the question of whether the dependence on Western theories obfuscated an understanding of Indian material and misrepresented its analysis. Later commentators took forward this question to ask whether the subsequent attempts at indigenisation further muddied and complicated the issue (Patel 2011). Satish Saberwal, who inaugurated this debate in India, discussed academic colonialism to imply the way local academics contribute via 'employment, contract research and through sheer publication—used by CIA, Pentagon and other overt and covert agencies of the United States government to advance its political objective of dominating Afro-Asian countries' (Saberwal 1968: 10). This financial dominance, Saberwal argues, leads to academic consequences, for it determines 'problem selection, research design, and modes of publication' (ibid.: 13). In turn, such knowledge helps influence local political processes.[1]

Uberoi carries forward her discussion on Indian sociologists' reflexive stance, particularly their concern about academic colonialism, by pointing out that today, that is, in 2000, 'one does not hear . . . a renewed call for intellectual self-reliance, or protests against academic neo-colonialism'. Surely, she argues, such an 'antediluvian protectionism would . . . be completely misplaced in a globalized culture of social scientific knowledge? Or would it?' (Uberoi 2000: 19). This volume answers Uberoi's query with a resounding yes by arguing that a discussion on academic colonialism is not misplaced even today. What is different today is the form the discussion has taken and the critique it offers to earlier conceptions of academic colonialism and its various solutions, one of which is indigenisation. The volume also contends that it is the current global discussion on this theme by various social scientists from the South including India (if not the mainstream sociologists) that has helped us to comprehend the contours of academic colonialism and the limitations of the indigenous approach.

The theme of academic colonialism found a new avatar within global sociological discussions after the publication of the 2007 book *Southern Theory: The Global Dynamics of Knowledge in Social Science* by Raewyn Connell. The book also initiated a new way of thinking about sociology as a discipline, its theories and its practices, and provided an assessment of the discipline's history. Connell agrees with Saberwal's contention that Afro-Asian social scientists are financially, politically and intellectually dependent on the First World, but she argues that this process was built into the origin of sociology and is moored in its episteme. Thus one has to evaluate the past to understand the limitations of the present scholarship.

Connell contends that the politics of unequal division between the metropole and the periphery (which she calls 'global difference') has organised the study of the discipline and its scholarship since its birth, leading to the universalisation of 'Northern theories' and 'its viewpoints, perspectives and problems' to the detriment of 'Southern theories' (Connell 2007: vii). In 1968, an introspection of Indian sociology had allowed a group of Indian sociologists to present a pre-theoretical position of the contemporary debates, which are now part of a global discussion on the sociology of sociology.[2] The current discussion has shifted the reflexive stance from merely elaborating the characteristics that organise academic colonialism (as Indian sociologists did) to an exploration of the epistemology that has structured sociological and, by implication, social science knowledge production since the nineteenth century and impacted not only India but also most of the ex-colonial countries in the South. The deliberations on this theme move at various scales—from global to regional, national and local.

So what is the nature of the new perspective that is organising a discussion on the political economy of the discipline of sociology and its intellectual representations? Why has Connell's text, together with earlier texts by Amin (1989) and Wallerstein (1996), played a noteworthy role? What implications do these texts and many others published since then have for a discussion on the history of sociology in India and Indian sociologists' reflexive stance?

Southern Theory introduces a perspective to assess the repertoire of practices organising the discipline of sociology. It argues that the production of knowledge and that of its disciplinary practices is enmeshed in 'relations of power', and an analysis of any knowledge system, in this case the discipline of sociology, alludes to 'authority, exclusion, and inclusion, hegemony, partnership, sponsorship and appropriation between intellectuals and institutions in the metropole and those in the periphery' (Connell 2007: ix). By suggesting that power is central to knowledge formation, Connell pushes the discussion of the discipline towards a critique of its European epistemology, thereby reformulating the debate inaugurated a decade earlier on reflexivity, modernity and the discipline.

This volume builds on this approach and initiates a discussion on this perspective with an introductory chapter titled 'Sociological Scholarship on India: The Epistemes of Colonial Modernity and Methodological Nationalism' by Sujata Patel. It presents an overview of sociological scholarship in India constituted during the colonial and post-Independence periods by interrogating the two trends that the scholarship has followed—an uncritical appropriation of Western/Northern concepts and theories (criticised by Saberwal earlier) and alternatively an endorsement of an indigenous sociology. Both trends, it argues are part and parcel of the binary of Eurocentrism (Amin 1989).

While accepting the argument that sociological scholarship in India has been diverse, given its many geographical locations and the varied influences that have organised it, Patel contends that it is still possible to understand the common assumptions that organically link the differences between scholars and their scholarship. She suggests that sociological scholarship in India is constituted within two epistemes, which she terms as 'colonial modernity' and 'methodological nationalism'. She uses the term colonial modernity to indicate the distinct ways in which Eurocentric assumptions were and are translated and transformed to organise the knowledge of the 'social' in India as 'traditional' when in fact the country was being imprinted by modernity, which in turn was being mediated through colonialism. The chapter argues that the colonial state stimulated deliberations on what it considered as three 'classic' themes germane to the constitution of the 'social' in India: the institutions of family, marriage and kinship; religion, in particular Hinduism; and the structures organising caste and tribe. These 'traditional' institutions and structures have been considered unique to India and its culture. This volume deconstructs this assumption and articulates how the episteme of colonial modernity and methodological nationalism organised the discussions and deliberations around these 'traditional' institutions and structures.

Drawing from studies done by Amin (1989) and Wallerstein (1996), Patel argues that this legacy is moored in the Eurocentric binary that divided the 'social' of the European/Western from the 'social' of the non-European/Eastern. It further legitimised these power divisions by organising the study of these two 'socials' into two separate and distinct disciplines—sociology and anthropology, with sociology studying modern societies and anthropology studying traditional or primitive ones. Though the discipline of sociology was formally institutionalised in India when teaching started in 1919, its approach remained anthropological, with nineteenth- and early twentieth-century anthropological theories, methods and methodologies used for studying contemporary India. As a consequence, the discipline used orientalist ideal types to excavate India's institutions and structures, presenting India as being steeped in its past, as being unique and distinctive, and as being peopled with pre-modern primitive groups. Thereby it eschewed efforts to make comparisons with processes and structures from other parts of the world including the ex-colonial regions. A reflexive questioning, which Uberoi (2000) has alluded to, did allow some Indian sociologists who were influenced by proto-nationalist positions to question this colonial construction of categories. This led them to frame a perspective of indigeneity.[3] This position, Patel argues, further reinforced the idea of India's uniqueness, of its philosophical moorings in its Hindu past and of its lack of fit for comparative analysis. This was contrary to the way sociology as a discipline grew and developed in the West.

Patel also contends that after Independence, the attempt by the Indian state to establish modern social sciences did not impact sociology as it did other social sciences. Even after Independence, the study of modern India continued to use nineteenth- and early twentieth-century anthropological theories and methods and interlaced these with modernisation theories that were imported from North America. As a consequence, the contemporary Indian 'social' remained etched within the frames of colonial modernity. Eurocentric positions were now integrated with the episteme of methodological nationalism that imagined the 'social' of the nation state through the prism of a universal model, thereby distancing itself from the diversity that characterised the practices of doing sociology during the colonial period. According to Patel, the organisation of knowledge through national institutions and its territorialisation has furthered endorsed the standardisation of a national curricula and determined specialisations and themes for research and teaching, allowing the official 'national' to coincide with the academic 'social'.

This volume brings together essays by sociologists who scrutinise this legacy. It assesses the theories and perspectives that have examined the 'traditional' institutions of family–marriage–kinship and religion together with the structures organising caste and tribe, and it offers new evaluations to comprehend these. In doing so, it suggests the need to assess the global discussions on each of these themes and to interrogate the way Eurocentric epistemes have operated to frame the received field of knowledge. It also asserts a need to desist from finding singular theories of change and transformation. Rather it contends that the intersection of received diversities and the current unevenness in the processes of transformation have made the appraisals of these processes highly complex and multifarious, which is why these need to be examined at various scales from global to regional, national and local. The essays in this volume initiate a discussion by elaborating the challenges facing the reframing of sociological scholarship on India. On one hand, they demand that the readers reflect on the ways hierarchies and practices of rule are imbricated in professional knowledge. On the other hand, they also argue for a need to empirically study the current manifestations of power and ideologies in organising the contours of everyday practices and social lives in India. In this context, the authors argue for a methodological focus that combines a discursive deconstruction, a historical sensitivity and an empirical focus on practices.

Debating the Sociology of 'Traditional' India

This section in the volume affirms the need to interrogate the discursive space on the themes of family–marriage–kinship, tribe–caste and religion in order to formulate alternative ways of thinking. Four chapters in this section make a critical assessment of the limitations of the earlier scholarship in the light of both empirical evidence and new theoretical and epistemological positions taken by contemporary social science scholarship. These chapters argue for a need to displace the received ideal typical positions formulated during colonial and nationalist phases and suggest instead that these institutions or structures be perceived through the lens of existing practices and secular processes, particularly those pertaining to domination and subordination.

We start this section with a chapter by Rajni Palriwala titled 'Confronting Disciplinary Practices: Rethinking the Sociology of Family, Marriage and Kinship'. The chapter assesses the reasons for the declining interest in kinship studies and suggests that this decline started within Indian scholarship with the division of the subject area into two: while kinship and marriage were studied through the prism of social anthropology, studies on family became the sole domain for scholars in sociology, who in turn placed family studies within modernisation theories and assessed the transition of joint families into nuclear ones. This fragmented an area or a field that needed to be perceived as being organically connected and that needed to include within itself not only the study of these three themes but also that of gender and sexualities, caste, endogamy and labour use, along with the sociology of emotions and that of violence. This integrated field, Palriwala argues, should be seen in terms of a matrix of power that manifests itself in unequal social relationships differentially across geographical areas, which while nurturing human beings emotionally and physically also uses norms and values to curb women's agency (as also that of children) through the practice of overt, covert and symbolic violence. (Almost 30 per cent of married Indian women between the age of 15 and 49 years have reported experiencing spousal violence at least once, according to the National Family Health Survey-4 conducted over 2015–16.) Thus if creating sociabilities of mutuality characterises this field, it also articulates, as Palriwala suggests, quoting Janet Carstens, 'differentiation, hierarchy, exclusion and abuse' (Carstens 2013: 247).

More importantly, she contends that today the scholarship in this area needs to combine the varied critiques that have emerged from different arenas in this field into a new perspective that unites a gendered interrogation with a methodological critique of the Brahminical moorings of the received ideal and normative models within Indian scholarship. She argues that these models need to be replaced with a practice-oriented approach that simultaneously analyses the impact of contemporary secular changes on women's agency and its dialectical engagement with historically received ideals or normative positions. Palriwala argues for a need to displace the 'naturalisation' that has organised the scholarship on the themes of family–marriage–kinship and to interrogate the 'the material, emotional and political investment' embedded in these institutions that arrange 'the most guarded cluster of social relationships' in order to contain 'chaos, multiplicity, change and critique'. Because this field discusses and deliberates the ways intimacies connect the everyday lives of women, men and transgendered people together with the old and young, it has faced and continues to face significant challenges in creating a new identity for itself within contemporary Indian scholarship. It is this that makes this field, Palriwala asserts, 'a field always in the making'.

Two essays—the first by Virginius Xaxa titled 'Tribes in India: Why Exclusions Persist' and the second by Surinder Jodhka titled 'How Not to Study Caste? Moving beyond the Avatars of the Orientalist Commonsense'—critically map out the history of scholarship on tribe and caste in India respectively. These chapters contend that these concepts came to be constructed during colonialism when the colonial administrator–ethnographer elaborated the attributes that characterised these two groups in terms of orientalist perspectives and in juxtaposition of each other. The cultural–historical characteristics of the groups subsumed under these categories have been fine-tuned to create a clear distinction between them by anthropological and sociological scholarship, which have over time become coded in the commonsensical understandings of what is caste and what is tribe and are reflected in the various policies designed for these groups by the colonial and post-Independence state.

Virginius Xaxa traces the history of the use of the term 'tribe' by colonial administrators. He argues that in its initial years of rule, colonial authorities lacked a clear understanding on what constitutes a tribe and had a tendency to sometimes mix it up with caste. However, by the early twentieth century, the term tribe had acquired clear connotations—it came to be identified with those who practised animism. Given that animism was associated with primitiveness, tribal groups came to be considered as primitive. Xaxa argues that the characteristic of primitiveness was never spelt out in clear terms, but its presence animated the subsequent debates within the scholarship on tribal groups: should these groups be protected in their natural habitat and kept isolated so that they could continue to practise their own ways of living or should they be assimilated through special policies and programmes in order to be integrated into the mainstream.

Xaxa argues that though there is no formal national policy on tribes, it is still possible to make an analysis of its principles through a reading of various programmes and policies such as affirmative action programmes, tribal development programmes and tribal sub-plans. These various programmes indicate that there has developed over time a commonsensical idea of how to deal with tribes, and Xaxa contends that this idea not only runs through the state's perceptions of tribes and organises the relationship of non-tribal people with the tribal but is also interspersed in academic writing on tribes. Today, he argues, the Indian state, academics and other professionals as also non-tribal people believe that tribes being backward need support and aid so that they can be integrated with the mainstream. As a consequence, tribal groups have suffered from the practice of double colonialism, first, from the state (both the colonial and the post-independent) and, second, from the outsiders who intervened in the name of development to displace them from their land and their access to forests. Increasingly large-scale developmental and extractive projects have been established by the state in tribal areas leading to the extensive displacement of tribal groups. Though the tribes of India have been given civil and social rights, according to Xaxa, these developmental projects have legitimised the expropriation of tribal resources of land and forests. This has led to not only an increasing gap between the tribal and non-tribal population of the country but also the former being dominated, discriminated and exploited.

If tribal groups have been characterised as being primitive and culturally exclusive, caste groups have been considered intrinsic to Hindu India. Surinder Jodhka argues that orientalist principles have organised the scholarship on caste. This scholarship assumed that caste was a pan-Indian system and was defined by Hinduism, which in turn was thought to be a 'as a cohesive faith system with a unified theological structure, without any variations in its social organisation and normative belief systems'. As a consequence, on the one hand, Hinduism was presented as a monotheistic faith system, and on the other, caste was reduced to a religious value associated with Hindu philosophy and rituals. Additionally, this scholarship privileged a Brahmin perspective of caste and thus argued that the principle of hierarchy was the core principle of caste system. Finally, the caste system was viewed as rigid in character and inhibiting changes in its organisation, which is why this lens of inquiry did not assess changes within the system and within its various groups.

Jodhka argues for a need to understand caste empirically and to assess its impact within the lives of people rather perceive it as a religious ideal type. If this is done, he contends, it will be possible to observe that though some hierarchies have waned, this is not true across all castes. As a matter of fact, caste-based material and political inequalities have increased in some cases given that discrimination has been practised overtly or covertly, thereby legitimising caste hierarchies. This, in turn, has further exacerbated caste-based inequalities. Jodhka thus questions the modernisation hypothesis that argues that caste would die out, and he suggests that its presence and footprints are visible in all arenas including urban areas. In these circumstances, for the deprived, having a caste identity matters and allows them paradoxically to use it to question domination. Jodhka thus suggests that caste permeates at all levels of life, both in macro and micro settings. Resonating what was earlier said by Xaxa with regard to tribes, Jodhka argues that caste relationships need to be analysed at three levels: first, as domination, when caste values/norms and institutions are used to perpetuate and legitimise caste-based power; second, as discrimination, when caste is used to effect disadvantages to individuals and to communities; and third, as exploitation, when lack of entitlements and resources create further disparities and inequalities between upper and lower groups.

Unlike the themes of family–marriage–kinship and caste–tribe, which are increasingly seeing new critical scholarship, the field of sociology/anthropology of religion remains caught in a received ideological and modular reading of Hinduism. A major challenge today is to comprehend the various religious expressions within India and more broadly in South Asia. How do sociologists and anthropologists reformulate the discussions on religion? Farhana Ibrahim's chapter titled 'Beyond State and Nation: The Anthropology of Muslims in South Asia' proposes ways to intervene in the discussions on faith and religiosities by examining the practices of Muslims in India in terms of how they see their own religiosities. She suggests that an emic approach may be best suited for a non-essentialised, contextual understanding of Muslim religiosities. Her chapter debates the need to transcend the deeply embedded structures of power/knowledge that have framed the study of religion in India, given that the sociological and anthropological gaze has for long rarely focused on non-Hindu religions and religiosities. The author argues that sociological scholarship has been impoverished as a consequence, with little to no conceptual tools to study non-Hindu communities.

Ibrahim initiates a discussion on this theme by applauding the shift in the sociology and anthropology of religion of India in late 1970s from a focus on Hinduism to a recognition of other religions, the most important being Islam. However, the author contends that despite the increasing interest in Islam, academics have continued to comprehend Islam in a monotheistic way. Moreover, they have incorporated discussions germane to the scholarship on Hinduism such as family–marriage and caste to the analysis of Islam, thereby averting investigations of Islam through its own practices. Additionally, the state, according to Ibrahim, has intervened in various ways to embed itself in the official discourse on Islam by arguing that Indian Islam has been syncretic in nature. Given the tendency to understand Muslim lifeworlds and everyday practices in terms of a universalistic understanding of Islam, Ibrahim argues that it is imperative to combine a practice-oriented approach with an emic perspective, that is, understand how Muslim communities understand Islam in their own terms. This will decentre the comprehension of Muslims from the state-centric definition of Islam.

Ibrahim asks academics to shift the focus of study from 'Indian Muslims' to 'Muslims in India/South Asia' and asks, 'Who are the Muslims of the subcontinent; *what* are their religious affiliations; how do they view their interactions within and across a domain of sociality and of belief that they deem to be Islamic; and who are the others against whom they identify themselves?' To answer these questions, she argues, our studies have to embrace both geography and history. Additionally, she also contends that anthropologists and sociologists need to examine the regional and global networks organising Muslim communities and thereby transcend the built-in methodological nationalism in the discipline and recognise the plurality and diversity of Muslim communities. The next section elaborates on how one can practise the prescriptions made by the authors in this section.

Family, Marriage, Caste and Religiosities in Contemporary India

How do we examine family–marriage–kinship, religion–belief and caste today? Section Two of the volume presents possible ways to evaluate the contemporary manifestation of these practices. The focus here is how modern globalising processes and national policies reconstituted institutions/structures. The chapters in this section argue that the institutions of family–marriage–kinship and religion–belief and the structures of caste must be analysed as being steeped in current power relations and must be perceived as being part of the processes of modernity organising contemporary India. The attempt here is not to provide universal models and theories to comprehend these 'traditional' institutions/structures. Rather the chapters argue against such universal models in order to avoid presenting one-size-fits-all theories and to ensure that contemporary scholarship acknowledges the diverse and varied practices that organise these institutions/structures across the country. These five chapters are based on an evaluation of primary and secondary evidence, and they map how social action is organised in the context of processes that create opportunities and those that constrain action.

The first chapter in this section, Kamala Ganesh's 'The Rebellious Woman and the Violence of Consensus: Contemporary Contestations of the Domestic Space' traces the impact of secular changes such as globalisation in creating new spaces of economic, geographical and educational freedom for women in contemporary India. Her focus is on young, unmarried, working women, a new category in the emerging field of 'middle classes' of India.

Like Palriwala earlier, Ganesh cautions the readers against hasty generalisations and asks them to be vigilant about differences in articulations about the processes structuring the freedom and action of women in India. Yet she sees a clear trend: the growth of new identity interventions that have mobilised families, kin groups and sometimes entire communities to constrain and control women, often through the use of violence, when the latter take up opportunities provided by secular changes. Women, she argues, are and remain crucial symbols of group differentiation, reinforcing the intrinsic linkage between women's conduct and community honour. And yet, she argues, individual choice marriage and inter-caste marriage, though few and far between, are threatening the social order, with families increasingly presented with a choice to strategise about whether they need to enhance status through gender performance or through the performance of modernity.

Ganesh's chapter uses secondary sources to highlight contradictory processes at work in modern urban India. On the one hand, families have encouraged young women to be educated, to migrate and to seek employment. This is reinforced by the aspirational cultures promoted by the middle classes in India. As a consequence, women from various castes, communities and income groups attempt to increase their space of action as they become educated, migrate (a tenth of all migrants are women) and find employment. And yet when it comes to exercising choice in finding one's own partner (5–10 per cent of all marriages in India are inter-caste), families foreclose individual choice and ensure endogamy is practised. She tries to unravel why this is so.

Ganesh contends that a feminist reading may help comprehend these contradictions. Family and kin groups, she argues, should not be perceived as a 'sealed, private, harmonious space' but one that can become 'patriarchal and violent' when challenged. Additionally, given that the family and kin provide material and emotional support in a context where there is little or no alternative support structure, individual women find their spaces of freedom constrained when it comes to choice in marriage or in continuing education and employment after marriage.

Though the absolute numbers are modest, statistics show that gender gaps in enrolment; dropout rates; performance levels; literacy; primary, secondary and higher education; and proportion of female teachers have decreased. These trends have been supported by policy interventions and bolstered by non-govermental organisations (NGOs). And yet there has been a decline in the female labour participation rate since the 1990s and particularly in the new century for those who have become partially educated. Why is this so? Ganesh quotes Papanek (1979) and later Afridi et al. (2016) to highlight how women's role in the production of the family's status is significant. Women do a 'basket of tasks' for the family, both 'traditional' (childcare, house care, networking with kin and community, meeting obligations and nurturing relationships) and modern ones (teaching children; helping them with homework; ferrying them for tuition, sports and hobby classes; and being part of their school activities). Ganesh points to the increasing role of women in what Afridi et al. (2016) refer to as 'home production'. In this context, if women work, part time or full time, or do income generation at home, this happens because of family support and not in spite of it.

Ganesh's chapter uses a feminist perspective to situate both the making of new freedoms and the structuring of these through new forms of domination. For Ganesh and many others including Parliwala, family and kinship remain the matrix through which power and domination need to be conceptualised. In the next chapter titled 'Deterritorialising Heteronormative Family and Kinship: Hybrid Existence and Queer Intimacies in Contemporary India,' Pushpesh Kumar argues that feminist positions that maintain the primacy of family and kinship as the site of domination and power obfuscate the possibilities of freedom and action available to individuals within these institutions. These positions thus may not provide us with frames to comprehend and examine the contours that organise desire and pleasure for individuals within households and families. The focus of his analysis is the queer community in urban areas and the way they organise their freedoms, independence and autonomy. An assessment of their transgressive acts, he argues, allows us to use distinct new perspectives to examine their actions and interventions.

Pushpesh Kumar combines two positions in his analysis—first, of Deleuze and Guattari who deconstruct the Oedipus complex and thereby displace the essentialising assumption of family and kinship being a site of organising sociabilities and, second, of Pierre Bourdieu's concept 'practical kinship' to comprehend various forms of sociabilities practised outside heterosexual ones in contemporary times. The chapter suggests that queer relationships are marked by hybridity and are not part of any ideal type alternative family and kinship arrangement. Based on ethnographic work on hijras and their lives within *kothi*s, Kumar's analysis suggests that these individuals place themselves in 'intermediate positions'.

Kumar argues that an analysis of hijras' everyday practices suggest that they mediate between their roles within kothis and those within heteronormative families and kin networks. Such hybrid conditions are possible, the author argues, if we accept that there is no one universal patriarchy and that distinct singular constrains organise norms within different families and kin groups. The chapter argues that the anthropological diagrams of triangles and circles cannot capture complexities within existing kinship arrangements. Further, it argues that such diversities are a 'viable and practical mode of being and becoming' in India for a large majority of the populace who do not challenge the ideal typical normative positions. The author suggests that unless we study the contradictory pulls that organise queer lives, we will not be able to examine the everyday practices that create possibilities for individuals to have hybrid existences without being oppressed necessarily by the ideologies of power inherent in kinships structures.

The complex nuances that structure caste domination is the focus of the next chapter titled 'Modernity without Alterity: Deshastha Brahmins and Hindu Cosmopolitanism in Mumbai' by Suryakant Waghmore. The chapter starts by asking whether caste domination and cosmopolitanism are antithetical. In order to answer this question, it asks readers to move beyond a Western liberal position on cosmopolitanism and situate its moorings within complex positions of domination–subordination that organise mobile groups within different intersecting geographies.

Waghmore argues that modern urban conditions generate a cosmopolitan cosmology among groups living in India. It is, he argues, 'a necessity of life in a metropolis', given the coexistence of cultures, ethnic groups and classes, which promotes individual liberty, creative dialogues and spontaneous sociabilities. In this context, received ideologies have lauded migration of deprived groups to urban arenas suggesting that city life would free oneself from discrimination and marginalisation.

The author argues that recent literature questions this assumption. He cites evidence from various secondary sources that assert how caste-based discrimination has created segmented and hierarchised communities within towns and cities in India. In fact, lower castes have been discriminated in terms of work and labour, access to housing, social and physical infrastructure, and everyday practices.

Does this mean, he asks, that there is no cosmopolitan ethos in urban India? No, he states, a cosmopolitan ethos is a compulsion, a strategy of survival for individuals who need spaces from being co-opted by the 'tyranny of cousins'. Waghmore asserts that cities articulate different kinds of cosmopolitanisms and these include and exclude the 'other' simultaneously. His chapter focuses on what he calls Hindu cosmopolitanism, a cosmopolitanism expressed by the Deshastha Brahmin, an upper-caste community in Mumbai. This cosmopolitanism, he argues, while celebrating caste as a community, helps individuals to negotiate modernity and democracy, bridge social distance between sub-castes, initiate social reform and organise cooperatives to nurture financial securities. Waghmore tries to comprehend the contours of upper-caste cosmopolitanism and how this cosmopolitaism helps give meaning to individualities and creates new selves as long as these do not wish to move into a negation of it.

The next two chapters are on religiosities. Sudha Sitharaman in her chapter titled 'Between Text and Practice: Reflections on

Sociological Study of Islam' follows the main contentions made by Ibrahim in this volume and states that it is unfortunate that the study of Islam remains calibrated through a discussion on communalism, community identity and Sufism/syncretism. Thus ethnographic accounts focus on dargahs and deliberate cultural mingling between Hindu–Muslim groups. However, when riots take place, the literature discusses the targeting of Muslims. These studies continue to gaze at the lifeworlds and everyday lives of Muslims communities in terms of Hindu–Muslim/majority–minority divides rather than comprehend the ways in which distinct Muslim communities are constituted through ecological, economic and cultural processes. In these circumstances, the author argues, sociologists and anthropologists need to follow the footsteps of historians of South Asia who have tried to move out from official/state-centric discourses to constitute new prisms of analysis.

A different take on community association is presented in the chapter titled 'Catholic Citizens: Faith as Activism in Mumbai' by Rowena Robinson and Nandini Paliyath. The chapter regrets that everyday concerns and practices of citizenship have not been given much attention in India. Robinson and Paliyath discuss individuals involved in lay Catholic associations. Calling these civil society organisations, the authors argue that an identity with Christian faith allows these individuals to become active citizens. They contend that a concept of citizenship is inherent in Christianity and this allows the individuals in this lay Catholic association to question clerical and religious authorities on many issues, including parish property, participation and decision making in parish matters, and gender discrimination issues. Faith, according to this chapter, breeds activism and allows it transcend the narrow community domain. The chapter suggests that when Christianity operates as a minority religion and when it needs to engage with multiple faiths and pluralism, on the one hand, and social and economic divisions of society, on the other, it can orient itself to become Christian citizenship.

On Education and Learning

This exploration leads to another question: given that these new academic interventions need institutional nurturance, can our contemporary higher educational institutions provide these? If today, the higher education institutions have a strong presence of marginalised groups within its institutional structures, these have also been the site of contestations in the context of received elite-driven casteist and patriarchal agendas. Additionally, there is a significant change in the way higher education has been reorganised in the context of reforms. Thus the question is: will the new perspectives opened up by the volume's authors have a future in teaching and research within higher education institutions, which are characterised by declining budgets, managerial principles organising their practices, increasing lack of institutional autonomy and freedom of expression, and an emphasis on instrumental research and courses at the expense of promoting exploratory and critical academic cultures? In its third and last section, the volume brings together essays that critique and explore the nature of contemporary educational institutions.

Satish Deshpande's chapter 'The Non-academic Uses of the Public University: An Optimistic Note' starts with a description of universities. Universities, he states, provide post-secondary education; advance scholarship and research in many disciplines, which go beyond solutions for practical problems; and have the autonomy to conduct these intellectual and academic activities.

Indian universities were, however, not modelled in this fashion, as N. Jayaram in his chapter 'Ritualising Higher Education Reforms in India' informs us. Though the first of Indian universities were established very early, in the mid-nineteenth century, these were affiliating and examining bodies with 'little intellectual life of their own', given that these were conceived to serve colonial interests. No wonder, as indicated in Section One of this volume, universities not only were closely aligned but also promoted the project of conceiving the 'social' that was organised by the colonial administrators.

The question that needs to be addressed is whether despite this origin, universities can and will promote new ways of thinking needed today to confront the challenges of framing the new 'social'? Jayaram argues that some efforts have been made since the colonial times to rescue the university from the consequences of its dependencies. However, these efforts remained muted, and by the time Independence arrived, Indian universities were in a crisis, characterised by low levels of enrolment together with its distorted and dysfunctional character. Since then, the system has expanded phenomenally and become the third largest in the world. By 2015–16, there were 753 universities, 41,435 college and 11,445 standalone institutes. The University Grants Commission (UGC) states that in the same year there were 14,37,753 teachers and 28,48,500 students, with the bulk of the student enrolment in higher education taking place in affiliated colleges in state universities in first-degree courses and in general education (arts, science, and commerce). Given that most of the teachers also work in these sites implies that the Indian educational system has not moved out of the shadow it was established under in the mid-nineteenth century. No wonder only a small number of central universities, standalone institutes and select departments have been able to promote cultures of research and independent and autonomous intellectual positions, though this is getting increasingly rare. Jayaram argues that despite the innumerable commissions and their recommendations, the educational system has not overhauled itself. Rather, over time, the system has ossified; it is 'drifting like a rudderless ship'.

But the last chapter in this volume, that by Satish Deshpande (mentioned earlier), is optimistic. While agreeing with many of Jayaram's analysis, Deshpande sees hope in the system because of its non-academic impact. The first such impact is the generation of employment within the various institutions that organise the system, though Deshpande accepts that, even here, contract jobs have increased and that there has been a steady decline in the recruitment for Class 3 and 4 jobs. For Deshpande, the next two non-academic implications are extremely significant: expanding student base and increasing participation of the lower castes within the educational system. This has led to the increasing presence of marginal groups in the educational system and thereby created enormous possibilities for mobility. However, Deshpande also highlights the fact that given the dominance of the upper castes and classes in the educational system in the previous decades, there has been 'stubborn resistance' to the inclusion of the marginalised groups. No wonder, caste and gender abuse and conflict have increased in these institutions. This leads him to the third non-academic impact of the university education system—the university as an enabling civil space. The university is a site for egalitarian and inclusive cultures to develop. Given the deep hierarchical society that India is, even if there are very few confrontations and struggles, what is most important is the 'social resonance' this inclusivity has on segregated communities.

Notes

1. Saberwal was not the only one in the Asian–African context to raise this issue. In early 1970s, the same position was taken by the Malaysian sociologist Syed Hussein Alatas, who contended that academic dependencies have led to defects and shortcomings in social science scholarship. The 'unreality' of Western basic assumptions has led to misplaced abstraction, ignorance or misinterpretation of data, and an erroneous conception of problems and their signification leads to superfluous knowledge systems. Hussein Alatas called this phenomenon the 'captive mind', that is, scholarship that uncritically emulates Western social science. The captive mind syndrome occurs when all major constituents of scientific thinking, such as problem setting, analysis, abstraction, generalisation, conceptualisation, description, explanation and interpretation, have been affected by this process (Alatas 1972: 10–12).
2. It is my argument that the debate initiated by Louis Dumont in *Contributions to Indian Sociology* on 'For a Sociology of India' and continued later in the New Series chases a red herring as it remains caught in the Eurocentric binary promoted in the scholarship of Dumont.
3. The project of indigenous sociologies emerges as a consequence of the growth of a proto-nationalist perspective. It expresses itself in many ex-colonial countries at different time periods. In India, ideas relating to indigeneity find articulation in the writings of some Bengali scholars

such as Benoy Kumar Sarkar (1887–1949) and later in some writings of D. P. Mukerji. See Patel (2015). For a different point of view, see Chatterjee (2007). A major intervention on indigenous sociology was made by the African sociologist Akiwowo Akinsola (1999) when he published a paper with a similar title in *International Sociology*. The elaboration of the concepts of indigeneity and indigenous have raised many questions. Critics have asked whether these sociologists created methods to examine the truth of particular indigenous concepts and their theories. If not, on what basis have they argued that these concepts are both effective and relevant? Would there not be alternativee concepts that are equally relevant, especially in regions where there are huge diversities, such as India or Africa? The latter query directs the question towards principles of science: how does one judge the merit of a theory? Contemporary scholars have asked whether indigenous sociologies have developed an understanding of science, of ways to interrogate its own assumptions and of creating an internal dialogue with itself. Any excursion into ethnophilosophy would necessarily involve testing contradictory claims and analysing the grounds of its own rigor. What are the tools available in various cultural/philosophical systems to do such testing? If such tools are not available, surely culturist readings such as these would fall into rightist political positions (Patel 2019)?

References

Afridi, F., T. Dinkelman and K. Mahajan. 2016. 'Why Are Fewer Married Women Joining Workforce in Rural India: A Decomposition Analysis over Two Decades', Discussion Paper Series, No. 9722, Institute for the Study of Labor (IZA), Bonn.

Akiwowo, A. 1999. 'Indigenous Sociologies: Extending the Scope of the Argument', *International Sociology*, 14 (2): 115–38.

Alatas, S. H. 1972. 'The Captive Mind in Development Studies: Some Neglected Problems and the Need for Autonomous Social Science Tradition in Asia', *International Social Science Journal*, 24 (1): 9–25.

Amin, S. 1989. *Eurocentrism*. New York: Monthly Review Press.

Carstens, J. 2013. 'What Kinship Does—and How', Comment on Sahlins, Marshall. 2011. *What Kinship Is—and Is Not, HAU: Journal of Ethnographic Theory*, 3 (2): 245–51.

Chatterji, R. 2007. 'The Nationalist Sociology of Benoy Kumar Sarkar', in P. Uberoi, N. Sundar and S. Deshpande (eds), *Anthropology in the East: Founders of India Sociology and Anthropology*, pp. 106–31. Ranikhet: Permanent Black.

Connell, R. 2007. *Southern Theory: The Global Dynamics of Knowledge in Social Science*. London: Polity.

Papanek, H. 1979. 'Family Status Production: The "Work" and "Non-Work" of Women', *Signs*, 4 (4): 775–81.

Patel, S. 2011. 'Ruminating on Sociological Traditions in India', in S. Patel (ed.), *Doing Sociology in India: Genealogies, Locations, and Practices*, pp. xi–xxxviii. New Delhi: Oxford University Press.

———. 2015. 'Colonial Modernity and the Problematique of Indigenous and Indegeniety: South Asian and African Experiences', in H. Sabea and F. Biegal (eds), *Academic Dependency: The Challenge of Building Autonomous Social Sciences in the South*. Mendoza: EDIUNC-SEPHIS.

———. 2019. 'Sociology through the "South" Prism', in E. Fiddian-Qasmiyeh and P. Daley (eds), *Routledge Handbook of South-South Relations*, pp. 31–47. London: Routledge.

Saberwal, S. 1968. 'Academic Colonialism. The Problem', *Seminar*, 112: 10–13.

Uberoi, P. 2000. 'Déjà vu?', *Seminar* ('Situating Sociology: A Symposium on Knowledge, Institutions and Practices in a Discipline'), 495: 14–19.

Wallerstein, I. 1996. *Open the Social Sciences: Report of the Gulbenkian Commission on the Restructuring of the Social Sciences*. Stanford: Stanford University Press.

1 Sociological Scholarship on India

The Epistemes of Colonial Modernity and Methodological Nationalism*

SUJATA PATEL

This chapter explores the way sociology as a discipline has been framed in India. It does so by excavating the moorings of the embedded systems of thinking in sociology in India (its episteme) in order to map the received ideas, institutions and practices that have organised the knowledge of this discipline in India. Drawing on the discussions and debates on social theory made in decolonial theories[1] and my earlier writings, I suggest that sociology in India has been constituted in three phases. The first two have been dominated by two distinct epistemes: colonial modernity and methodological nationalism respectively. The third phase is evolving as we speak about it, and its history can only be written post facto. However, it is still possible to use a critique of the first two phases to outline the contours of the new episteme being framed and discuss its patterns.

I use two master concepts to comprehend the history of sociology in India. The first is colonial modernity, sometimes referred to

---

* This is a shortened version of a paper titled 'Colonial Modernity and Methodological Nationalism: The Structuring of Sociological Traditions of India' presented as the presidential address at the Indian Sociological Society conference in Tezpur, December 2016. Originally published in *Sociological Bulletin*, Vol. 66, No. 2.

as Eurocentrism. It is a discursive term/concept, that is, it is about not only modernity experienced in the colony or in the period of colonialism but also the way ideas, ideologies and knowledge systems were organised within the colony to refract and invisibilise the 'modern' contours of the everyday experience of the people who were colonised by constructing these experiences as non-modern. Methodological nationalism is the naturalisation of the nation state by the social sciences. Scholars who share this intellectual orientation assume that countries are the natural units for comparative studies; equate society with the nation state at the expense of local, regional or global concerns; and conflate national interests with the goals of social science. Methodological nationalism reflects and reinforces the identification that many scholars maintain with their own nation states (Patel 2011a).

This chapter suggests that the episteme of colonial modernity defined the identity of sociology as it was organised within academia in the early twentieth century. It also suggests that notwithstanding some criticisms to this position, the former was institutionalised after Independence through its association with another episteme, that of methodological nationalism. The chapter opens up a discussion on how we displace these embedded traditions in order to constitute a comparative sociological vision that integrates the local/regional and national concerns of the subaltern with the decolonised and denationalised theoretical and methodological practices that can be generalisable across the globe.

The chapter is divided into four sections. The first section maps out the perspective through which the sociology of epistemology is analysed. The next three sections elaborate the three phases of the growth and legitimation of sociological traditions within India. In the second section, I outline how the discourse of colonial modernity marked out the discipline's identity as anthropology and the subsequent propagation of the use of its theories and methods, which promoted a colonial understanding of the patriarchal, upper caste and upper class discourse of sociabilities. In this phase, we also see a challenge emerging to this discourse with the growth of an anti-Western, indigenous sociology, influenced by trends within nationalism and rooted in 'Indian' values. I suggest that notwithstanding its anti-Western/anti-colonial orientation, there was little attempt in this approach to displace the caste, class and gender orientation of the discipline whose discourse was organised and interpellated through the episteme of colonial modernity.

In the third section, I elaborate how this orientation becomes enhanced as the discipline that is redefined as sociology/social anthropology gets recognition with the nationalist modern project of the post-independent state. The discipline articulates itself as a political project of the nation state, in the context of the expansion of the higher education system and the standardisation of a 'national' sociology. One part of sociology becomes 'social anthropology', utilising the methods of ethnography and 'field view' to study the defining character of the Indian structure, i.e., the caste system. The focus of social anthropology shifts to the study of the micro—the village and its tradition(s)—and to assess incremental changes within a civilisational perspective without releasing itself from its received patriarchal, upper-caste and upper-class perspective. While a Marxist critique of this theoretical position made an attempt to break its domination by suggesting that the nation and class intersected with each other, this critique did not break the received episteme of methodological nationalism.

The fourth section, which is the conclusion, gives a brief overview of the challenges facing contemporary sociology.

The Discourse of Colonial Modernity and the Constitution of Anthropology in India

Contemporary Indian sociology's moorings are in nineteenth-century anthropology whose main contours were framed by colonial administrators in the context of the growth and spread of the orientalist position in Europe, which was institutionalised in India a century earlier, first through the study of India's languages and through this the study of its society. It is thus no surprise to note that such orientalist studies became the frame of reference for administrators 100 years later, when enjoined by the colonial state to create knowledge about Indian society. This is how Eurocentric assumptions were transformed and implemented to frame the social within India.

The disciplinary identity of anthropology in India was shaped by the Eurocentric assumption that groups in India could be understood and categorised on the lines of spatial–cultural structures as groups were in the West. This assumption not only created a distinction between groups living in India but also constructed these groups in terms of an internal hierarchy. Following orientalist/racial principles, British civil servants and anthropologists and later Indian anthropologists placed the debate of identifying and designating these groups as 'castes' or 'tribes' within the discussion of 'stocks' or 'races' in relation to other 'stocks' and 'races' in the Western world. In order to formulate these categories, they took the help of evolutionary theory as well as Victorian social thought associated with 'race science'. In this, they were aided by a theory of the 'Aryan' (white or fair-skinned) invasion of India, which grew out of the discovery of the Indo-European language family in the late nineteenth century. Hence linguistic classification merged with racial classification to produce a theory of the Indian civilisation being formed by the invasion of fair-skinned, civilised, Sanskrit-speaking Aryans, who conquered and partially absorbed the dark-skinned savage aborigines (Patel 2006).

This theory was critical in producing the basic division of groups in India into Aryan and non-Aryan races, now termed as 'castes' and 'tribes'. What is of interest is the fact that while 'castes' were defined, in the context of Hinduism, as groups who cultivated land, had better technology and a high civilisational attribute, 'tribes' were defined in contrast to castes as those who practised primitive technology, lived in interior jungles and were animistic in their religious practices. Such a classification and categorisation were not peculiar to India. They also found manifestation in the African continent, as British officials used this knowledge to construct categories of social groups in Africa and retransferred the newly constructed classification back again to India, as happened in the case of the term 'tribe' being defined as a lineage group based on a segmentary state.

In the process, 'caste' and 'tribe' were made out to be far more pervasive, totalising and uniform concepts than ever before and defined in terms of a religious order, which it was not always so empirically. In fact, ancient and medieval historiographers now inform us that those whom we identify as castes and tribes were groups that were shaped by political struggles and processes over material resources. In pre-colonial India, multiple markers of identity defined the relationship between groups, and these were contingent on complex processes, which were constantly changing and were related to political power. Thus we had temple communities, territorial groups, lineage segments, family units, royal retinues, warrior sub-castes, little as opposed to large kingdoms, occupational reference groups, agricultural and trading associations, networks of devotional and sectarian religious communities, and priestly networks. Those who came under the name 'caste' as defined by the colonial powers were just one category among many and constituted as one way of representing and organising identity (Dirks 2001).

The categories of caste and tribe were further defined once the colonial authorities organised the revenue settlements to facilitate an agrarian taxation system. British officials searched for a new classification to understand and assess the material conditions that organised groups within the Indian subcontinent. On the one hand, the rulers needed to create spatial units for the maintenance of law and order as well as for the regular collection of taxes once these were assessed. Simultaneously, on the other hand, they needed to ensure proper collection and thus created new positions, which they did on the basis of their knowledge of the way taxation worked in England.

Three units were created in India—villages, estates and properties, with positions such as zamindars, patels, chaudhuris, *talukdars*, chiefs, rajas, nawabs and princes, while in Africa, the spatial units were hamlets, lineages, clans and tribes and the positions headmen, elders and chiefs (Cohn 1987: 206). The village was attributed a boundedness, making it almost like an 'island society' (first theorised by Radcliffe-Brown) in which communities of castes lived in harmony. Since colonialism, this perception came to be firmly embedded as it resonated in many ways both with nationalist thought and with the sociological imagination. Thus when empirical research in the social sciences developed in the 1950s and 1960s, sociologists made the village the locale for understanding the caste system (Patel 2006). Colonial conquest and knowledge both enabled ways to rule and to construct what colonialism was all about—its own self-knowledge. The British played a major role in identifying and producing Indian 'tradition', that is, the beliefs and customs of those living in the region. Thus Cohn states that

> In the conceptual scheme which the British created to understand and to act in India, they constantly followed the same logic; they reduced vastly complex codes and associated meaning to a few metonyms.... [This process allowed them] to save themselves the effort of understanding or adequately explaining subtle or not-so-subtle meanings attached to the actions of their subjects. Once the British had defined something as an Indian custom, or traditional dress, or the proper form of salutation, any deviation from it was defined as a rebellion or an act to be punished. India was redefined by the British to be a place of rules and order; once the British had defined to their own satisfaction what they constructed as Indian rules and customs, then the Indians had to conform to these constructions. (Cohn 1997: 162)

This classificatory schema, that is, using the attribute of race to divide the people of the world found its own 'local' legitimation, its own articulation and its 'voice' once colonial authorities imposed it to divide the 'natives'. Thus this project found an expression (ironically and paradoxically) in the work of indigenous intellectuals in the subcontinent, which was in search of an identity against colonialism. For them, the immediate necessity was to locate 'our modernities'. Thus unlike the Europeans for whom, 'the present was the site of one's escape from the past' (Chatterjee 1997: 20), for the indigenous Indian intellectuals 'it is precisely the present [given the colonial experience] from which we feel we must escape' (ibid.). As a result, the desire to be creative and search for a new modernity is transposed to the past of India, a past ironically constructed by orientalist colonial modernity. Thus Chatterjee argues that 'we construct a picture of "those days" when there was beauty, prosperity and healthy sociability. This makes the very modality of our coping with modernity radically different from the historically evolved modes of Western modernity' (Chatterjee 1997: 19). The past was now rarefied to understand the present and the future, and an orientalist imagination came to define the so-called indigenous expression.

In a different way, the historian Sumit Sarkar makes a similar argument when he suggests that while modern Western history writing has generally been state oriented (with an understanding of the nation as a reflection of the nation state), the historical consciousness of the Indian intelligentsia in the late nineteenth and twentieth centuries was oriented to the valorisation of culture against the state. He states:

> In this period *samaj* (society, community) came to be counterpoised to *rashtra* or *rajshakti* (state, the political domain). The real history of India, it was repeatedly asserted, was located in the first, not the second, for *samaj* embodied the distinctive qualities peculiar to the genius, culture and religion of the Indian people. (Sarkar 1997: 21)

He further argues that '*samaj* was simultaneously all too often conceptualised in Hindu, high caste gentry, and paternalistic terms' (ibid.: 23). Obviously racial constructions of 'difference' found a new legitimacy within a Brahminical, casteist, patriarchal ideology as the two overlapped with each other to organise the study of social sciences through newly reconstructed majoritarian and or/casteist positions (Patel 2007).

Was there no intervention to displace this episteme? We can note some attempts made by Indian scholars from the 1930s and 1940s as they started becoming anthropologists and sociologists. One of the key influences in their work was two trends of nationalism, which Bhikhu Parekh (1995) identifies as modernist and modernist-traditional. The Marxist sociological interventions of A. R. Desai were articulated through an engagement with the modernist current, while those of certain scholars in the Lucknow school were moored in modernist-traditional nationalist currents. There was one other attempt to conceptualise society, this was in and through the anti-Brahminical movements that emerged in the mid-nineteenth and early twentieth centuries in today's Maharashtra and Tamil Nadu. However, neither of these movements made a significant impact on the framing of the discipline in the post-1950s period. This was because of the overwhelming domination of the traditional nationalist current in the constitution of sociology and the valorisation of its key thinker G. S. Ghurye as the father of sociology by subsequent sociologists.

Let me explain this argument. In an earlier paper (Patel 2011a), I have drawn from Bhikhu Parekh to indicate how three different currents, that of the modernists, the traditionalists and the modern-traditionalists influenced the framing of Indian society. Parekh has argued that there was little disagreement between the three on the causes of the nation's degeneration and decadence. All three agreed that this was related to colonialism, domination by the British, the extraction and control for imperialist purposes of India's rich material resources, and the destruction of its vitality and ideas by the colonial elite. They also agreed in the necessity of a strong state to ensure a transition to modernity. However, there were differences regarding the possible solutions, and these differences, I suggest, affected the subsequent identity of the discipline.

Partha Chatterjee (1997) has argued that all the three currents were steeped in Eurocentric epistemes. He draws to our attention that '(t)here is no promised land of modernity outside the network of power' (ibid.: 19) and, one may add, outside its discourse. Colonialism brought together for the once colonised two promises: the struggle for 'dreams of freedom' and, at the same time, the experience of being its victims. Its episteme organised both the 'desire for power' and the 'resistance of power'. No wonder, the discussion on modernity in India has been steeped in ambiguity, given colonialism's framing of modernity as a discourse simultaneously of freedom and of subjugation. Nationalism structured an understanding of being both unfree and free to change the world. In so doing, it now reconstructed the colonial binary in a new context, that of the nation. This ambiguity played itself out in context with the framing of nationalist sociology, and it can be seen in all the three trends mentioned earlier.

The 'modernists' wanted India to identify with the future and with progress. They argued that the problems that India faced were tied to its past, that is, to Indian culture that had made 'Indian' people passive, lifeless and non-productive. These scholars had ideological affiliations to left-liberal, socialist and Marxist positions, advocated the path set by Europeans earlier and wanted India to have a new industrial economy, free from agrarian dependencies. A. R. Desai's early work, which elided a discussion on caste and patriarchy, is an example of this approach within sociology. The 'modern-traditionalists' envisioned society through syncretic and culturist positions. The goal of modern-traditionalists was to understand the present and construct a social science language best suited to transforming the specific culture that they were studying: India. These influences can be seen in the work of sociologists such as D. P. Mukerjee. In that sense, the modern-traditionalists remained trapped in the colonial episteme.

It was the traditionalist current that was most influential in the subsequent identity of sociology. These scholars argued for a need to draw out concepts and theories from the past, that is, from India's rich histories and its civilisation. They suggested that though the Indian civilisation had suffered a decline, it was essentially and fundamentally sound and was embodied with much strength. These strengths had kept the 'Indian' people together over centuries, and these ideas would continue to bind them together in the future. The traditionalists also contended that Indian society had a distinct character and history, which had evolved in interaction with its people and its institutions. Indians, and the social sciences in India, needed to mobilise their society's creative resources for its regeneration, without losing its coherence and inner balance. The traditionalists also cautioned Indians not to imitate the West by taking on its language and its values. They believed that India had to work out its own salvation in its own terms—its temperaments, traditions and circumstances. This set of ideas framed the sociological language in India and can be best seen in the work of G. S. Ghurye who used an orientalist methodology to discuss indigenous concepts, such as caste, tribe, family and Hinduism, which organised Indian traditions (Patel 2013).

The episteme of colonial modernity thus became part of the 'background understandings' and 'beliefs' of doing anthropology and later sociology. Specifically, in the case of India, this knowledge had the following traits: (i) it was produced as part of the colonial politics of rule; (ii) it was expressed and organised in terms of values that were in opposition to modernity; (iii) it used disciplinary practices such as Indology and ethnography to elaborate these positions; (iv) it was codified with the help of native intelligentsia, especially the Brahmins; (v) it reflected the social order as represented by the native intelligentsia both in its expressed articulations (in anthropology and later social anthropology) and in its silences; (vi) it mitigated an examination of the way classification systems of the state organised new forms of inequalities in the colonial territory (Patel 2011a).

Methodological Nationalism and the Formation of Sociology

In its most straightforward usage, methodological nationalism implies coevalness between 'society' and the 'nation state', that is, it argues that a discussion on modern society (which sociology does) entails an implicit understanding of the nation. In other words, the nation is treated as 'the natural and necessary representation of the modern society' (Chernillo 2006: 2). Methodological nationalism is the taken-for-granted belief that the boundaries of nation states are natural boundaries within which societies are contained. Sociology, according to Ulrich Beck, 'assumed that humanity is naturally divided into a limited number of nations, which on the inside, organized themselves as nation-states, and on the outside, set boundaries to distinguish themselves from other nation-states' (Beck 2007: 287). This outside limitation and the competition between nation states constitute 'the most fundamental category of political organization' (ibid.).

Thus sociology's visions of culture and politics, law, justice and history represent those of individual nation states (ibid.). Wimmer and Schiller (2002) suggest that there are three different strands of methodological nationalism. The first is ignorance and/or blindness in recognising that modern societies are structured the way nation and nationality are organised. As a result, sociologists ignore the study of nation and nationalism in each country and do not frame their theories to understand the interface between modernity and nationalism. The second strand, following the aforementioned point, is mode of 'naturalisation'. Sociological theories take for granted official discourses, agendas, loyalties and histories without problematising them. They study groups and cultures as being unitary and organically linked to territories, thus reproducing the social world as bounded, culturally specific spatial units. The third strand is that of territorialisation of the social science imaginary and its reduction to the boundaries of the nation state. There is an obsession to comprehend all aspects of life in terms of territory rather than seeing social interconnections between territorial boundaries.

All social sciences in India including sociology were framed through the lens of methodological nationalism. Unlike Europe, wherein methodological nationalism is not associated with self-conscious nationalist agendas, in the case of India, sociologists and other social scientists were self-conscious in their support of the nation state's project to use higher education and the social science professions in the service of the nation and the state. In this context, what kind of sociology found an expression in India?

I have argued earlier that the Eurocentric episteme divided the disciplines that study the 'social' into sociology and anthropology and defined their theories, methodologies and methods in terms of the modern–traditional binary. Notwithstanding the project of the Indian nation state to create knowledge of and about modern India, sociology in India carried forward the colonial knowledge systems constituted as anthropology in the shape of sociology. The promotion of methodological nationalism in sociology allowed anthropological positions to merge into sociological ones as a consequence of three processes discernible in the post-1947 decades, which I will discuss next.

First, the university became the main (and the only) site for organising the practices of the discipline. Thus there was huge investment in university education. Second, there was an attempt to standardise and make uniform the contours of the knowledge governing the discipline, wherein three institutions played a key role. The first of these was the University Grants Commission (UGC), which initiated the process of standardisation through the organisation of syllabi across universities within the country. The second was the Indian Council of Social Science Research (ICSSR), which introduced the idea of doing bibliographic surveys of sociology and social anthropology (as other social sciences) in India in order to chart out the specialisations in the discipline and aid research in these areas. The last was the Indian Sociological Society, which emerged after its merger with the Lucknow-based All India Sociological Conference, as a strong pan-India professional organisation of sociologists, with its own journal (Patel 2002). Henceforth, all sociological knowledge was organised to discuss, debate and represent social changes occurring within one nation and territory—India.

Third, in this context, it is no coincidence that when the state demanded that sociologists together with other social scientists develop and organise systematic knowledge about contemporary society as it responded to planned social change, most sociologists affirmed the need to have a sociological language that can comprehend the uniqueness of the Indian nation, its culture and its civilisation. Sociologists in India saw their project as analysing one's own society (India) in one's (indigenous) 'own terms', without colonial and neocolonial tutelage. This project allowed for the institutionalisation of a particularistic problematique—an assessment of the changes occurring within India's characteristic institutions, that is, caste, kinship, family and religion. This particularistic problematique had much in common with the notions of India embedded within elite and mainstream nationalism. Thus, if colonial heritage was a key element that structured this effort, the need to examine how modernity and modernisation (in the context of nation building) were organising the changes occurring within the institutions of family, caste, kinship and religion fuelled its energy (Patel 2011a).

But how was this sociology defined and identified? Very early in his career, M. N. Srinivas argued that there was no distinction between sociology and social anthropology. Instead, he suggested, there needs to be a distinction between sociology/social anthropology and anthropology. The latter should deal with physical anthropology and ethnology and study the primitives, while the former should use a functionalist perspective to study castes as jatis. This approach found acceptance within the growing sociological community as many of those trained in Bombay went on to make careers in Delhi, Pune, Mysore and Bangalore and as the University of Delhi became the key centre for sociological thinking. Of the many alternatives that the discipline inherited from its early twentieth-century experiences, what was ultimately institutionalised as a standard and uniform language to examine and assess social change in modern India, was the perspective provided by M. N. Srinivas. In this form, the episteme of colonial modernity was not displaced, but it found a new vibrancy in Srinivas' perspective as it became a standard variant.

Srinivas' sociology/social anthropology was constituted as a modern discipline, though it did not study the 'social' in its modern variant—it continued the earlier ethnographic approach of studying 'communities' but now viewed as segmented groups of jatis/castes. Its modern orientation, however, was reaffirmed because it promoted the 'field view' (empirical investigations) against the 'book view' (Indology), which was associated with colonialism. And because it was indigenous in so far as it introduced participant observation as an 'insider's perspective' of doing sociology, it also affirmed a nationalist position. Lastly, it remained closely aligned to elite nationalist visions of society and therefore found resonance with the new ruling groups managing the nation state.

The key leadership role that Srinivas and his colleagues at the Department of Sociology of University of Delhi took in the various institutions mentioned earlier also legitimised the universalisation of his sociological vision, with other positions, such as those of sociologists from Lucknow, of Marxist sociologists such as A. R. Desai and of structural functionalists like Y. B. Damle, being pushed to the margins. The diversity in perspectives, which was the feature of the colonial period, was now substituted by a master narrative. Srinivas' perspective was designed to represent the language of sociology (Patel 2011b).

As a consequence, the episteme of colonial modernity translated itself within the discipline of sociology to conceive the nation as consisting of discrete groups called castes, to view the diverse manifestations of caste as the nation's signature, and to regard economic development and planning as key to reframing the social and the cultural for modern India. Groups that were not castes, such as tribes (both in central India and the northeast) and the religious minorities, were relegated to being backward and/or undeveloped. Henceforth, the hegemonic, imagined visions of the state's ruling groups and their practices and dispositions became the frames of doing social science, thereby not only denying the recognition of marginalities of all kinds but also advocating its virtual disappearance in its language in the first few decades after Independence. If one attribute of inequality was recognised by the new nation state, it was that of income. This attribute was related to a diffuse concept: poverty. It is no coincidence thus to note that the sociological language remained muted on the political moorings of this project, imbricated as this was with its close linkages with metropolitan advanced capitalism and its embeddedness in the dynamics of capital accumulation on a world scale. It took for granted state and elite/ruling class discourses, agendas, loyalties and histories without problematising them. Additionally, methodological nationalism made it possible to take for granted the nation state's boundaries, making these appear as natural boundaries, which had to be protected militarily and fought for by its people. Sociological language naturalised and territorialised class, caste and gendered elite visions of the nation as it was articulated in the colonial episteme and represented it to comprehend groups within the post-independent nation state.

This orientation stamped the extensive production of sociological literature in India after Independence. This literature was promoted by many institutions such as universities, research institutes and funding organisations, which came up with the state expanding the system of higher education. This reinforced the close functional relationship between Indian academics and the system of higher education and by extension between the project of knowledge creation and the elite/upper class and savarna conceptions of nationhood. No wonder, what developed in India was a culture of professionalisation that equated the social sciences and sociological knowledge with the state's policy orientations. This was unlike Europe where the social sciences developed through a reflective and/or public intervention and their professionalisation was related to these two orientations (Burawoy 2004).

Lastly, this nationalist perspective legitimised the idea that if Indians do research, they are rid of the colonial moorings of social science research and that nationalist regulations will constrain any further inequities in knowledge production. However, Eurocentrism is not only an episteme but also a way to organise the production, distribution, consumption and reproduction of knowledge unequally across different parts of the world. The Malaysian thinker Syed Hussein Alatas (1972) and the African philosopher Paulin Hountondji (1997) have discussed these aspects of knowledge production through the concepts of 'captive mind' and 'extraversion' (or externally oriented knowledge) respectively. They argue that the syndrome of 'captive mind' and 'extraversion' can be seen in teaching and learning processes, in the way the curriculum and syllabi are framed, and in the processes of research—design of research questions, methods and methodologies used, formulation of criteria for accepting articles for journals and books, and ultimately defining what and where one publishes and what constitutes academic excellence. The argument here is that the trenches of this episteme are deep and layered. Thus this episteme cannot be merely replaced through cognitive supplants of concepts, theories and methods, which was what the best in nationalist sociology attempted to do.

In what ways did sociologists in India react to these processes? By the late 1970s and early 1980s, it was clear (at least to some sociologists) that the discipline was caught up in problems. For many, this problem was related to the methodology being used—that of participant observation. Saberwal (1983) was one of the first to criticise the sole reliance on participant observation to study social change in India. This methodology, he argued, does not allow its practitioner to present a theoretically and methodologically robust perspective to assess and examine the complex processes of conflict and consensus at work in India. The discipline needed a language that could study the complex macro interfaces between groups and processes that were often in a relationship of involution. Oommen (1983) continued this argument by highlighting how the unit of analysis is critical to understanding contemporary modern processes. It is possible to examine family, caste and kinship through small units of study. But this is not so in the case of critical issues of contemporary salience, such as the impact of Partition on the Indian nation or the question why untouchability continues to be practised in contemporary India. The same argument was reiterated by Dhanagare (1980: 25), who contributed to this debate through his critique of functionalist theory, which he argued could not assess conflicts and contestations that were becoming part of the Indian experience of modernity. Sociology, he argued, needs to be understood as social criticism. If historical analysis is used to assess changes, then sociologists would be able to grasp the interrelationship between macro and micro processes.

For Saberwal (1983), the problem was also related to the way the method of participant observation was conceptualised and institutionalised across departments within the teaching and learning processes. With non-trained teachers as interlocutors of the teaching process, increasingly description rather than analysis dominated the teaching of this method. This pattern got inflated with simultaneous expansion of departments. In the 1950s, he stated, an idea gained currency, that modernity can be organised through the expansion of universities rather than first creating a group of professionals that would understand the strengths and weaknesses of the perspectives and methodologies being used, and then transmit these in professional ways. To Saberwal, the problem thus was related to the Indian notions of modernity.

The expansion of universities bred its own contradictions, such as those mentioned in the preceding discussion. These contradictions were reinforced due to disparities in accessing physical and human resources as well as differential structures of academic autonomy, which were dependent on the university's legal character in terms of whether it was a state or a central university. Central universities were better funded, more autonomous and had a 'national character'. State universities needed to project a regional identity, and had less funding and low staff strength. This process became more complicated with further expansion of state universities and the growth of a new state elite demanding that state universities teach in the language spoken in the region. Unfortunately, there was little to no intellectual investment in creating a vocabulary of the social sciences in regional languages. In these circumstances, such a demand further impinged on the quality of the learning process and implicated what got taught and what was researched. Thus the problem confronting the discipline was not merely that of its own language but also of the limitations inherent within the modern institutional structures that sustained its practices. Increasingly, the sociologist–ethnographer–teacher within departments encouraged doctoral students to use 'insider' descriptive perspectives to generate monographs of 'my village' and/or 'my community'. Overtime, the learning of sociology became a 'soft experience' (Saberwal 1983: 308). If sociology in India could boast of some of the best in the field, it was also producing a large mass of professionally untrained students and thus teachers and researchers.

Towards a Conclusion

What has been the legacy of these trends? Currently, we can note three tendencies. First, there is a new energy among a small group of sociologists in India to rethink earlier themes, such as marriage, family, caste and religion, and reframe these in novel ways, for instance, through the theoretical lens of intersectionality, exclusions, distinctions, identities and queer positions; by engaging with new perspectives such as those framed by Pierre Bourdieu, Ulrich Beck or John Urry, and reframing old or recent ones, such as Marxism, Weberian sociology and feminism; by conceptualising new areas of interdisciplinary investigation such as popular cultural studies, northeast studies, Partition studies, violence studies, media and film studies and sexuality studies, and reframing earlier ones such as urban studies, environmental studies, science and technology studies, Dalit studies, tribal and Adivasi studies; and by using new methodologies such as grounded theory and triangulation and/or combining historical and ethnographical methods in research and study. Theoretically, these sociologists have moved away from the debate of the indigenous and have embraced global theoretical perspectives.

The gaze of these sociologists is now towards the present. Their focus is on identifying and interrogating contemporary processes that are organising sociabilities and creating new groups. They wish to excavate the linkages between the past and the present of inequalities and exclusions. They assert a need to evaluate state programmes and policies and assess how these are disrupting lives and displacing the cultural moorings of individual and group identities. In sum, they want to unravel the complex and contradictory processes structuring current processes of modernity in India.

As a consequence, a new litany of concepts and theories are being articulated as old ones are being recalibrated to examine and comprehend how contemporary social imaginaries are being constituted. Today's sociologists are respecting subaltern voices and allowing these to help them reorganise their knowledge.

This recognition has also helped in creating distantiation from earlier elite visions promoted in the 1960s and 1970s. No wonder, slowly and steadily, the earlier assumptions associated with the epistemes of colonial modernity and methodological nationalism are being chipped away. There is a now a new affirmation to frame a sociological language that can assess the organic relationship between formal/institutional and non-formal forms of organisation of the 'social'.

Second, notwithstanding the fact that contemporary sociological discussions in India have moved away from framing research in terms of binaries—for instance, of societies (modern and traditional), disciplines (anthropology and sociology), theories (indigenous versus Western), methodologies (ethnography versus survey; qualitative versus quantitative research)—the geographical compass of research and discussion has remained focused on the local and regional and on examining cases or case studies defined by administrative boundaries: village, districts, wards, towns and cities.

Though India is a vast country with diverse processes and uneven patterns of sociabilities, the methodological tools that sociologists have used has neither allowed them to compare these diversities in local and regional processes in various parts of the country nor given them the tools to assess similarities and differences between regions. Thus it will be no surprise to note that it is rare to find sociologists comparing processes and attributes across nation states. At this juncture, it is important to recall Satish Saberwal raising the question of how to examine the intersection of the micro, meso and macro to assess the causes and consequences of contemporary sociabilities.

The continued methodological dependence on using cases and focusing on administrative sites as a locale of constituting sociabilities raises two issues: First, with contemporary processes creating new geographies, under what conditions can we still use the case study method as it was fashioned in twentieth century? At that time, case studies were used to generalise for the regional and national scale. If we were to use this methodology today, how do we rethink case studies in order to make them comparative and to represent other/larger scales? Second, it is critical that we ask why we continue to use administrative boundaries as sites for doing sociological work. If administrative boundaries represent political projects, should sociologists be using them to understand social space? Why are sociologists reducing the social to a space of power? Given that these methods are associated with the epistemes of colonial modernity and methodological nationalism, it becomes extremely crucial that there is a discussion on these issues.

It is necessary to recognise that since the late 1970s and particularly after the 1990s, the dynamics of the world have changed—the nation can no longer be equated with the nation state and is recognised and evaluated through the prism of the global. At one level, the world has contracted. It has opened up possibilities of diverse kinds of transborder flows and movements, of capital and labour and of signs and symbols, organised oftentimes in intersecting spatial circuits. However, even though we all live in one global capitalist world with a dominant form of modernity, inequalities and hierarchies are increasing and so are fragmented identities. Lack of access to livelihoods, infrastructure and political citizenship across the world now blends with exclusions relating to cultural and group identity, which are organised in local and/or regional spatial and temporal zones. Many sociologists are wondering whether we need to search for a new framework that moves beyond the nineteenth and early twentieth century social science language and addresses the new challenges posed by contemporary processes and its new geographies. These trends need a global conversation. Are we ready to initiate such conversations?

The two issues discussed indicate a renewed energy among some sociologists to self-reflect, to assess the reasons for the uneasiness regarding the discipline's future and to comprehend the subject's contemporary angst, all of which are directing a small group of sociologists to ask new questions about their own language. The question that needs to be addressed today is the following: Are sociologists as a group and as a community concerned about the future of their subject and their discipline? Do they recognise that they have lost their earlier common vision regarding the profession and its goals? Do they recognise that today there is no consensus on what should be taught, what should be researched, and what should be the theoretical and methodological tools to do sociological research? There is neither consensus on these matters nor an urgency to debate these issues. Does this trend signify lethargy in thought and in goals? Are sociologists completely unconcerned about the declining standards of professionalism that abjure principles of rigour and discard interpersonal respect and civility within the community?

There is a deep divide in our community. This divide has grown to become hierarchical and has a negative impact on the profession at large. On the one hand, there is a small elite (mentioned earlier) that is oriented to the language of a global professional culture and that is internationally networked through its use of the English language. On the other, there is a large mass of practitioners who are locally and regionally networked through the vernaculars, who promote a sociology that uses descriptive analysis, combining these with uncritical case study methods, and whose sociological visions have a naïve commonsensical perspective of the subject. This divide has led to the growth of two models of learning the subject: one promotes a sociology defined by Western social science, which is held out as typical for the world and has led to brain drain and the second popularises another culture, which promotes an 'infantilisation' of scientific and professional practices, and a lethargy and disdain towards professionalism, with little to no connect with the politically creative work done in the vernaculars of the region. And because the mass of sociologists are in the second group, this has an impact on the entire subject.

To be sure, there are structural reasons that have supported this trend. Since the late 1980s, the nation state's understanding of the role of higher education institutions in the country's growth has changed. Unlike the past when education was part of the development goal of the state, today it is considered to be an economic service to be consumed by individuals. Thus it has to be accountable in terms of the immediate economic benefits it can accrue to individual(s) and the state. These shifts along with the fiscal crisis suffered by the states and the Centre have created the conditions for a radical change in the university structure. These changes have affected the social sciences exponentially, given that the contemporary position does see any economic value in the social sciences. Consequently, there has been an uneven growth of colleges and education, huge investment in education by the private sector, and a thinning of resources for public universities and within them for the social sciences. Simultaneously, the change in the state's orientation towards higher education has also led to the demise of a liberal understanding of what the university is and what its role in developing critical thinking is. This is the heritage of the modernist trend of nationalism, and this heritage of nationalist culture is slowly being eroded as the state questions what we should speak, when we should do so and in what manner we should do so. In the 1980s, sociologists inaugurated a debate on its crisis; today we need to once again analyse the moorings of the present crisis.

Should the growing censorship on what we can write about, the decrease in human resources, decay in physical infrastructure, and decline in financial support for research and for upgrading knowledge tools become incentives to challenge policies of the state so that we can reconvene as an community and re-energise our professional culture? Has not the moment arrived once again when the community of sociologists needs to reflect on how it should go forward? And when this is done, it is important to remember that sociology as a subject was established and institutionalised to study the problems faced by the exploited and the poor. It draws on its legacy of using scientific practices to promote a critique of those in power and on its repertoire of theories and practices to understand the complex processes that subject people to the machinations of the dominant. This is the reason why sociology is and remains a modern social science.

In this chapter, I have tried to show that sociological traditions in India had a different heritage. The heritage of the epistemes of colonial modernity and methodological nationalism entangled our scientific practices and professional culture in non-modern practices and legitimised traditionalist perceptions and practices. There is a need to constantly look at the past to define the present. Today, more than ever, there is a need to look at the future to understand the limitations of the present.

Note

1. I use the concepts of 'decolonial' and 'decoloniality' in the way these have been theorised within Latin American scholarship. It uses these to critique the theory of modernity from a post-structuralist and critical theory perspective. Decolonial in this sense does not valorise the pre-colonial as it is done by scholarship associated with Hindutva positions but rather is an epistemic intervention that questions the 'coloniality of power', a theory elaborated by the sociologist Anibal Quijano (2000).

References

Alatas, S. H. 1972. 'The Captive Mind in Development Studies', *International Social Science Journal*, 24 (1): 9–25.

Beck, U. 2007. 'The Cosmopolitan Condition. Why Methodological Nationalism Fails', *Theory, Culture and Society*, 24 (7–8): 286–90.

Burawoy, M. 2004. 'Public Sociologies: Contradictions, Dilemmas, and Possibilities', *Social Forces*, 82 (4): 1–16.

Chatterjee, P. 1997. *Our Modernity*. Rotterdam/Dakar: SEPHIS and CODESRIA.

Chernillo, D. 2006. 'Social Theory's Methodological Nationalism: Myth and Reality', *European Journal of Social Theory*, 9 (1): 5–22.

Cohn, B. S. 1987. 'African Models and Indian Histories', in B. S. Cohn, *An Anthropologist among Historians and Other Essays*, pp. 200–23. Delhi: Oxford University Press.

———. 1997. *Colonialism and Its Forms of Knowledge: The British in India*. Delhi: Oxford University Press.

Dhanagare, D. N. 1980. 'Search for Identity', *Seminar*, 254: 23–26.

Dirks, N. 2001. *Castes of Mind: Colonialism and the Making of Modern India*. Princeton: Princeton University Press.

Hountondji, P. 1997. 'Introduction', in P. Hountondji (ed.), *Endogenous Knowledge: Research Trails*, pp. 1–39. Dakar: CODESRIA.

Oommen, T. K. 1983. 'Sociology in India: A Plea for Contextualisation', *Sociological Bulletin*, 32 (2): 11–36.

Parekh, B. 1995. 'Jawaharlal Nehru and the Crisis of Modernisation', in U. Baxi and B. Parekh (eds), *Crisis and Change in Contemporary India*, pp. 21–56. New Delhi: Sage Publications.

Patel, S. 2002. 'The Profession and Its Association: Five Decades of the Indian Sociological Society', *International Sociology*, 17 (2): 269–84.

———. 2006. 'Beyond Binaries: A Case for Self-Reflexive Sociologies', *Current Sociology*, 54 (3): 381–95.

———. 2007. 'Sociological Study of Religion: Colonial Modernity and Nineteenth Century Majoritarianism', *Economic and Political Weekly*, 42 (13): 1089–94.

———. 2011a. 'Ruminating on Sociological Traditions in India', in S. Patel (ed.), *Doing Sociology in India: Genealogies, Locations, and Practices*, pp. xi–xxxviii. New Delhi: Oxford University Press.

———. 2011b. 'Sociology in India: Trajectories and Challenges', *Contributions to Indian Sociology*, 45 (3): 427–35.

———. 2013. 'Orientalist-Eurocentric Framing of Sociology in India: A Discussion on Three Twentieth-Century Sociologists', in J. Go (ed.) *Decentering Social Theory* (*Political Power and Social Theory: A Research Annual*, Vol. 25), pp. 105–28. Bingley, UK: Emerald Group.

Quijano, A. 2000. 'Coloniality of Power, Eurocentrism, and Latin America', *Nepantla: Views from South*, 1 (3): 533–80.

Saberwal, S. 1983. 'For a Sociology of India. Uncertain Transplants: Anthropology and Sociology in India', *Contributions to Indian Sociology*, 17 (2): 301–15.

Sarkar, S. 1997. 'The Many Worlds of Indian History', in S. Sarkar, *Writing Social History*, pp. 1–49. New Delhi: Oxford University Press.

Wimmer, A. and N. G. Schiller. 2002. 'Methodological Nationalism and Beyond: Nation Building, Migration and Social Sciences', *Global Network*, 2 (4): 301–24.

SECTION ONE

Debating the Sociology of 'Traditional' India

2 Confronting Disciplinary Practices

Rethinking the Sociology of Family, Marriage and Kinship

RAJNI PALRIWALA

The sociology of India, from its beginnings in anthropology, has taken four institutions for granted as constituting India as an object of analysis, a society and a nation. These institutions form a core of first papers on the Sociology of India across universities in India: kinship–marriage–family, caste–tribe, religion and village. It is crucial that we re-examine these institutions from contemporary perspectives, developments and processes. Crucial in shaping the contemporary have been the paradoxical experiences of India as a nation state—a colonial past that remains present, economic development but increasing unevenness, an expanding middle class and growing inequalities, centralisation of governance with greater demands for autonomy, political movements for social justice and the denial of the right to politics, women's movements for equality and emancipation contested by concerted affirmations of patriarchal traditions and violence against women, demands by youth to make their own life choices but louder attempts to control and deny them, diversity and homogenising assertions, and a deepening neoliberal globalisation with identity movements, increasing militarisation and new and old violences between communities and by the state. The many socialities and cultures that make this object of study have to be retrieved in any sociology of contemporary India. The insistence of a contemporary perspective, however, cannot be only to diversify our empirical contexts and questions but to ask whether our frameworks enable us to ask the questions that need to be asked and to address these questions.

Thus, our questions, as sociologists, may be how and why do gender, class and caste inequalities persist? Why do we, even sociologists, hold on to our caste identities and assert our religious beliefs in our marriage practices and as the primary features that make us human; try and practice the dominant norms of gendered behaviour and age; assert our middle-classness and insist on hierarchical acknowledgements by those not as fortunate as us? What has a rethinking of kinship and marriage and family to do with this?[1] It is with these concerns that I question whether existing perspectives enable an understanding of 'social problems' being witnessed today. Is new research a mere accumulation of empirical knowledge, an outcome of 'new' practices and social dynamics, and/or is it emerging from and leading to conceptual and theoretical shifts to that critical edge that our discipline must claim?

This chapter can cover only the periphery of these concerns, focusing on how our sociological scholarship has or can help address them or obstruct us. In doing so, it will touch on aspects of a very rich sociological tradition in the domain of marriage–kinship–family, through critiques that have had greater or lesser impact. These include the acknowledgement of the significance of gender, of a shift from norms to practice in understanding social life and of the diversity of cultures and complexities of meaning and practice that make and are made in the materialities of everyday life. These shifts not only affect the study of marriage–kinship–family but also are central to understanding persistent and fluid inequalities mentioned earlier. The focus of the chapter, however, is on the hows of the former more than the latter. All this entails questions of method and methodology, particularly in the study of change. Through this, the chapter traces the directions that we have and may take if sociology in India and elsewhere is to be capable of moving beyond its own present limits and enable us to understand contemporary social life. It develops on well-enunciated critiques that abjure the idea of family–kinship–marriage as a basic, given and necessarily privileged institution. It turns to the idea of relationship and relationality as the basic social and sociological unit and, thence, of family–kinship–marriage as a field always in the making, socially and sociologically, a simultaneously powerful and fragile, desired and oppressive, continuing and changing cluster of intersecting relationships.

Questioning the Axiomatics of Family and Kinship Sociology

As already indicated, family–kinship–marriage studies in India were central to the development of sociology in India, which was made through its interface with social anthropology. In this disciplinary history, a striking tendency was that anthropologists studied kinship and marriage and sociologists the family. This could have much to do with anthropologists finding that in the societies and cultures they were studying, intimate relations were not limited to or in keeping with the norms and assumptions about the family unit in the societies from which they originated. Sociologists, on the other hand, were studying their own societies. These two strands came together subsequently in important studies by anthropologists of their own societies (cf. Schneider 1968; Strathern 1992, 2005) and, thence, in a sociology of India. Over time, however, kinship and marriage moved out of focus, and family was made the institution of interest, often embedded in a framework of tradition and modernity and a concern with the 'joint' and 'nuclear' family. While the first Indian Council of Social Science Research (ICSSR) review of sociology had a volume on kinship by Leela Dube (1974), in the review of 40 years later—otherwise a magnificent three-volume effort edited by Yogendra Singh (2013)—kinship, marriage and family had disappeared. There was no chapter on kinship–marriage or family; apparently they were no longer matters of significant sociological study or interest!

The blame for the diminished scholarship on kinship (and family) in Euro-American academia was laid at the door of Schneider's 1984 critique (Stone 2001). In demolishing its biological premises and the ethnocentrism of the idea that 'blood is thicker than water', Schneider explicated how and why kinship had been central to the discipline, problematising three axioms that he saw cutting across social anthropology and sociology in the making of these disciplines. The first was that four institutions—economics, politics, religion and kinship—were basic and bounded systems, 'each of which is conceived to be a natural, universal, vital component of society' (Schneider 1984: 187), from among which 'kinship is the specially privileged of the privileged institutions' (ibid.: 188). The privileging of kinship rests on the second axiom that kinship is about human reproduction and relations between human beings deriving from sexual and biological processes. This leads to the third axiom that the relations so created have a special quality as they derive from pre-social and pre-cultural biological links. True, the sociologist/anthropologist studies the social and cultural facets of kinship, but its power is already given to them, by a natural biology. Schneider's critique was developed through a re-examination of his own earlier analyses of kinship. While he suggested that these axioms have cut across theoretical stances and epistemic shifts, it was also a call to move from functionalist and Eurocentric framings in the scholarship, which we see reified further in Parsonian sociology–of the natural, universal, division of society into four domains/institutions as modernity comes into being. According to Stone (2001), Schneider's refusal to assume a universal idea of kinship, leave aside one rooted in biological reproduction, left scholars with no object of study.

Yet, significant studies on kinship, such as Strathern (1992) and Carstens (1997), were written, which in their own ways addressed the concerns that Schneider had raised. Nor was Schneider's critique the causal factor in kinship, marriage and family studies receding in the Indian context. Parallel to that critique had been significant cultural analyses of the biological constructions of kinship and familial relations in India (cf. Das 1976; Khare 1975; Inden and Nicholas 1977), but as with Schneider's earlier work (1968) on American kinship, these writings did not explicitly question the biological and universalising axioms of the discipline. Most studies on the family proceeded as if the last was a non-issue. Instead, one could trace the growing absence of kinship–family studies to the growing denial of social anthropology in sociology departments and more so to the shadow cast over them by one problematic. This was the idea of *one* Indian family, the joint family, and the debates as to whether the joint family would persist or not in the face of modernity, its functionality for a developing nation (cf. Madan 1976). The implicit assumption (linked to the absence of the very critiques discussed in this chapter) seemed to be that all else that needed to be known about family–kinship–marriage in India was already known. Rarely was this problematic related to the very conceptualisation of the unit of the study. The family as a *basic institution* with the joint family as the Indian cultural form has remained central to sociological pedagogy across universities. Within this, the biological, normative and functional premises of scholarship on the family, kinship and marriage and the assumption of four bounded institutional domains have persisted. This is where radical rethinking is required.

Recognising Gender, Practice and Diversity

The growing invisibility of family–kinship–marriage studies may also have been despite or because of the questioning of the disciplinary tradition—both in India and in sociology and the social sciences more globally—from other vantage points. A pivotal critique pertained to the absence of gender as an analytical category, despite the deeply gendered nature of all arenas of social life, these in particular. That the experiences of the worlds of kinship and marriage were gendered was not unrecognised. It was seen as early as in Irawati Karve's magnum opus (1953) that mapped kinship patterns and organisation in India or later in Khare's 1975 analysis of male and female views of kinship/familial worlds and Das' 1976 analysis of Punjabi kinship. The gendered nature of the family was acknowledged widely but in a frame that essentialised culture and naturalised and normalised it rather than questioned it, despite Irawati Karve's brilliant reading of the Mahabharata in *Yuganta* (1968).[2]

The call for a unified analysis of gender and kinship (Yanagisako and Collier 1987; Rubin 1975) and the wide-ranging feminist troubling of kinship studies have perhaps had the most profound effects—both in terms of shaking the foundations of much of kinship and family studies but also in reviving them globally.[3] Undoubtedly, there was also significant work on gender and kinship in India in the last decades of the twentieth century, the arguments of which are touched upon at various points in this chapter and which are critical in pointing to new directions in kinship studies.[4] However, this also led many in India to decide that the domain of family and kinship was to be left to 'gender' scholars to do, if at all. After all, gender meant women and the family was women's sphere!

A second critique, again both theoretical and substantive but unfortunately less pervasive across the discipline, has been that analyses of kinship, marriage and family have been based on stated rules and values, that too of upper and middle castes and classes, such that the latter continued to provide the grid for understanding this domain of social relations. This has carried a double distortion. One is the presentation of normative models to the exclusion of an analysis of kinship practice—elaborately critiqued by Bourdieu (1977) in his theory of practice. This obscured the 'conflict between ideal model and everyday experiences' (Morgan 1970: 143) that a range of scholars writing on family for undergraduates had highlighted. It hid the messiness of the everyday, which, with observations on the exercise of agency, was taken as evidence of deviancy and change rather than a constant of social life. It reified homogenising, hegemonic and structuralist models, obscuring diversity and the making of inequalities. Thus, the ideal value of the 'joint family' in the Brahminical law books was misread to conclude that most people lived in joint households in the past and that there was a decline in contemporary times when people failed to live by norms as they had in the past.[5] Gendered, domestic violence was advocated in dominant social norms, especially to keep wives in order, but the assumption that people lived according to ideal norms led to pronouncements that deviance and thence domestic violence were marginal. The ubiquity of violence in patrilineal and patriarchal familial settings and its significance in enforcing familial power relations were obscured. Durkheim's argument that the socially pathological is not sociologically pathological was insufficient in this regard as it could just be noted that there was a 'normal'—read necessary—rate of violence. It was women's movements and feminist critiques of the 'anti-social family' (Barrett and McIntosh 1982) that drew attention to the everyday inequities within familial life both in accordance with and contrary to normative rules and values, a theme Karve presented but did not seem to be able to look beyond in her telling of the Mahabharata.

The second distortion that this methodological and theoretical framework resulted in takes us to another critical vantage point, which has received more attention in other sociological fields. Consequent to taking values and rules of Hindu upper castes to be descriptive of practice was the elision over practices, preferences and rules of groups beyond them, be they Dalits, non-Brahmins, non-Hindu religious groups or regions wherein upper-caste Hindus are not the mirror in which people search for themselves.[6] This is not to say that the study of kinship–marriage–family practices of communities other than Brahmins and other Hindu upper castes were not undertaken; they were even viewed as necessary to understand the central structures of Indian society and not only the margins. This was as early as in the work of Dumont (1957) on the Pramalai Kallar or Gough's (1959) comparison of Brahmin and non-Brahmin marriage. Gough's analysis was in the nature of a disaggregation and synthesis, looking at different communities to understand each. Dumont argued that there was a structured pattern in the simultaneous variations in descent, residence, marriage and caste hierarchy and that this was important in understanding the practices of all the castes discussed. He suggested that sub-castes could emerge from marriages that were secondary or not strictly according to the rules. His discussion hinted at the co-constitution of caste and marriage. However, the Indological and Brahminical framing of his theorisation of caste (1970) meant that caste could continue to be viewed as primarily an ideational structure, its dominance meaning that marriage and family strategies were ways to fit into it. It did not contest sociological ideas that took the values and norms of the upper caste as the ideal model of living for other groups. The co-constitution of kinship, marriage and caste was not pursued in sociology in India till much later and then through examining endogamy and exogamy.[7] Ambedkar's more direct argument regarding the co-constitution of Brahminism, endogamy and oppressive gender relations and the continuing dependence of the caste system on endogamous marriage and the control of women (Palriwala 2016; Rege 2013) was barely acknowledged. This silencing had much to do with disciplinary conceit as also with his simultaneous critique of Brahminism as a religious and caste system (Ambedkar 2014 [1916], 2014 [1944]).

The disquiet with the overarching shaping of family and kinship studies through upper-caste normative ideals is in part about social and cultural diversity and plurality—of differences and commonalities between and within castes, religions, regions and classes. The response, at times, was simply to assume that non-Brahminic practice was that which was denied by dominant Brahminic ideals and that a strategy to claim status was through practices assumed as Brahminic. Analysing and understanding diversity is, of course, first an issue of recognition and disaggregation—of values, rules and practices among religious minorities, 'peripheral regions', dominated castes and the working poor. Documenting diversities is a crucial step in reconfiguring the meanings and practices of social, cultural, political and economic life in general and not just of kinship, marriage and family. Yet, even studies that did not collapse diversity into 'deviancy', as in studies of widow remarriage (Kolenda 1992 [1982] Chowdhry 1994), while noting female agency, tended to stop with the mapping of community rules and ideals of kinship, marriage and family, noting implicitly or explicitly the differences from dominant norms and other communities. Given the dominant discourse within the discipline and beyond, the idea of marginal practices could prevail or they were so read, as with the collection on life at the margins of Hindu marriage edited by Harlan and Courtright (1995), Dube's 1997 comparative work or Kapadia's (1993) regendering of the ego of kinship studies. Their ideas were not pursued to rethink the dominant sociological theory and practice.

The problematic emerges more clearly when we look at studies of women and of gender. While disaggregation of data on male and female characteristics has become a regular feature in many studies, these do not provide an analysis of women's lives, leave aside a gender analysis. After the disaggregated data is presented, perhaps in a table, articles continue as if this disaggregation is of no great import unless women are the focus of the study. If the latter is the case, studies have proceeded as if what men do and possess have no bearing on women and vice versa and on understanding gender—gendered kinship is natural! There are too many such studies to be able to list them, and the same holds true when we look at the manner in which non-upper-caste Hindus enter the sociology of family and kinship. The disaggregation of caste or class data or an elaboration of non-elite community practices may have little bearing on the subsequent analysis. Reconfigurations of the meaning and elaboration of kinship, marriage or family are not undertaken, determined as present knowledge is by studies of the normative ideals of socially dominant groups or reified disciplinary frameworks. The direction that the discipline needs is not only of centring male–female or caste and class divisions in the worlds of kinship or even of thinking of multiple sexualities but also of thinking of how community, gender, sexuality, family and kinship–marriage, on the one hand, and caste, class and other inequalities, on the other, construct each other, co-constitute each other. As many writers have suggested, 'Neither gender, kinship, marriage, nor sex can be demonstrated to be a prior term logically, temporally, or sociologically' (Borneman 1996: 222; cf. also Butler 2002). Cross-cultural studies show clearly that marriage, kinship, sex, gender norms and gender relations and the experience of family vary greatly across and within cultures and social formations.

Dominant representations as well as frameworks insensitive to the aforementioned dimensions or to inequalities and power relations may hide more than they explain. Their continuing shadow is also tied to a question of method. What research techniques would enable understandings of contemporary kinship–family? Everyday practice, diversity and contradictory behaviours are often evaded in normative statements of ideals, values and rules, especially when pertaining to the intimate. Interview and questionnaire research can only partially elicit the responses that enable the analysis to go beyond the surface and the normatively correct. That the last does influence practice cannot be denied but intensive ethnographic fieldwork a la social anthropology is required to capture meanings and practices in the everyday that are not readily spoken of, because they are not in keeping with the approved. Unfortunately, such intensive fieldwork, requiring the sociologist to move out of her/his comfort zone—physically, socially, mentally—is shrinking rather than increasing despite the huge growth in the profession in contemporary times. One-off conversations and interviews, especially with questionnaires that ask for answers that are to be directly tabulated, have become the methodological orientation. This orientation is not conducive to the rich and complex detail necessary to study kinship–marriage and family relations in all their messiness. These are arenas of intimate relations, worries and joys as well as of the making of social and cultural status in most societies, leading to the reiteration of (hierarchised) norms in formal conversations. An understanding of the conflicts within and between models and everyday practices, group and individual strategies, diversity and variation requires intensive ethnographic data collection, which becomes more evident as we turn to a fourth critique pertaining to the problematic of change.

Studying Change

Elaborating on a confusion that is embedded in the Indological orientation and in current sociological practices brings us directly to the problematics of studying the contemporary. Comparing normative values as educed in Indological studies with current practice or politically correct statements may be interpreted as transformation or as signs of deviancy when neither is the case. Let us take the case of endogamy. There has been a long and denied history of both flexibility in and violation of marriage norms and rules that have been 'normalised'. Dumont's study of the Pramalai Kallar, referred to earlier, pointed to the formation of sub-castes following secondary marriages across caste lines. Chowdhry (1994) explicated both the practice of remarriage by widows of non-Brahmin castes in Haryana and their refusal of remarriage to the point of being perceived as 'unchaste'. Abraham (2014) points to shifts over time and context in the prescribed circle of endogamy as well as in the modes and violence of the enforcement of endogamy. Observations on the practice and advocacy of marriages across sub-castes and across regions (that can obscure caste-crossings) have led to arguments that caste endogamy is weakening. However, these studies or observations do not show that the ideology of endogamy or hypergamy, including lay arguments of their importance for a happy family life, is seriously threatened. Along with the long-standing process of sub-caste formation and shifts in the boundaries between castes, we find old and newly emergent ways of making, practising, obscuring and upholding caste boundaries in marriage strategies.

In a similar manner, a conclusion drawn from the sheer visibility of self-choice or 'love marriage' and the documentation of 'honour' killings is that arranged marriage and the strength of caste, final truths in earlier writings, have been fundamentally shaken. Yet, even apparently cosmopolitan youth opt for arranged, intra-caste marriages. True, many (possibly more than in the past) young women and men 'enjoy' a free, transgressive life for a period, before they settle into their properly arranged conjugal families and domesticity.[8] One could argue that Indian youth are less fooled by stories and ideologies of everlasting marital romance! Simultaneously, perhaps more than women, young men wish to enforce caste endogamy, and in areas where the sex ratio is particularly adverse, their difficulties in ensuring marriage is a factor in their holding on to caste. It goes beyond this. Upper-caste men have attacked sisters and lineage kin for inter-caste and inter-religious marriages in north India, while in the south, young educated men of the middle castes organised a 'Campaign Against Inter-Caste Marriage Movement' in the Kongu region of Tamil Nadu, directed against marriages and relations between their female kin and Dalit boys. Undoubtedly, 'honour' killings are a weapon of caste and kinship patriarchs to reassert their power and control, perhaps necessitated more now than in the recent past, but probably caste rules and power could never have been taken for granted. Marriage rules, status, masculinity practices and the caste system continue to sustain each other.

These brief examples show that delineating and understanding processes and recognising directions of continuity and change in family, marriage and kinship—'fixing' the contemporary—is not simple, not least when the diversity of norms and practices and persisting inequalities are also factored in (Kaur and Palriwala 2013). This is evident in other dimensions of this social domain. It can be shown that across the apparent shifts, the conjugal contract remains embedded in an earlier gender contract, with some slight modifications in some social groups and strata. Marriage and domesticity continue to be framed in and shape unequal gendering, despite the small shifts induced through female agency with a rising age at marriage and education and with a political and cultural economy of a new middle class and new hopes, growing inequality, poverty and the desperate search for and loss of livelihood among households and men. New/old processes, such as sex selection, the domestic division of labour and women's unpaid work, domestic violence and inheritance practices, all point to the complexity with which norms and practices shape each other and maintain a structure not very different from what has supposedly changed—a women unfriendly and status-seeking family. An issue that I will turn to comes into relief—the family in India is a cluster of relations that rests on women accepting the patriarchal contract in which their primary responsibility is to be good daughters, wives and mothers. The naturalisation of the gender contract in family and marriage and the preservation of the idea of the traditional family are lynchpins in a social structure and a cultural–ideational system that rests on class, gender, caste and political inequalities. The continuing naturalisation of family and the assumption of its biological basis in sociology play no small part in this.

Two analytical pathways may be drawn out. As elaborated earlier, too often, change is assumed by placing glimpses of present practice next to an 'ought to be' of the past—the normative model—not even against the troubles of familial and kinship life that we find in mythology. Shah (1973) had pointed out that the study of change in the family requires a historicity that moves the analysis from such 'ought to be' to practice and process. The study of 'what is' requires a separation of 'what ought to be' and 'what is' (Giddens 2009: 335), though it may threaten the dearest-held values. Feminist anthropologists and sociologists have long argued that family is essentially a conceptual and ideological construct, significant in people's lives and in motivating them towards family, not least because it masks the realities of inequalities and oppressions and the variety of experiences within family–households (Rapp et al. 1979; Barrett and McIntosh 1982). This directs us to the second path compatible with the first—a rethinking of marriage, kinship and family that moves our analysis from institutional form and rule to relationship and relatedness, both institutionalised and fluid. It is to this that I now turn.

Moving from the Normative Family to Social Relationships

The starting remark made in the first chapter in a thesis, article, lecture or chapter on family, marriage or kinship in India is often that the family is the basic unit of society. Perhaps made unthinkingly, it suggests a naturalisation and ideological construct of a sociological problematic. It surprises me when I find this statement continues to be made by sociologists or anthropologists of our times, despite our studies and everyday experiences that who or what we speak of as family and the relations that we encompass in it are constantly expanding, diversifying and contracting, in an apparently random fashion with the idiosyncrasies of individual lives, *but also in a patterned manner.* The diversity of 'family' forms, relations and ideas are becoming ever more evident, leaving us uncertain as to what the basic unit is, if that is what it is.

Is the idea of the family as the basic unit linked to the idea of biological reproduction, for which the normative and/or legally sanctioned family is in fact not required, as IVF shows?[9] Is it the idea of a clearly demarcated unit (like a brick), which the family is not, especially in South Asia with its layering of relationalities? Is it linked to the idea that we are not humans until socialised, though we may be socialised to be inhuman to our fellow citizens and even though socialisation studies suggest that the process is much more complex than what the neat division into primary (familial) and secondary socialisation assumes? Or is it essentially an ideological and political statement that enables the status quo, of which the ideological and political moorings should be studied rather than asserted?

It is good to recall not only feminist questionings but also Schneider's critique of the biological and ethnocentric fallacies of kinship theory, which imbue family studies too. The critique was a also a dismissal of the Parsonian four sub-systems and functionalist framework and of the biological family as a basic and universal institution. Levi-Strauss had earlier asserted (in a not unproblematic 1956 article) that there is no natural law that makes the family universal and that a non-dogmatic approach is necessary if the problem of the family is to be addressed. Morgan (1970) too warned against taking the normative ideal of the family as an actually existing institution; many undergraduate sociology textbooks have included such alerts. Why are such critiques and warnings skipped when family is introduced in teaching India or in thesis chapters? Morgan's explanation is pertinent—it reflects a difficulty of objectivity consequent to the sociologist's embeddedness in a social context that stresses family values. The methodological implication is that self-reflexivity among sociologists is a necessity in pushing the boundaries of understanding—a self-reflexivity regarding ideas of family but necessarily also of the privileges and normative rules of their caste, class and gender that tie into values of family.

Central to a rethinking of family–kinship–marriage is the recognition that the axiom 'family is the basic unit of society', meaning that family is *the basic* institution of society, is an ideological statement or a theological one but not a sociological statement. As a range of scholars have shown—feminist, Marxist and/or Foucauldian—the family enables a naturalisation of the hegemonic order. However, the persistence of the assertion that the family is the basic unit is not only because it is a political bulwark against uncontrolled change but also because family—as continuous, intense and normatively valued intergenerational relations and as officially sanctioned sexual and reproductive relations—has material and emotional meaning for people, a meaning that can define their lives productively or through depletion and limitation. The desire to speak of significant everyday relations of intimacy as family keeps appearing (Weston 1991), not least because of state and legal systems. In other words, we need to understand the material, emotional and political investment that make ideas and practices of marriage, kinship and family among the most guarded cluster of social relationships—or institution if it is so designated—brought out against chaos, multiplicity, change and critique.

Despite an oft-belied hope for security, the ideal family model is perhaps the most normalised of social arenas. It is a mask to much that happens in the everyday. Studies of intra-household discrimination and sex ratio, ageing and widows, child abuse, dowry, marital and domestic violence, assertions of intertwined caste and class power through family power and the denial of value and voice have all pointed to the fact that the great Indian family—and indeed the family across the globe—is not always or even often or for many the happy place it is supposed to be. Our analyses cannot start from a statement that makes widespread experiences, realities and structural consequences into marginal notes or natural and thence inevitable and necessary to accept. Perhaps the reason why earlier warnings regarding the gap between the ideal model and realities of family–kinship–marriage were not taken sufficiently into account was to do with the continuing acceptance of the axiom that the family is the basic institution and the first unit of analysis; the drive was to protect the family against deviant individuals and ideas or to expand its connotations, rather than go beyond it or bring its injuries to the fore. It has been a catch-all category for diverse and diverging ways of organising everyday life.

Strathern, in many insightful writings (e.g., 1992, 2005), has marked relations and relationality to lie at the heart of kinship and also social anthropology. If we are to rethink family, how people live and make and are made by kinship and marriage, it is important that we move from the concept of family to the concept of 'relationship' as the basic unit of sociology and society—whether the sexual relationship, the relationship between co-hunters and the animals they are hunting as food providers, and between the carer, biological parent or otherwise, and the child, those who share a home and hearth, parents, women transplanting paddy together, co-worshippers at a roadside shrine, the person being disallowed entry into a temple and those who claim the right to worship, the man and those against whom he is asserting control over land or forest, and those who make waste and those who are supposedly by birth and/or gender and in fact by economic and political control meant to remove their waste. These multiple relations are apparently interpersonal ties and interactions in separate and diverse domains of life, but they are more than that. They pertain to how sociality, intimacy, personhood and meaning are made and structured into institutions, in and through inequalities, dominations and solidarities—dimensions we need to take apart in our analyses.

Carstens (1997) has argued for an approach to kinship that does not assume that we know a priori what defines kinship or family in any and all societies. She posits a framework of relatedness and recognition of the significance of the dimension of temporality, where relationships accumulate or dissolve over time—the idea that relations are always in the making such that kinship (and family) is to be viewed as a process. Subsequently, in another attempt to escape the naturalising, biological and procreative premises of kinship concepts that Schneider critiqued (as outlined earlier), Sahlins put forward the idea of 'mutuality of being', in which the transmission of life capacities among persons and the meaning of participating in one another's life are central (2011: 13). These directions would move the analysis from the family as a natural and basic institution into which people need to fit to clusters of intimate relationships made by and making the participants in the bareness or fullness of their lives, shaping relations of procreation rather than being shaped by them, fluid and with institutional effect. Carstens also emphasised that the processual dimension was given insufficient attention in kinship (family) studies, but many who argued a similar framework, including Sahlins, continued to concentrate on the positive, warming aspects of family–kinship, passing lightly over the negative, chilling dimensions—the 'differentiation, hierarchy, exclusion, and abuse [that] are ... also part of what kinship does or enables' (2013: 246–47)—noted by feminist scholars as well as a range of anthropologists whom she cites (including Veena Das, Michael Peletz, and Michael Lambek). The diverse writings on gender and women in India have all drawn attention to these very dimensions of family, marriage and kinship.

If analyses of kinship–marriage and family are to be revitalised and move forward productively, rather than remain stuck in reiterations of past conclusions and the limitations of methodological nationalism (Patel 2016), sociologists have to acknowledge painful truths, however difficult and threatening of one's self-conception and extant sociological frames this acknowledgement may be, truths that sociology has not shirked from confronting. Family is not a basic, universal institution but a cluster of intersecting relationships, variously shaped and experienced and with diverse meanings, which are value and emotion laden and carry institutional force in their very fragility, not least in their imbrication in hegemonic structures and ideologies of oppression and inequality. What societies and communities see as family and kinship encompass intimate relationships of amity and enmity, sharing and caring, hierarchy and exclusion, livelihood and deprivation, of all together and variously over time. Despite its injuries and ephemeral security, people and especially women invest in relations named as family and kinship for they are most often their only path to resources, status and power in an unequal world.

With relationship rather than family as our entry point, we are immediately warned that we do not know what the institution of family is—we have to work to understand the relationships we call family in time and place and in conjunction with other institutions and processes. We cannot assume that family as we think it is or should be ever existed or exists. Importantly, it implies that it is not blood that makes family but what we name as family that makes blood (and bloodshed). This is also a recognition that kinship, marriage and family are not just about rules and structures but rest on emotion, interest, practice and the practical. As mentioned earlier, too often, dimensions of the emotional and the interpersonal relationship are mapped through ideal and reified claims made in responses to surveys, whether of conjugal love or parental/maternal love. Ethnographic studies, such as that of Trawick (1990), Abraham (2007) or recent theses by Bapna (2015) and Chaudhry (2016), show that the practice of emotion in marriage and family is not always nice and saccharine sweet, even as women strive to maintain these relationships. Meanings and desires of intimacy are complex and historically and culturally specific, to be known in part through the stuff of everyday life and relationships. These are not just interpersonal or idiosyncratic, but orientations, practices and negotiations framed by structures, community-endorsed values and collectivities; indeed, these are also shaped by formal rules and classifications as Hardenberg (2009) argues. We need to study the latter too.

It is important to reiterate the necessity to question which rules and whose rules were the focus and became the frame of analysis and the taken-for-granted if we are to move from the colonial construction of India as an object of study and a society and if we are to explicate the paradoxes of our postcolonial present. Critically, this entails a move out of culturalist arguments to integrate the materialities of political economy into the cultural economies through which intergenerational relations shape sexual and gendered constructions and practices of 'family', as with the adverse sex ratio, ideas of son preference and daughter aversion, and control of marriage by elders. Importantly, we have to constantly remind ourselves that the social and personal projects of family and kinship reproduce structural inequalities and oppressions and accept that extant family and kinship institutions may fall or stand with those inequalities and oppressions. Investment in the social, economic and social order or resistance to it calls on and demands investment in or resistance to the social and cultural order of family, marriage and kinship, including the violence and discriminations it rests on. It means that we rethink family as having always been shifting, produced and constraining, patterned and yet idiosyncratic, clusters of relations that people see as significant in their lives, in particular phases of their lives, and in cultural and historical specificities.

In conclusion, following Borneman, I point to empirical themes that remain understudied or underanalysed, not least because of the frameworks that have shaped the field and thence marred our analyses of marriage–kinship–family. Borneman argues that a world ideology of marriage giving the right to found a family, linking marriage to birth, life and freedom of choice, has occluded 'the connections of marriage [and I add family] to the assertion of privilege, to closure, death, abjection, and exclusion. . . . The non-married, siblingship, same-sex ties, friendships, divorce and widowhood are taken as supplementary rather than central to understanding kinship, family and social structure in general' (1996: 216, 222). It is important to warn ourselves that sociologists can add to the stigmatisation of the right to choice, widowhood, divorce and non-marriage if marriage and the family based on marriage and community continue to be taken as the natural social bases of society and of understanding society to even denying social processes and if we do not interrogate the ways in which privilege, order and hegemony are made through marriage and family.

Notes

1. These questions, unfortunately, are pertinent to experiences and observations at conferences of the Indian Sociological Society and other gatherings of sociologists. I wish to thank those who asked questions of my presentation and colleagues from Mumbai and Hyderabad, who sent me relevant course outlines and reading lists, which, along with discussions with colleagues at various universities, broadened my understanding of the teaching of family–kinship–marriage.
2. Irawati Karve's retelling of the Mahabharat foregrounds the women of the epic—Satyavati, Gandhari, Kunti, Draupadi—whether to the actions that were done to them or did not take them into account, their own actions and strivings, and their plaint against the feudal social order, an order made through kingship, lineage, patriarchy and caste. Her narrative analysis draws out the changing discourses and fortunes of kingship and kinship and points to later interpolations, even as her own normative ideas on correct behaviour enter. She reminds us that the structural and cultural context in which the women lived shaped their choices, hopes and desires, experiences, emotions and fears, such that though they were far from complaisant, they did not contest the structures of kingship, caste and 'women's duty' in which they were born. She also focuses on other persona, such as Vidura and Karna, who were positioned as marginal in the ethos of kingly caste and manly power, indicating the injustices against them and their actions and motives. Her love for and deep engagement with the epic as a literary work and social key (to understand ideas and practices of lineage, marriage, family and rule) and in which all characters are in shades of grey are striking.
3. Only a few of the influential writings on kinship–gender that emerged globally are cited here.
4. Among the many works that directly examined gender and kinship/family in the last decades of the twentieth century, especially if we take South Asia as our location rather than the Indian nation state, and which suggested critiques of extant kinship–family studies and engaged with some of the issues discussed later in this chapter are: Bennett (1983) on Nepal; Das (1975) on Hindu marriage; Dube's various comparative writings as well as her work on Lakshwadeep; Fruzetti (1990) on Bengali marriage; Jacobson (1977) on women's residential practices in north India; Jeffery (1979) on Muslims in Delhi; Jeffery and Jeffery (1996) on rural Uttar Pradesh; Kapadia (1993) on marriage and kinship among non-Brahmin castes in Tamil Nadu and the implications of considering the ego as female rather than male against the prevalent practice; Kolenda (1982) on widow remarriage among Dalits and on varied marriage rituals (1984); Levine

(1988) on polyandry in the Himalayas; Nongbri (1988) on property and family among the Khasis; Palriwala (1991, 1993) on residential practices and intra-household consumption and authority; U. Sharma's various studies (1980, 1986) on women's work and family in north India; Standing (1991) on Bengali middle class women and family; Singh and Uberoi (1994) and Uberoi (1998) on popular magazines and films; Sharma (1984) on dowry; and Vatuk (1975) on marriage prestations. Most of the studies from before the early 1990s are discussed in Palriwala (1994), which suggests that a larger range of very rich studies on gender and on kinship could be drawn on to rethink and understand the intertwining of kinship–family and gender. There were many writings on dowry, social reform (Uberoi 1996) and widow remarriage. Edited anthologies such as Palriwala and Dube (1990), Palriwala and Risseeuw (1996) and Risseeuw and Ganesh (1998) brought together many of the concerns regarding the gendering of kinship/family studies. After a plethora and then a distinct ebb, a whole range of writings have again emerged from across the social sciences that, starting from gender, focus on kinship, marriage and family, including the arranged/love marriage dynamic, post-marriage residence and wedding practices (Abraham 2013), popular culture (Uberoi 2009) and intra-familial relations and conjugality (Grover 2011; Chaudhry 2016).

5. See Shah (1973) for an early contestation of this view.
6. Studies of 'tribal' groups in different parts of the subcontinent have had a long, albeit uneven, history, including those of family–marriage–kinship among such groups. These studies tended to put 'tribal' groups in a separate compartment and/or viewed them through an upper-caste Hindu lens as the 'other' rather than stimulating a rethink of the conceptualisation of this domain.
7. See Abraham (2014).
8. Akanksha Awal (2019) speaks of the idea of 'enjoying' as a life phase among young, urban, college-going women.
9. But which the new surrogacy law in India reasserts.

References

Abraham, J. 2007. 'Gender, Status and Class: A Sociological Study of the Thiyyas', doctoral thesis, Department of Sociology, University of Delhi.

———. 2013. '"Why Did You Send Me Like This?" Marriage, Matriliny and the "Providing Husband" in North Kerala, India', in R. Kaur and R. Palriwala (eds), *Marrying in South Asia: Shifting Concepts, Changing Practices in a Globalised World*, pp. 293–310. Delhi: Orient Blackswan.

Abraham, J. 2014. 'Contingent Caste Endogamy and Patriarchy', *Economic and Political Weekly*, XLIX (2): 56–65.

Ambedkar, B. R. 2014 [1916]. 'Castes in India: Their Mechanism, Genesis and Development', in *Writings and Speeches*, Vol. I, pp. 3–22. Delhi: Dr. Ambedkar Foundation, Government of India.

———. 2014 [1944]. 'The Annihilation of Caste', in *Writings and Speeches*, Vol. I, pp. 23–96. Delhi: Dr. Ambedkar Foundation, Government of India.

Awal, A. 2019. 'Ghaziabad's Daughters: Educated Subjectivity and Social Haunting in North India', doctoral thesis, School of Anthropology and Museum Ethnography, University of Oxford.

Bapna, G. 2015. 'Contemporary Meanings of Marriage', doctoral thesis, Department of Sociology, University of Delhi.

Barrett, M. and M. McIntosh. 1982. *The Anti-social Family*. London: Verso Press.

Bennett, L. 1983. *Dangerous Wives and Sacred Sisters: Social and Symbolic Roles of High-Caste Women in Nepal*. New York: Columbia University Press.

Borneman, J. 1996. 'Until Death Do Us Part: Marriage/Death in Anthropological Discourse', *American Ethnologist*, 23 (2): 215–35.

Bourdieu, P. 1977. *Outline of a Theory of Practice*. Cambridge: Cambridge University Press.

Butler, J. 2002. 'Is Kinship Always Already Heterosexual?' *Differences: A Journal of Feminist Cultural Studies*, 13 (1): 14–44.

Carstens, Janet. 1997. *The Heat of the Hearth: The Process of Kinship in a Malay Fishing Community*. Oxford: Clarendon Press.

———. 2013. 'What Kinship Does—and How', Comment on Sahlins, Marshall. 2011. *What Kinship Is—and Is Not, HAU: Journal of Ethnographic Theory*, 3 (2): 245–51.

Chaudhry, S. 2016. 'Lived Experiences of Marriage: Regional and Cross-Regional Brides in Rural North India', doctoral thesis, University of Edinburgh.

Chowdhry, P. 1994. *The Veiled Women: Shifting Gender Equations in Rural Haryana*. Delhi: Oxford University Press.

Das, V. 1975. 'Marriage among the Hindus', in D. Jain (ed.), *Indian Women*, pp. 71–86. New Delhi: Publications Division, Government of India

———. 1976. 'Masks and Faces: An Essay on Punjabi Kinship', *Contributions to Indian Sociology*, 10 (1): 1–30.

Dube, L. 1974. *Sociology of Kinship: An Analytical Survey of the Literature*. Bombay: Popular Prakashan.

———. 1997. *Women and Kinship: Comparative Perspectives on Gender in South and South-East Asia*. Tokyo: United University Press and New Delhi: Vistaar.

Dumont, Louis. 1957. 'Hierarchy and Marriage Alliance in South Indian Kinship'. Occasional Papers of the Royal Anthropological Institute of Great Britain and Ireland 12, Royal Anthropological Institute, London.

———. 1970. *Homo Hierarchicus: The Caste System and Its Implications*. Chicago: University of Chicago Press.

Fruzetti, L. M. 1990. *The Gift of the Virgin: Women, Marriage and Ritual in a Bengali Society*. Delhi: Oxford University Press.

Giddens, A. (revised and updated with P.W. Sutton). 2009. *Sociology* (Sixth Edition). Cambridge: Polity Press.

Gough, K. 1959. 'Brahmin Kinship in a Tamil Village', *American Anthropologist*, 8 (5): 826–53.

Grover, S. 2011. *Marriage, Love, Caste, and Kinship Support: Lived Experiences of the Urban Poor in India*. Delhi: Social Science Press.

Hardenberg, R. 2009. 'Categories of Relatedness: Rituals as a Form of Classification in a Central Indian Society', *Contributions to Indian Sociology* (n.s.), 43 (1): 61–87.

Harlan, L. and P. Courtright (eds). 1995. *From the Margins of Hindu Marriage: Essays on Gender, Religion and Culture*. New York: Oxford University Press.

Inden, R. B. and R. W. Nicholas. 1977. *Kinship in Bengali Culture*. Chicago: University of Chicago Press.

Jacobson, D. 1977. 'Flexibility in Central Indian Kinship and Residence', in K. David (ed.), *New Wind: Changing Identities in South Asia*, pp. 263–83. The Hague: Mouton and Co.

Jeffery, P. 1979. *Frogs in a Well: Indian Women in Purdah*. London: Zed Press.

Jeffery, P. and R. Jeffery. 1996. *Don't Marry Me to a Plowman! Women's Everyday Lives in Rural North India*. Colarado: Westview Press.

Kapadia, K. 1993. 'Marrying Money: Changing Preference and Practice in Tamil Marriage', *Contributions to Indian Sociology* (n.s.), 27 (1): 25–51.

Karve, I. 1953. *Kinship Organization in India*. New York: Asia Publishing House.

———. 1968. *Yuganta: End of an Epoch*. Hyderabad: Orient Longman.

Kaur, R. and R. Palriwala (eds). 2013. *Marrying in South Asia: Shifting Concepts, Changing Practices in a Globalised World*. Delhi: Orient Blackswan.

Khare, R. S. 1975. '"Embedded" Affinity and Consanguineal "Ethos"': Two Properties of the Northern Kinship System', *Contributions to Indian Sociology* (n.s.), 9 (2): 245–61.

Kolenda, P. 1992 [1982]. 'Widowhood among "Untouchable" Chuhras', in A. Ostor, L. M. Fruzetti and S. Barnett (eds), *Concepts of Person: Kinship, Caste, and Marriage in India*, pp. 263–83. Delhi: Oxford University Press.

Kolenda, P. 1984. 'Woman as Tribute, Woman as Flower: Images of "Woman" in Weddings in North and South India', *American Ethnologist*, 11 (1): 98–117.

Levine, N. E. 1988. *The Dynamics of Polyandry: Kinship, Domesticity and Population on the Tibetan Border*. Chicago: University of Chicago Press.

Levi-Strauss, C. 1956. 'The Family', in H. L. Shapiro (ed.), *Man, Culture, and Society*, pp. 261–85. New York: Oxford University Press.

Madan, T. N. 1976. 'The Hindu Family and Development', *Journal of Social and Economic Studies*, 4 (2): 211–31.

Morgan, D. H. J. 1970. 'The Family', in P. Worsley, R. Fitzhenry, J. Clyde Mitchell, D. H. J. Morgan, V. Pons, B. Roberts, W. W. Sharrock and R. Ward, *Introducing Sociology*, pp. 115–51. Harmondsworth: Penguin Books.

Nongbri, T. 1988. 'Gender and the Khasi Family Structure: Some Implications of the Meghalaya Succession to Self-Acquired Property Act, 1984', *Sociological Bulletin*, 37 (1&2): 71–82.

Palriwala, R. 1991. 'Transitory Residence and Invisible Work: A Case Study of a Rajasthan Village', *Economic and Political Weekly*, 26 (48): 2763–77.

———. 1993. 'Economics and Patriliny: Consumption and Authority in the Household—A Rajasthan Case-Study', *Social Scientist*, 21 (9–11): 47–73.

———. 1994. *Changing Kinship, Family, and Gender Relations in South Asia: Processes, Trends and Issues*. Leiden: Women and Autonomy Centre, University of Leiden.

———. 2016. 'Understanding Dr Babasaheb Ambedkar's Writings on Caste and Gender', *Women's Equality*, April–September: 2–6.

Palriwala, R. and L. Dube (eds). 1990. *Structures and Strategies: Women, Work and Family in Asia*. New Delhi: Sage Publications.

Palriwala, R. and C. I. Risseeuw (eds). 1996. *Shifting Circles of Support: Contextualising Kinship and Gender Relations in South Asia and Sub-Saharan Africa*. Delhi: Sage Publications.

Patel, S. 2016. 'The Challenge of Doing Sociology Today', *Economic and Political Weekly*, LI (46): 33–40.

Rapp, R. R., E. Ross and R. Bridenthal. 1979. 'Examining Family History', *Feminist Studies*, 5 (1): 174–200.

Rege, S. 2013. *Against the Madness of Manu*. New Delhi: Navayana

Risseeuw, C. I. and K. Ganesh (eds). 1998. *Negotiation and Social Space: A Gendered Analysis of Changing Kin and Security Networks in South Asia and Sub-Saharan Africa*. New Delhi: Sage Publications.

Rubin, G. 1975. 'The Traffic in Women: Notes on the Political Economy of Sex', in R. R. Reiter (ed.), *Toward an Anthropology of Women*, pp. 157–210. New York: Monthly Review Press.

Sahlins, M. 2011. 'What Kinship Is' (Parts one and two), *Journal of the Royal Anthropological Institute* (n.s.), 17: 2–19 and 227–42.

Schneider, David M. 1968. *American Kinship: A Cultural Account*. Englewoods Cliffs, N.J.: Prentice-Hall.

———. 1984. *A Critique of the Study of Kinship*. Ann Arbor: University of Michigan Press.

Shah, A. M. (1973) 1974. *The Household Dimension of the Family in India: A Field Study in a Gujarat Village and a Review of Other Studies*. Berkeley and London: University of California Press.

Sharma, U. 1980. *Women, Work and Property in North-West India*. London and New York: Tavistock.

———. 1984. 'Dowry in North India: Its Consequences for Women', in R. Hirschon (ed.), *Women and Property—Women as Property*, pp. 62–74. London and Canberra: Croom Helm; New York: St. Martin's Press.

———. 1986. *Women's Work, Class, and the Urban Household: A Study of Simla, North India*. London: Tavistock Publications.

Singh, A. T. and P. Uberoi. 1994. 'Learning to "Adjust": Conjugal Relations in Indian Popular Fiction', *Indian Journal of Gender Studies*, 1 (1): 93–120.

Singh, Y. 2013. *ICSSR Research Surveys and Explorations: Indian Sociology*, Vols 1–3. Delhi: Oxford University Press.

Standing, H. 1991. *Dependence and Autonomy: Women's Employment and the Family in Calcutta*. London: Routledge.

Stone, L. (ed.). 2001. *New Directions in Anthropological Kinship*. Boulder: Rowman and Littlefield Publishers.

Strathern, M. 1992. *After Nature: English Kinship in the Late Twentieth Century*. Cambridge: Cambridge University Press.

———. 2005. *Kinship, Law and the Unexpected: Relatives Are Always a Surprise*. Cambridge: Cambridge University Press.

Trawick, M. 1990. *Notes on Love in a Tamil Family*. Berkeley: University of California Press.

Uberoi, P. (ed.). 1996. *Social Reform, Sexuality, and the State*. New Delhi: Sage Publications.

———. 1998. 'The Diaspora Comes Home: Disciplining Desire in DDLJ', *Contributions to Indian Sociology* (n.s.), 32 (2): 305–36.

———. 2009. *Freedom and Destiny: Gender, Family, and Popular Culture in India*. New Delhi: Oxford University Press.

Vatuk, S. 1975. 'Gifts and Affines in North India', *Contributions to Indian Sociology* (n.s.), 9 (2): 155–96.

Weston, K. 1991. *Families We Choose: Lesbians, Gays, Kinship*. New York: Columbia University Press.

Yanagisako, J. and J. Collier. 1987. 'Towards a Unified Analysis of Gender and Kinship', in J. Collier and J. Yanagisako (eds), *Gender and Kinship: Essays towards a Unified Analysis*, pp. 14–50. Stanford: Stanford University Press.

3 Tribes in India

Why Exclusion Persists

VIRGINIUS XAXA

Conceptualising Tribes

The use of the term 'tribe' to describe certain types of societies had become well established in European writings by the nineteenth century. In these writings, the term was restricted to designate people considered as savage and barbarous. More popularly, the term came to be associated with the idea of primitiveness. This idea had been well ingrained in the use of the term by the time the British consolidated their rule in India. Yet, when the British began writing on Indian society and its people, they hardly introduced the idea of primitiveness in their descriptions of tribes, though it may have been implicit. This may have been mainly to do with the complexity of Indian society. The people of India in general could not be associated with the idea of primitiveness as they had had a long history of civilisation dating many centuries before Christ. At the root of this civilisation, there have been varied religious traditions, Hinduism being the most dominant one. The people of India have been primarily associated with these religious traditions and their social organisations. One of the important markers of social organisation has been the institution of caste. Though caste has been more discernible in Hinduism, the other religious traditions have not altogether been free from it, though they may have been relatively less rigid. These distinctive features of the region seem to have led the British away from focusing on the idea of primitiveness and instead looking for different elements in the delineation of tribes.

The British, however, did realise that not all the population under their rule was part of religious traditions and their social organisation. There was a population that was outside of these traditions. It is this segment of the population that the British delineated and classified as tribes at a later stage. However, even before the delineation took place, the British were aware of the differences of this segment of the population from the rest. This can be inferred from the nature of administration in vogue in tribal and non-tribal areas at the time. The two sets of population had, by and large, different administrative setups. Laws in force with respect to the general population were usually not applicable to groups called tribes. More often than not, special laws, that is, laws believed to be in consonance with the tribal system of administration, were framed for their governance. In colonial administrative parlance, the nature of such administration was described by terms such as non-regulation tracts, scheduled areas or excluded and partially excluded areas. The difference in administration was invariably linked to the conception of tribes as being different from non-tribes. However, this was conceived more in terms of ethnicity rather than tribe–caste.

To begin with, there was a lack of clarity in the conceptualisation of tribes. This was evident in the interchangeable use of the terms caste and tribe. In fact, the early writings of colonial administrator–ethnographers made no distinction between tribe and caste. Instead the two terms were used synonymously. Later, they were even used in a cognate manner as one can see in Risley's work (1903) on castes and tribes of India. The two were, in fact, seen as stages in the socio-economic and political evolution of communities in India. This shows that the colonial administrator–ethnographers were far from clear in their minds as to what the terms tribe and caste stood for. They had difficulty differentiating one from the other because they found considerable overlaps among these groups on the ground. Nowhere, has this been more obvious than the way in which the administrative-cum-census officials handled the two categories in the census reports of 1881. In the census, the term used was not tribe but forest tribe and that too as a subheading under the broader category of agricultural and pastoral castes, placing tribes thereby as parts of caste (Xaxa 1999). Since 1901, however, a somewhat clearer criterion began to evolve. Tribes were identified and described as those who practised animism, a term that was later substituted by the expression 'tribal religion'. The criterion so introduced was continued in the subsequent census enumeration, but other descriptions were added as well. Thus the 1921 census report referred to the hill and forest tribes, and in 1931, when Hutton was the census commissioner, tribes were also referred to as 'primitive tribes'. Through descriptive criteria such as these not only was differentiation being introduced among tribes but also geographical/ecological setting and stage of development were taken into consideration in making a distinction between tribes and non-tribes. These criteria were, however, never explicitly employed in delineating tribes in the census enumeration. What was explicitly employed was the criterion of religion, that is, tribes were those who did not adhere to existing established religions, Hinduism being the most dominant among them. If a group was shown to be Hindu in its belief and religious practices, it was identified as a caste. On the other hand, if a group practised animism, it was believed to be a tribe. This distinction was, however, not satisfactory because caste Hindus too had elements of animism in their religious practices. Since the list of tribes had been drawn with a view to give these groups certain political and administrative benefits, the application of suitable criteria to define tribes had to take a back seat. The list of Scheduled Tribes included in the schedule of the Constitution had its genesis in this list. It is obvious then that the list was drawn more on the basis of administrative and political expediency than well-thought-out criteria. With the listing of the schedule in the Constitution, a distinction has been drawn between tribes and Scheduled Tribes. And it is only the latter that are entitled to avail the benefits of state policies and programmes. The two categories overlap but are not necessarily coterminous. Following the distinction, there has been an increasing demand for Scheduled Tribe status, leading to a need for greater clarity on the conception of tribes. Accordingly, the Lokur Committee (1965) was constituted to look into the matter. The committee recommended five criteria for identification of tribes: (1) primitive traits, (2) distinct culture, (3) geographical isolation, (4) shyness of contact with the community at large and (5) backwardness (Lokur 1965).

Perspectives on Tribes

More than the question of conceptualisation, it was the situation of tribes that attracted greater attention on the tribal question in British India. The tribal question in colonial India was seen from two perspectives. These two perspectives were most evident in the debate between Verrier Elwin and G. S. Ghurye. The debate had its genesis in the publication of the book *The Aboriginals* (1943) by Elwin, which made certain suggestions regarding the approach to be adopted towards tribes. The issue at the centre of the debate was whether tribes should be kept in a state in which they had been living, viz., in isolation from the larger Indian society, or whether they should be drawn into the larger society and given the fruits enjoyed by this section of the society. Elwin was charged with advocating the policy of isolation. The charge, Elwin wrote later in his article in *Seminar* (1960), was a result of suggestions badly put forth by him and the unfortunate connotation of the expression 'national park' that was used by him. The suggestion, he said, was made in desperation as the Baigas, a tribal group he worked on, were deeply impacted socially, culturally and economically and had lost the zest for life at the time he wrote the book *The Baiga* in 1939. It was not so much about preserving their culture as keeping them alive and away from exploitation and oppression, the only 'development' that was occurring among them (Elwin 1943). As against this, Ghurye advocated the policy of assimilation. His view was that tribes were Hindus or, what he referred to as, backward Hindus. He thought of tribes as inferior and backward because they remained cut off from the large mass of the Indian population. He also identified them as standing at a stage lower in the evolutionary scale, in fact not very different from the large mass of the Indian population—in terms of the values and attitudes that marked their lives—at the eve of Independence. He considered it best that they be assimilated with the larger society in order to be lifted out of their abject poverty and 'base' lifestyle (Ghurye 1943). Clearly, this view placed tribals lowest on the tribe–caste–class continuum, a conceptual paradigm used to understand the processes of change in tribal life. For Ghurye, this continuum suggested a movement of tribals from tradition to modernity, from pantheism to a higher form of religion, from a base and crude way of life to a life morally and ethically superior (ibid.). Both Elwin and Ghurye later abandoned their early positions and espoused for a policy of integration.

The two perspectives on policy that Elwin and Ghurye articulated were part of a wider thinking prevalent in the colonial period. Elwin's line of thinking had an echo among the colonial administrators and Ghurye's among the nationalist leadership. These two lines of thinking, prevalent on the eve of Independence, found space in the Constituent Assembly debates and deliberations, shaping the overall approach towards tribes in post-Independence India. This is reflected in provisions enshrined for tribes in the Indian Constitution. The provisions, if one were to examine them carefully, move neither in the direction of isolation nor towards assimilation. They are aimed at protecting and safeguarding the distinct identity of tribes but at the same time address the problem of isolation with which tribal social backwardness has been associated. The recognition of tribes' distinct identity is reflected in provisions such as statutory recognition (Article 342); proportionate representation in the parliament and state legislatures (Articles 330 and 332); restriction on the right of non-tribals to move freely, settle or acquire property in tribal areas (Article 19[5]); conservation of tribal languages, dialects and cultures (Article 29) and, more importantly, in the somewhat special treatment of tribal administration. In administrative parlance, tribal areas are known as Fifth or Sixth Schedule areas (Articles 244 and 244[a]). Provisions of the Fifth and Sixth Schedules in the Constitution are in line with administrative practices in vogue during the colonial period

(Verma 1990). Isolation and social backwardness are addressed in the provision for reservation in general (Article 14[4]) and in jobs and appointments in particular (Article 16[4]). There is also the directive principle of the Constitution that requires the educational and economic interests of the weaker sections of society including tribes to be especially promoted (Article 46).

It is interesting to note that though there has been an overriding concern to address the tribal question in post-Independence India, there has been no formal enunciation of a tribal policy. What comes out as a tribal policy in pronouncements and writings is a statement of integration. Of course, if one were to look carefully into the kinds of provisions enshrined in the Constitution, these do point towards an approach of integration. Paradoxically, there has been no clear formulation of the statement of integration. Some form of explication could of course be discerned in the five principles that Nehru listed in his foreword to the book *A Philosophy for NEFA* (1959) by Elwin. In a sense, the five principles were a step towards the concretisation of the idea of integration inherent in the Constitution. However, these principles have been more rhetoric than reality. The five principles make a plea for respecting tribal rights in land and forest; the development of tribal people along the lines of their own genius and refraining from imposing anything on them; avoiding the entry of too many outsiders into tribal territory and building teams of tribal people for administrative and development work; avoiding over-administration in terms of introducing too many programmes and instead working through tribal social and cultural institutions; and judging results not by statistics and the amount of money spent but the quality of character produced (Nehru 1959).

The Location of Tribes in Indian Society

In post-Independence India, integration is thought as the panacea of all tribal problems. Whatever the problem, it is attributed to the lack of integration. The emphasis on integration lies in the prevailing and overriding conception of tribes. There was, of course, an alternative conception in the form of 'Adivasi', meaning original inhabitants. In fact, 'tribal' people in self-reference identified themselves more as adivasis than as tribes. However, it was the idea of tribe that dominated the thinking of colonial administrators and nationalists. The driving idea underlying the term was primitiveness or general backwardness to be more moderate. The idea was not only a political construction but also deeply social and cultural. Nationalist scholars and leaders attributed this conceptualisation to the isolation of tribal people from the so-called civilisation comprising advanced technology and the corresponding economic, political and social structure coupled with a distinct cultural ethos. The fact that the breaking of isolation had also led to exploitation and dispossession of tribal people from their land, forest and other resources, which Elwin had highlighted, was peripheral if not completely glossed over. It is the idea of primitiveness that has shaped the discourse on tribes in India.

It is worth noting that the process of integration/assimilation has been at work even before the interventionist policy of post-Independence India. In fact, much of the sociological thinking on tribes and their trajectory of change and development has been in the direction of tribes' absorption into the larger Indian society. In other words, the transformation of tribes is invariably located in the form of caste. Thus, the difference between tribes and the wider Indian society is recognised in sociological thinking. Tribes remain the 'other' of Indian society. However, the two have not been without interaction with each other, which then opens up the space for inclusion of the tribal population into the larger Indian society. Indeed, Kosambi (1975) refers to the growth and expansion of Indian society through the fusion of elements between tribes and what constituted then, if one may say so, the larger Indian society. Bose (1941) draws attention to the process of how tribes were attracted to the larger Indian society by drawing themselves into the social organisation of its production system, which invariably provided protection and security. This was how, according to him, tribes got absorbed into the larger Indian society. He called it 'the Hindu method of tribal absorption'. Sinha (1962,

1987), too, points to the process of sanskritisation and Hinduisation, but, for him, these take place invariably within the framework of state formation. Following these seminal publications on the transformation of tribes, a plethora of publications came up, which drew on Srinivas' concept of sanskritisation. Srinivas (1977) talks of the process of sanskritisation by which castes lower down the hierarchy emulate the lifestyle of castes above them. Although sanskritisation has been mainly used to understand the process of social mobility within the caste hierarchy, it has been extended to understand the process of transformation even in the context of tribal society (Xaxa 1999).

Now, in this understanding of Indian society and its social transformation, tribes as entities with a distinct language, culture, custom, tradition and, above all, social organisation are invariably recognised as outside of the larger Indian society. And yet they are in interaction with this wider society. This interaction has been differently conceptualised by different scholars. Sinha, for example, has viewed tribes as a dimension of little tradition that cannot be adequately understood unless it is seen in relation to great tradition (Sinha 1958). As against this, Béteille sees tribes as remaining outside the state and civilisation (Béteille 1986). But even when tribes have been living outside the state and civilisation, they have not been outside the influence of civilisation. By virtue of this location, they have stood at the lowest end in the hierarchical structure of Indian society. They have been treated as savages and beasts. They could overcome this status only by absorption into the larger Indian society. In other words, tribes had no other option of change and mobility but through absorption into the larger Indian society.

The Nature of Inclusion under the British

With the advent of British rule, there was an incorporation of tribes into the colonial state structure through war, conquest and annexation. This was followed by the introduction of new and uniform civil and criminal laws as well as establishing an administrative structure that was alien to tribal tradition and ethos. Like in many other parts of India, the British imposed upon tribes the notion of private property and landlordism in place of lineage- or community-based ownership. Revenue collectors/administrative officials were converted into owners and landlords, which they were not. All these developments led to the large-scale eviction of tribes from their land and the installation of non-tribes in their place. In places where tribes still had control over land, massive transfers of land took place from tribes to non-tribes through measures such as fraud, deceit and mortgage. Since tribes had no practice of record-keeping and did not have the knowledge of reading and writing, non-tribes took advantage of this by forging evidence and documents in their favour. The local administration, which was manned by non-tribes, worked hand in hand with their ethnic kin to ensure the smooth transfer of land from tribes to non-tribes. The court language was alien to tribes, and they had absolutely no idea of what was going in the court. Moreover, the colonial state took over the rights to the forest, thereby denying tribes the right to collect fuel and other daily necessities of life for which they were heavily dependent on forests (Singh 2002; Bosu Mullick 1993). Such processes at work continued all through the colonial period in different scales, causing havoc in tribal society. Tribes lost autonomy over their control over land and forest. They lost autonomy over the way they governed and regulated themselves as a society. The response of tribes to this loss of self-rule or *swaraj* invariably took the form of armed struggle. In fact, in almost every tribal territory, the entry of colonial rule met with stiff resistance. The early encounters of the British with groups/communities that later came to be described as tribes was characterised by revolts and rebellions all through the late eighteenth and nineteenth centuries (Raghavaiah 1979; Bosu Mullick 1993).

The British rule thus brought tribes and non-tribes under one single political and administrative authority. With some exceptions here and there, they were subjected to the same laws, rules, regulations and administrations. The same was the case in the economic sphere. Through land, labour, credit and commodity markets, tribes and non-tribes were all brought under a single economic order. Tribes thus came to be part of the same political and economic system that the larger Indian society was part of. However, the position tribes came to occupy in the new politico-administrative system was one characterised by a steady erosion of their control over and access to land, forests and other resources. Both the colonial administration and the non-tribal population, especially traders, merchants and moneylenders, were responsible for this. Tribes thus underwent a process of twin colonisation—one by the British rule and administration and the other by the non-tribal population. Tribes that had control over land, forest and other resources and enjoyed the autonomy of governance got pushed to the margins of the new political and economic system. Thus the process of integration/inclusion of tribes into the larger system under colonial rule came to be intertwined with the process of exclusion in the form of loss of access to and control over livelihood (economic rights) as well as loss of control over decision-making processes (Xaxa 2011).

The Policy of Inclusion in Post-Independence India

Though tribes have been integrated into the larger political and economic system, this integration or inclusion is far from complete. Tribes still live in relative geographical and social isolation. Indeed, much of the problems of tribals are still thought of as being linked to the phenomenon of isolation.

To draw tribals out from their existing isolation and social backwardness and to integrate them in the larger Indian society, many provisions were made for tribal people in the Indian Constitution. As a part of the process to ensure their integration and thus build an inclusive society, tribals were, to begin with, given the same rights and status as those accorded to members of the larger Indian society in the form of citizenship rights. Citizenship is a status, which entitles an individual full membership of a community. It confers on individuals an array of rights and obligations. In this sense, the status of an individual as a citizen is contrary to the general notion of status, which is invariably associated with hierarchy and inequality (Béteille 1996).

Affirmative action programmes are interventions that aim to primarily address the issues faced by disadvantaged groups. Possible interventions according to Myron Weiner (1993) are broadly of four types: One, a wide range of policies that aims to reverse social inequalities but is racially/ethnically neutral. Two, policies directed at eliminating barriers to entry into jobs and universities by ending legal and official barriers. Three, interventions to improve the quality of the pool from which individuals are recruited. And finally, reservations or quotas for the disadvantaged.

All these possible interventions have been at work in different measures in the context of India. However, what has received wide attention and generated public debate is reservation. This debate has been not so much on political reservation as reservation in government employment and in admission to institutions of higher learning, especially medical and technological institutions. Reservation in employment and educational institutions has been at work for over 50 years. Tribes have no doubt taken advantage of these provisions. This is evident from the fact that they are now found at all levels of government services. It is a different story that in terms of their share or quota, the position is far from adequate, especially at the upper echelons of government services. In fact, in 1999, the share of tribes in Class I and II central government services stood at a mere 3.39 and 3.35 per cent respectively. Even in the case of Class III (6.07 per cent) and IV (7 per cent) services, the percentage fell short of the stipulated 7.5 per cent (Government of India 2001). What is important to note here is that tribals are yet to approximate the quota stipulated for them. The scenario is the same in the sphere of higher educational institutions as well.

There have been other forms of affirmative action programmes as well. These programmes are geared towards improving the economic and social condition of tribal people. They are based on the assumption that improvement in the economic and social well-being of tribes would help them take advantage of the benefits extended to them by the state. To this end, special considerations were made for the welfare and development of tribal people and special allocation of resources were made in the plan outlay of the First Five Year Plan (1951–56). As a first step towards developmental initiatives, special multipurpose development projects were introduced in tribal areas as supplementary to the community development projects in 1954. It is to be noted that the general development programmes in the case of tribes were so designed as to adequately address their special needs, and special provisions were used for securing their additional and more intensified development. Accordingly, the community development programme approach—the general approach to development in India—was reoriented, keeping in mind the special problems of tribal people. This approach continued till the Fourth Five Year Plan. Since the approach failed to serve the interests of tribal people, a new approach in the form of the tribal sub-plan was adopted in the Fifth Five Year Plan, which continues till date. The tribal sub-plan approach stipulates the allocation of resources for the development of tribes in proportion to the size of their population. It is a different story that the allocation has fallen far short of the stipulated 7.5 per cent all through the planned phases. Another big push forward for development came in the form of the Provisions of the Panchayats (Extension to the Scheduled Areas) Act, 1996 and the Scheduled Tribes and Other Traditional Forest Dwellers (Recognition of Forest Rights) Act, 2006. The initiatives, popularly known as PESA and the FRA respectively, are important departures from the past. The former provides for empowerment and development through self-governance. The latter aims to address historical injustice by restoring the rights of tribes over land and forest. The implementation of PESA and the FRA from the very outset has met with difficulties because of the centralised administrative structure in the country. The spirit and provisions of PESA have been compromised in most state acts, thereby defeating the objective and spirit of the central act. The effective functioning of panchayats has been constrained by bureaucratic control and the paucity of resources at the disposal of panchayats. There are contradictions between the laws of self-governance such as PESA and other laws. The latter give power to various departments to control resources and many other functions, a control that should have been vested in panchayats in the changed regime of self-governance. The current system of governance, still largely colonial in nature, has been unable to accept the radical change that self-governance entails (Xaxa 2016)

In case of the FRA too, the implementation has been poor till date. There is a big gap between the land claimed and the actual extent of the titles issued to the claimant. The key bottlenecks for actualisation of the provision have been varied. To begin with, there is a conflict between the national or state agenda of development that seeks to exploit or divert mineral and forest resources and the recognition of rights under the FRA. The Forest Rights Committee has to play the crucial role of assisting gram sabhas in determining claims of individuals by receiving, consolidating and verifying claims. The committee has fared poorly in this respect. The act protects forest-dwelling communities from eviction and removal from forest land under their occupation till the process of recognition and occupation of their rights is complete. However, there has been enough evidence from different states/regions with regard to the violation of this provision of the act (Xaxa 2016).

The impact of the two legislations and their bearing on the development status of tribes is yet to be systematically examined. However, whatever studies are available on the subject are far from encouraging. The development schemes under the tribal sub-plans have been at work for over 40 years now. Further, PESA has been in force for over 20 years and the FRA for over a decade. Yet the results are still depressing. In 1993–94, the proportion of the tribal population falling below the poverty line was 51.14 per cent, compared to 35.97 per cent for the country as whole. By 2004–05, the share of the tribal population living below the poverty line had declined to 46.5 per cent, compared to 27.6 per cent for the population as a whole (Mathur 2008). Thus, although there has been a decline, the level of poverty in the tribal population is still much higher than the national average and the gap between the two continues to be one of the major issues of concern in the poverty discourse in India. The same is the case with regard to other indicators of social development such education and health. In 1991, the literacy rate of Scheduled Tribes was 29.60 per cent, compared to 52.21 per cent for the general population. The gap between the two was as high as 28.09 per cent. By 2001, the literacy rate for the general population had jumped to 65.38 per cent, compared to 47.1 per cent for the tribal population. The gap between the two has been somewhat bridged but the difference of 21.71 per cent is still very large (Government of India 2007). The literacy rate of the general population as per the 2011 census was 73 per cent, compared to 59 per cent for the tribal population, reducing the gap to 14 per cent (Government of India 2013). The picture is no different with respect to the health of the tribal population as seen from the figures of the National Family Health Survey (NFHS). The infant mortality rate as per NFHS-2 was 84.2 for the tribal population, compared to 67.6 for the total population, the child mortality rate 46.3 compared to 29.3 and the under-five mortality rate as high as 126.6 compared to 94.9. The figures as per NFHS-3 were 62.1, 35.8 and 95.7 for the tribal population and 57.0, 18.4 and 74.3 for the total population respectively. The percentage of institutional deliveries was a mere 17.1 and 17.7 per cent in the case of tribes, compared to 33.6 and 38.2 for the total population, as per NFHS-2 and NFHS-3 respectively. As for antenatal check-ups, the figure was 56.5 per cent for the tribal population and 65.4 per cent for the total population as per NFHS-2. It increased to 70.5 per cent, compared to 77.1 per cent for the total population, as per NFHS-3 (Government of India 2007, 2013).

Broadly, there are three lines of explanation for the poor development status of tribes in India. Geographical isolation resulting in lack of or inadequate development of infrastructure such as educational, health and other related institutions is one explanation. This is often coupled with allocation of inadequate resources for the development of tribes. The second line of argument finds fault with ineffective implementation without probing into the reasons for the persistence of ineffective implementation. The third set of argument is built around the traditional socio-cultural aspects of tribal life, that is, the poor development status of tribals is attributed to their tradition and style of life. So in the third explanatory framework, the way out of the problem is believed to be through the adoption of new ideas, knowledge and values. This is the modernisation perspective, which has been in currency world over in the discussion of so-called traditional societies.

The issue, however, is not so much the failure to push through development programmes in tribal areas on account of inadequate resources, ineffective implementation or tribal traditions and social structures but the larger question of development in the form of large-scale projects such as dams, irrigation, power plants, roads, railways, industry and mining. The latter has invariably taken the form of appropriation of tribal land, forests and other resources, a process that begun under colonial rule and has continued in the post-Independence era in the garb of national and regional development. The benefits of such development projects, which Jawaharlal Nehru, the country's first prime minister, described as the temples of modern India, have not accrued to tribal people. Such development interventions have been detrimental to the interests of tribal people and have even affected their access to affirmative action programmes. For no fault of their own, tribal people are being denied control over and access to land, forest and other resources due to state-sponsored projects of national development, on the one hand, and alienation of land to non-tribes, on the other. Between 1951 and 1990, a little over 21 million people are estimated to have been displaced by development projects (dams, mines, industries and wildlife sanctuaries) in India. Of the total displaced population, over 16 million have been displaced by dams, while about 2.6 and 1.3 million have been displaced by mines and industries respectively. A little over 1 million people have been displaced by other projects, wildlife sanctuaries being the most important among them. Of the total displaced, as large as 8.54 million have been estimated to be tribals. Tribals have thus come to constitute as large as 40 per cent of the displaced population, though they comprise less than 8 per cent of the total population. Their share in displacement from projects such as mines, wildlife sanctuaries and dams has been to the tune of over 52, 75 and 38 per cent respectively. It is only in respect of industrial and other unspecified projects that the size of their share does not exceed 25 per cent. And yet, even here, the proportion is much higher than the proportion of their population to the total population of the country. Of over 21 million people displaced, only 5.4 million have been resettled, out of which 2.12 million are stated to be tribals. This means that only about 24.8 per cent of displaced tribals have been rehabilitated. For a very large chunk of the population, rehabilitation still remains an elusive phenomenon (Government of India 2001). Further, land alienation from tribes to non-tribes, an endemic phenomenon for centuries, continues on a wide scale even to this day. As per the information available with the Ministry of Rural Development in January 1999, 4.65 lakh cases of alienation of tribal land, covering an area of 9.17 lakh acres, have been registered in the states of Andhra Pradesh, Assam, Bihar, Gujarat, Himachal Pradesh, Karnataka, Madhya Pradesh, Maharashtra, Orissa, Rajasthan and Tripura (Government of India 2001).

Besides dispossession from land, tribes had to also face greater restrictions on access to forests in post-Independence India. Tribes were greatly dependent on forests for their day-to-day needs, including food, shelter, instruments, medicine and even clothing in some cases. But as long as tribes were in control of forests in the sense of unrestricted use of forests and their produce, they had no difficulty meeting these needs. The entry of the British, however, drastically altered this relationship. For the British, forests were an important source of revenue and commercial exploitation. Hence the forest policy enunciated by the British introduced state control over forest resources and imposed curtailment of rights and privileges over forest resources. The policy pursued by the British was continued in the post-Independence era of economic development, with even stricter regulation and enforcement. This was justified on the grounds of wider and national public interest. However, this has had serious consequences on access to basic necessities of life such as food and shelter for tribals. Moreover, the forest laws have turned tribals into encroachers who have to live under the constant threat of eviction and violence.

Nature and Terms of Exchange

There have thus been two kinds of interventions in post-Independence India with regard to tribes—affirmative action and development projects. What has been the net result of these two kinds of interventions? One kind of result is the widening gap between tribes and the rest of population with respect to the fruits of development. There is no doubt that there has been increase in the literacy rate, decrease in the proportion of people below poverty line, increase in school enrolment, decrease in the school dropout rate, and so on. Yet the gap between tribes and the general population is widening. Since affirmative action programmes are meant to address the problems of the disadvantaged, the least that could be expected from these programmes is to bridge existing gaps. Yet, efforts in this direction have not borne results.

Large-scale development projects and the policy of denying access to forest resources are interventions of a greater magnitude and scale than reservation and other affirmative action programmes developed for the welfare of tribal people. Such interventions offset all that is desired to be achieved by affirmative action programmes. The state displayed the latter as the signpost of development. On introspection, however, affirmative action in the case of tribes tends to no longer be affirmative action, as it does not uplift them from the social base in which they have been traditionally located. It has instead been pushed alongside the processes that further deteriorate the existing social base of tribes, thereby exposing their vulnerability.

The way development has been pursued in tribal India other than the northeast region can be best captured by borrowing

Thorner's concept of 'built-in depressor', which he used in his work to understand the agrarian problem in post-independent India. In dealing with the reasons for India's agricultural underdevelopment, Thorner argued that a number of factors endemic in the rural situation served to constitute a 'built-in depressor' of agricultural stagnation in India (Thorner 1957). In a similar vein, one can articulate the developmental problem of tribal people other than those in the northeast. Though subjected to much state violence as a part of the agenda to contain self-determination movements, the northeast region did not witness the scale of dispossession from land, forest and other resources that the mainland tribes have gone through after Independence. The dispossession is evident in the scale of alienation of land from tribes to non-tribes, on the one hand, and massive displacement of tribal people from state-driven infrastructure development projects such as dams, hydraulic projects, industries and mineral exploitation, on the other, since India's planned development. Such dispossession, the northeast has historically not experienced. This largely explains as to why social development indicators are so poor among the tribes of mainland India as compared to those in northeast India. Hence there is nothing affirmative about the affirmative action programme in mainland tribal India. The dispossessions that tribal people have been through far outweigh gains they have made by way of the affirmative action programme. In a way, affirmative action in case of tribes, especially of mainland India, is a myth.

Thus, the reason why the gap between tribes and non-tribes has remained intact or is even widening lies inherently in the way tribal problems have been articulated by the state and state apparatuses. The tribal problem has primarily been couched in terms of social and economic backwardness arising from tribals' geographical and social isolation. Hence the whole discourse on tribes has been around the question of integration through the extension of civil, political and social rights via affirmative action programmes. Yet the economic rights that tribes traditionally enjoyed and which was their critical asset has been usurped by the state in exchange of the aforementioned rights. In fact, the extension of civil, political and social rights and affirmative action has become the arena of legitimising the expropriation of resources of tribal people. Hence the terms of exchange between the state and tribals in India has been steeped in expropriation, domination and discrimination. Integration, which has been seen as the panacea of tribal problems, has diverted our attention from looking into the nature and types of integration. If one looks at the nature of integration, one finds that the relationship between tribes and non-tribes and even the state has been one that is overwhelmingly interspersed with domination, exploitation and discrimination. This is an issue that is conveniently overlooked and hence needs to be problematised and explained.

The key to understanding this issue lies in the relationship between tribe, state and the larger society. The state in India, both at the level of the union and the region, cannot compromise with the interests of the numerically, economically and political dominant communities. The interest of these communities can be better served only at the expense of tribal societies. The larger society, at the union or state level, has always viewed tribes as alien outsiders and hence there is an overall indifference towards the cause and development of tribes. The relationship between tribes and non-tribes has historically been one of appropriation of resources of the tribal community by the larger society, a trend which continues even today. The state administration too is not untouched by such an attitude. This explains as why there has been a failure to adequately address tribal problems in India including the implementation of schemes under the affirmative action programme.

References

Béteille, A. 1986. 'The Concept of Tribe with Special Reference to India', *Journal of European Sociology*, 27 (2): 297–318.

———. 1996. 'The Mismatch between Class and Status', *The British Journal of Sociology*, 47 (3): 513–25.

Bose, N. K. 1941. 'The Hindu Method of Tribal Absorption', *Science and Culture*, 77: 188–94.

Bosu Mullick, S. 1993. 'Jharkhand Movement: A Historical Analysis', in M. Miri (ed.), *Continuity and Change in Tribal Society*. Shimla: Indian Institute of Advanced Study.

———. 2003. 'Introduction', in R. D. Munda and S. Bosu Mullick (eds), *The Jharkhand Movement—Indigenous Peoples' Struggle for Autonomy in India*. Copenhagen: IWGIA.

Elwin, V. 1939. *The Baiga*. London: John Murray.

———. 1943. *The Aboriginals*. Bombay: Oxford University Press.

———. 1959. *A Philosophy for NEFA*. Shillong: The Advisor to the Governor of Assam.

Ghurye, G. S. 1943. *The Aborigines So-Called and Their Future*. Bombay: Popular Prakashan.

Government of India. 2001. *Report of the Steering Committee on Empowering the Scheduled Tribes for the Tenth Five Year Plan (2002–2007)*. New Delhi: Planning Commission

———. 2007. *Report of the Working Group on Empowerment of Scheduled Tribes for the Eleventh Five Year Plan (2007–2012)*. New Delhi: Ministry of Tribal Affairs.

———. 2013. *Statistical Profile of Scheduled Tribes in India*. New Delhi: Ministry of Tribal Affairs.

Kosambi, D. D. 1975. *The Culture and Civilization of Ancient India in Historical Outline*. Delhi: Vikas Publishing House.

Lokur, B. N. 1965. *Report of the Advisory Committee on the Revision of the Lists of Scheduled Castes and Scheduled Tribes*. New Delhi: Government of India, Department of Social Security Department.

Mathur, A. 2008. 'An Overview of the Jharkhand Economy and Perspectives for Human Development', Background Paper, National Seminar on 'Growth and Human Development in Jharkhand—Perspectives and Policies', Ranchi, 4–5 July.

Nehru, Jawaharlal. 1959. 'Foreword', in V. Elwin, *A Philosophy for NEFA*. Shillong: The Advisor to the Governor of Assam.

Raghavaiah, V. R. 1979. 'Tribal Revolts in Chronological Order: 1778–1971', in A. R. Desai (ed.), *Peasant Struggles in India*, pp. 12–26. Bombay: Oxford University Press.

Risley, H. H. 1903. *Census of India Report*. Simla: Government of India Press.

Singh, K. S. 2002. *Birsa Munda and His Movement 1872–1901: A Study of a Millenarian Movement in Chotanagpur*. Kolkata: Seagull Books.

Sinha, S. 1958. 'Tribal Culture of Peninsular India as a Dimension of Little Tradition in the Study of Indian Civilization: A Preliminary Statement', *Journal of American Folklore*, 71: 504–18.

Sinha, S. 1962. 'State Formation and Rajput Myth in Tribal Central India', *Man in India*, 45 (1): 35–80.

———. (ed.). 1987. *Tribal Polities and State Systems in Pre-colonial Eastern and North Eastern India*. Calcutta: Centre for Social Sciences and K.P. Bagchi & Company.

Srinivas, M. N. 1977. *Social Change in Modern India*. New Delhi: Orient Longman.

Thorner, Daniel. 1957. 'Prof Dantwala on "The Agrarian Prospect in India". A Note', *The Economic Weekly*, 9 (23): 705–06 & 723.

Verma, R. C. 1990. *Indian Tribes through the Ages*. New Delhi: Ministry of Information and Broadcasting, Government of India.

Weiner, M. 1993. 'Summary Comments on the Affirmative Action Workshops', *Development and Democracy*, September: 81–86.

Xaxa, V. 1999. 'Transformation of Tribes in India: Terms of Discourse', *Economic and Political Weekly*, 34 (24): 1519–24.

———. 2011. 'Tribes and Social Exclusion', Occasional Paper, No. 2, Centre for Studies in Social Sciences Calcutta and the United Nations Children's Fund (CSSSC-UNICEF), Social Inclusion Cell.

———. 2016. 'The Global Indigenous Peoples Movement: It's Stirring in India', *Journal of Law, Property, and Society*, 2: 141–56.

4 How Not to Study Caste

Moving Beyond the Avatars of the Orientalist Commonsense

SURINDER S. JODHKA

Among all the social science disciplines, those from sociology and social anthropology have researched and written the most on the subject of caste. These two disciplines were the first to engage with the subject and have continued to do so over the decades. The subject of caste has also enjoyed a place of prominence in the teaching of sociology in India. It has been among the core topics of discussion in a range of courses, such as social stratification, political sociology and Indian society, taught across the country in schools, colleges and in postgraduate departments of sociology and social anthropology.

Around the middle of the twentieth century, when the twin disciplines took shape in India, researching on caste and village was seen as the natural entry points for a sociologist or a social anthropologist into the empirics of Indian society. Village studies, which marked the arrival of the twin disciplines on the academic scene of the Indian social sciences, almost universally recognised the centrality of caste in the social structure of the Indian village and, by implication, of the Indian society. The village, for the social anthropologist of the 1950s, was not simply a demographic unit of settlement, 'not merely a place where people lived; it had a design in which were reflected the basic values of Indian civilisation' (Béteille 1980:108). And almost everyone agreed that the foundational institution of this design of village life was the caste system. Even those who researched on subjects like family and kinship, religion and culture or economy and politics tended to see caste to be the most obvious and important mediating institution. Everything Indian was presumably organised around caste.

Interestingly, this had not been the case with other social science disciplines, particularly during the early decades of their practice in India. For example, mainstream economists and historians almost completely ignored the subject of caste in much of their research writings and teaching practices for a long time. Even political scientists in India began to take caste seriously only when their disciplinary orientation intersected with sociology. It was during the second half of the 1960s, with the writings of the Rudolphs who explored the sociology of electoral politics empirically and its working on the ground that the dynamics of caste began to be recognised as a significant aspect of Indian democracy (Rudolph and Rudolph 1967; also see Kothari 1970). It took much longer for historians to recognise the value of researching on the subject of caste. Though some historians had been researching and writing on aspects of caste all along, it was only with the publication of Nicholas Dirks seminal work *Castes of Mind* (Dirks 2001) that researching on the subject acquired respectability among historians. Economists were the last to recognise the continued relevance of looking at caste in the spheres of their discipline, for instance, in the manner in which it shaped or influenced labour markets, occupational mobility and business practices in the present-day economy, beyond the village agrarian systems (Munshi and Rosenzweig 2006; Thorat and Newman 2010; Deshpande 2011).

Why did these disciplines take so long to recognise the significance of caste in their disciplinary practices? In the early decades after Independence, a large majority of Indian social scientists and the middle class elite approached the subject of caste with a certain degree of disdain, seeing it as an undesirable cultural hangover of the past, and they mostly believed that with India moving on the path of modernisation and development, caste would/should die out on its own. They saw themselves as bearers of modernity and progress and practised their disciplines with a mission to take India forward through economic development and secularisation of its cultural traditions (see Jodhka and Prakash 2016). They had deeply internalised the colonial and orientalist conceptions of India's past. A large majority of them came to accept the colonial view that interpreted caste as a signifier of India's persistent backwardness and ignorance. Even researching on caste would have been viewed by many of them as an act aiding to its persistence.

What then was different about sociologists and social anthropologists? Why did they take the subject seriously even when many among them too would have shared the mainstream middle class elite assumptions on the future of caste? Unlike economists and political scientists, whose disciplinary concerns were largely shaped by the normative framework of economic growth and nation building, sociologists and social anthropologists largely practised their disciplines by undertaking empirical studies of the ground realities of the 'Indian social'. However, the empirical is never out there to be captured only through observations and fieldwork. It is also framed through categories and available conceptions of a given society. Empirical questions are shaped by such conceptions and available theoretical paradigms.

Quite like the nationalists and practitioners of other social sciences, the early generation of sociologists and social anthropologists also uncritically accepted the orientalist view on the distinctive nature of Indian society, represented through categories such as village, caste and joint family. They too accepted the need for India to modernise its economy, polity and social life. However, given their preoccupation with the empirical, they pursued their craft primarily through ethnographic fieldwork, mostly in the pervasive worlds of the Indian village. The 'field view' had to produce nuanced details of what was already believed to be the core feature of traditional Indian life, particularly its rural life. Even though economists and historians too engaged extensively with the 'rural', they mostly focused on the 'land economy' or its 'revenue regimes', where the category of class and peasantry provided an obvious frame of reference. In the received West-centric theories of social and economic change, working with 'class' was also viewed as being 'politically correct' and 'progressive', an analysis that would be suitable for aiding positive social change. Such a language was to enable India to move on the path of becoming a modern society. A class analysis of the rural was also a popular project for Marxist and left-wing scholars as a way of assessing and strategising India's revolutionary potential.

As indicated in the preceding discussion, the post–Second World War ideas of modernisation and development played a critical role in shaping the disciplinary practices of sociology and social anthropology in India. Such theoretical frames reinforced the mainstream middle class and academic attitude towards caste. While caste as a signifier of traditional social life became the bread and butter of Indian sociologists, they were also quite taken in by the idea of evolutionary change as advocated by modernisation theory. Thus, interestingly, even when they argued for the recognition of caste as a persistent reality on the ground, the leading sociologists and social anthropologists of the time mostly viewed its future from a modernisation–evolutionary perspective.[1] They too believed that caste would eventually fade away with time, on its own, as the modernisation process progressed. The only point of difference they had with their fellow social scientists was on its continued relevance. In other words, while almost everyone agreed on the *imperatives of its disappearance*, sociologists and social anthropologists underlined caste's robustness and sticky nature.

The Contemporary Context

The social science research on caste has moved a long way since the days of 'village studies'. Beginning with the late 1980s and early 1990s, the subject of caste re-emerged in the Indian political scene in a fundamentally different way, mostly from below in the form of the social movements of those on the margins of the social order of caste. These movements demanded the recognition of caste as a reality that continued to matter for them as it reinforced their marginality. The neo-Dalit activist and caste warrior of the post

1990s pointed to the resilience of caste and its ability to actively intersect with the evolving realities of India's social and economic life, its culture and its political processes.

Today, caste is clearly among the most engaging and intensely researched subjects among a wide range of scholars from diverse disciplinary traditions. The subject of caste today also presents itself in far more diverse and complicated forms. However, the popular perspective on the subject within the disciplines of sociology and social anthropology has not seen much change, particularly in the manner in which it is taught in the classroom. This is evident from the continued popularity of orientalist formulations of the subject, presented most effectively in the writings of the French scholar Louis Dumont, particularly his book *Homo Hierarchicus* (1971). Further, much of the sociological research on caste still works within what I have described earlier as the 'disappearance imperative'. Such an understanding of caste thus keeps us tied to an evolutionary view of history. The next section of this chapter elaborates this point through a critical overview of the manner in which caste has been studied by sociologists and social anthropologists.

Sociology and the Study of Caste

As mentioned earlier, the dominant view of caste approaches it from a position of Indian exceptionalism, that is, a social arrangement unique to the Hindus of India. This perspective sees the traditional caste system as a system of social hierarchy that operates through the categories of varna and jati. While varna provides a normative model, jatis are concrete social or empirical groupings. The idea of varna as spelt out in the *Manusmriti* divided Hindus into four mutually exclusive categories: Brahmin (priest), Kshatriya (warrior), Vaishya (trader) and Shudra (peasant/artisan/labourer). Beyond the four varnas is the category of *achhoot* (untouchable). These four or five categories occupy different positions in the status hierarchy, with the Brahmins at the top, followed by the other three varnas in the same order as mentioned and the achhoots occupying a position at the very bottom. Jatis are groupings of kinship communities that maintained their symbolic border by strictly following rules of exogamy and endogamy in marriage practices. They are further divided into subgroups, which have localised names and systems of classifications. Unlike the fourfold or fivefold model of varnas, jatis and their subunits are numerous, going into hundreds in every linguistic region and into thousands across the entire subcontinent.

According to the popular and dominant view, even when the details and names of jatis varies across regions and time, the structure of hierarchy remains the same everywhere, and it has been intact for centuries. According to this view, everyone accepts the varna model of hierarchy and every jati places itself within the all-pervasive and pan-Indian Hindu order of hierarchy. Even religious conversions, such as to Islam or Christianity, have made little difference to the hierarchical minds of Indians (read Hindus). Similarly, local movements that have articulated critiques of the hierarchal system and offered alternative views on transcendence have failed to erase the value of hierarchy from the lay minds of the local communities. Further, this simplistic and popular view of caste also proposes that it was only during the British colonial rule, when modern ideas originating in the West were infused into Indian life through the introduction of Western-style secular education, modern technology and urban life that the reality of caste began to loosen its grip. The post-Independence Nehruvian state, with its emphasis on development, modernisation and economic growth, further reinforced this process, hoping for its eventual disappearance from the mental and social landscapes of Indians.

A wide range of critical scholarship has quite convincingly shown that this popular view of caste and Hinduism is founded on several untenable assumptions (Frykenberg 1989; Smith 1989; Thapar 1989; Oberoi 1994). First of all, it constructs caste as a singular, pan-Indian reality and Hinduism as a cohesive faith system with a unified theological structure, without any variations in its social organisation and normative belief systems across geographical regions and vertical hierarchies. By implication, Hinduism is presented as a monotheistic faith system, comparable to other religious systems, such as Christianity and Islam, which are similarly presumed to be monotheistic in their ideological moorings.

Second, this scholarship views caste purely as a religious value, the structural logic of which lies almost exclusively in Hindu religious philosophy and ritual practice, which alone is believed to have shaped the Indian mind and everyday social and economic life. While it is true that much like many other social institutions, such as marriage and family, caste too has an ideational dimension, which finds its articulation in Hindu religious philosophy, the diverse realities of caste cannot be entirely reduced to religious ideology or ritual practice (Jodhka 2015). Reducing caste to the logic of the ritual life of Hindus has also meant that the materiality or the politics of caste is viewed as either irrelevant or of less significance. Third, in such a view of India, Hinduism or the caste system and village life allows no agency to the Indian people and negates any possibility of change through internal processes and critiques (see Inden 1990; Cohn 1996).

As mentioned earlier, this view of caste and the Hindu social order attributes all changes in the system solely to its encounter with Western modernity during the colonial period. The postcolonial state through its policies of development has been trying to further accelerate this process of modernisation, albeit with several shifts and 'compromises'. How did this view come to be so hegemonic? Historians of caste have traced the origins of the present-day social science conceptualisations of caste to the early writings on India by Western writers (Indologists), travellers and colonisers. Though the source of their interest varied, they all tended to look at the social and cultural life of the region as being fundamentally different from that of Europe. Over the years, India and the rest of the 'Eastern' world came to be viewed in the dominant Western discourses as the 'other' of the West European societies. Scholars like Edward Said (1985) and Ronald Inden (1990) have described this as orientalism, a discourse that tries to present oriental culture as being different from and inferior to that of the West. Caste served as a good example of an institution of the 'peculiar orient'.

Given that these writings became a source of knowing about India for the early social science scholarship in Western Europe, the latter tended to produce similar kinds of imaginations and arguments about the social and cultural life in the region. Examples of this can be found in the writings of scholars like Hegel, Marx and Weber. Marx, for example, wrote on the positive effects of colonial rule on India, arguing that it could break the traditional village community structured around caste (Marx 1853). Along the lines of this early imagination of caste as a rigid and static institution of the Hindus, Max Weber too approached India from an ideological perspective and underlined the static and otherworldly nature of its religious system based on the ideas of karma and rebirth.

However, unlike others, Weber also looked at caste from a comparative perspective and saw it as an example of a specific type of inequality, which could be found in all cultures/societies. For him, caste was an example of a status group. Caste groups were like ethnic communities, completely closed to outsiders. Recruitment to a caste group, like an ethnic group, was based exclusively on birth. Unlike other ethnic communities, castes were hierarchical and the order of hierarchy was acceptable to those lower down in the system (Weber 1946). While Weber accepted the orientalist view on the rigid and unchanging nature of caste, he did not think that the presence of caste-like status groups was peculiar to India or Hindus.

Looking more closely on the subject in this evolving framework, Louis Dumont reworked the orientalist view on caste in his well-known book *Homo Hierarchicus: The Caste System and Its Implications,* first published in French in 1967, and its English edition appearing in 1971. Drawing mostly from the classical Hindu scriptures, Dumont constructed a well-integrated theory of the caste system. As was the case with much of the classical orientalist writings, Dumont conceptualised caste as emanating from the Hindu religious system. According to him, the structural logic of caste lay in the 'Hindu mind', as an ideological construct, which divided and hierarchised social groups on the basis of the ritual purity or impurity of their occupations. Dumont's thesis on caste was, in many ways, an extension of the argument put forward by another French scholar, Celestin Bouglé.

In an essay first published in 1908, Bouglé argued against those who looked at caste merely as a system of occupational specialisation. He defined caste as a system consisting of hierarchically arranged hereditary groups, separated from each other in certain respects (caste endogamy, restrictions on eating together and on physical contact) but interdependent on each other as well (traditional division of labour). The word 'caste', he emphasised, not only involved a hereditary specialisation of occupational groups but also differential rights. Different occupations were arranged in a hierarchical order that made their members socially unequal. Inequality was an essential feature of the caste system. Along with inequality, he also underlined the element of pollution as an important feature of caste. Different groups, in a caste society, tended to 'repel each other rather than attract, each retired within itself, isolated itself, and made every effort to prevent its members from contracting alliances or even from entering into relation with neighboring groups' (Bouglé 1971: 65). Bouglé identified three core features of the caste system, viz., hereditary occupation, hierarchy and mutual repulsion.

While Dumont agreed with Bouglé's identification of the core features of the system, he argued that for a proper theoretical explanation of caste, it was important to identify one common element, 'a single true principle', to which the three features of the caste system suggested by Bouglé could be reduced. Such a principle, Dumont argued, was 'the opposition of the pure and the impure'.

> This opposition underlies hierarchy, which is the superiority of the pure to the impure, underlies separation because the pure and the impure must be kept separate, and underlies the division of labour because pure and impure occupations must likewise be kept separate. The whole is founded on the necessary and hierarchical coexistence of the two opposites. (Dumont 1971: 43)

Another important and extremely contentious aspect of Dumont's theory is his assertion about the superiority of the Brahmin over the king. India was different from the West because in India, status was not determined by the logic of political economy, as was the case with the West. In a caste society, status as a principle of social organisation was superior to power. Status encompassed power, as Dumont would assert.

While Dumont's theory of caste has been very influential, it has also been widely criticised. He has been accused of presenting an ideologically biased view, an account that looked at caste upside down as the Brahmins would wish to present it. Given that his sources were mostly textual and that these texts were all written and retained by the upper-caste Brahmins, he constructed a theory that presented a Brahminical perspective on the subject, that is, an uncritical celebration of tradition. He has also been accused of ignoring the available empirical accounts of caste's functioning on the ground, produced by professional social anthropologists in form of village studies and monographs (Gupta 2000: 114). Some have accused him of also being selective in the choice of textual sources (Das and Uberoi 1971).

In his defense, Dumont would argue that he had only tried to construct an ideal type of caste that theorised the underlying structure of the system and not the way caste was practised in everyday life. However, this is not what he does. If caste is an ideal type, a scale or conceptual category, it should be available for a comparative study of structures of hierarchies in other cultures and societies as well. Dumont, however, repeatedly underlines an exceptionalist position—the uniqueness of caste as an Indian and a Hindu ideological system.

As Berreman has pointed out, caste did not exist except empirically, that is, in and through the lives of people as they interacted with each other. The lived experience of caste was very different from what Dumont seems to suggest. Berreman argues, 'The human meaning of caste for those who lived it was power and vulnerability, privilege and oppression, honour and denigration, plenty and want, reward and deprivation, security and anxiety. As an anthropological document, a description of caste, which failed to convey this was a travesty in the world today' (Berreman 1991: 87–88; also see Gupta 1984). Similarly, Joan Mencher, who conducted fieldwork among the lower castes in a village in south India, reports that 'from the point of view of people at the lowest end of the scale, caste had functioned and continued to function as a very effective system of economic exploitation' (Mencher 1978). Fuller makes a related point in his criticism of Dumont's theory. He points that Dumont's notion of caste not only undervalues relations of power but also undermines the obvious facts about inequalities in material life and the role played by caste in their reproduction. In his study of the redistributive system prevailing in pre-colonial India, Fuller shows how the village-level system of caste relations was integrated into a larger political authority, beyond the village (Fuller 1977).

Another point of contention in Dumont's theory has been his argument that constructs Indian and Western societies as binaries where India is presented through categories of holism and hierarchy and the West through individualism and equality (Béteille 1986). Such a construct tends to ignore the internal differences within societies and regions. The actually existing realities have never been so simple, in the West or in India. We can also find echoes of this argument in the historical scholarship on caste. As Bernard Cohn argues, the textual view of caste constructed through orientalist categories is fundamentally flawed because it constructs a picture of Indian society as

> being static, timeless and space-less. Statements about customs, which derived from third century A.D. texts and observations from the late eighteenth century, were equally good evidence for determining the nature of society and culture in India. In this view of Indian society there was no regional variation and no questioning of the relationship between prescriptive normative statement derived from the texts and the actual behavior of individuals and groups. Indian society was seen as a set of rules, which every Hindu followed. (Cohn 1968: 7–8)

Following the works of Bernard Cohn, some other historians of modern India have done important work on the subject. Perhaps the most important and influential of this scholarship has been the work of Nicholas Dirks. In his well-known book, *Castes of Mind* (2001), Dirks convincingly shows how the colonial rulers through a process of enumeration and ethnographic surveys raised the consciousness about caste. They also produced social and intellectual conditions where 'caste became the single term capable of expressing, organizing, and above all "synthesizing" India's diverse forms of social identity, community and organization' (Dirks 2001: 5). Dumont's theory of caste is a restatement of the same colonial and orientalist formulation.

The fallacy of the orientalist view of caste is also evident from the fieldwork-based writings on the Indian village. Field studies of the Indian village tend to present a much more diverse picture of caste. Many of these studies question the superiority of Brahmins and place landowning castes at the centre of village social life. While some emphasise reciprocity and interdependence (Wiser 1936; Dube 1955; Srinivas 1955), others point to the coercive nature of power in caste society. F.G. Bailey, for example, questions even the idea of interdependence in caste society: 'The system works the way it does because the coercive sanctions are all in the hands of a dominant caste. There is a tie of reciprocity, but it is not a sanction of which the dependent castes can make easy use' (Bailey 1960: 258).

Similarly, Beidelman points to the exploitative nature of the relationship between the landowning, politically dominant *jajmans* and those who provided them services of various kinds, that is, those belonging to landless caste groups called *kamins* (Beidelman 1959). Some of these writings also raised wider theoretical questions regarding the relationship between status and power and the validity of the claims made by Dumont on the encompassment of power by status. Gloria Goodwin Raheja, for example, argues that

> [T]he relationship between a hierarchical order of castes, with its focus on the superior position of the Brahman, on the one hand, and a conception of sovereignty focused on the Hindu

> king or the royal functions of the dominant caste at the level of the village, on the other, has been a central reverberating issue in the anthropological and historical study of South Asian society.... Virtually all of the major contributions to the anthropological, indological and historical study of Hindu South Asia have been concerned in some fashion with this relationship, and have seen it to be constitutive of the fundamental aspects of social life, polity, and religion. (Raheja 1988: 497)

Based on her study of village in northern India, Raheja offers an alternative theory of caste and ritual practices, a theory that places 'dominant caste' at the centre of the caste system. She also questions the dominant 'Western view of Hindu society', which sees hierarchy as 'the sole ideology defining relations among castes' and reduces the role of the king and the dominant caste to a residual level (Raheja 1989: 79). Instead, she argues that

> [T]here are several contextually shifting ideologies of inter-caste relationships apparent in everyday village social life. Meanings and values are foregrounded differently from context to context, and they implicate varying configurations of castes. Detailed data on prestation patterns and language use from the Gujjar dominated north Indian village ... indicate that aspects of inter-caste relationships, that ... I call 'centrality' and 'mutuality', are distinguishable from the ranked aspect that is usually called 'hierarchy'.... Among these configurations of caste, both the ritual centrality of the dominant caste ... and the mutuality among the castes of the village prove to be more significant in social intercourse than the hierarchical pre-eminence of priestly Brahmans. (Raheja 1989: 81–82)

These wide-ranging contestations of the popular Western view of caste point to the diversities that have been part of social and cultural life in the subcontinent. They also represent the diverse ways in which an institution like caste can be and has been approached.

Caste and the State

Besides the crafting of its conceptual frames and theoretical formulations that enabled caste to fit into the grand theories/

narratives of social transformations evolving in Western societies around the same time, the British colonial administrators also deployed caste in their administrative narratives, particularly after the introduction of the colonial census in the late nineteenth century. This had far-reaching implications (see Cohn 1996; Dirks 2001). Perhaps the most important of these was the process of classification of caste communities into an all-India schema. For example, the British clubbed together the so-called untouchable communities into an administrative category, initially as 'Depressed Classes' and later as 'Scheduled Castes' (SC) under the Government of India Act of 1935. The post-Independence state continued with the same category but has over the years expanded the list of communities and the scope of state action for their welfare and development. Though SC communities are identified at the state level, they are listed in the Constitution of India, with the authorisation of the president of India. This classification became an important medium for the postcolonial Indian state in its administrative strategies of transforming the institutionalised hierarchies of caste into an open social and economic order with a level playing field.

The postcolonial state also legally abolished the practice of untouchability and initiated several other administrative measures for the development and inclusion of the historically marginalised caste communities. The first and most important of these measures was the quota system, that is, reservation of seats in government-run educational institutions and for employment in government and public-sector jobs. Second, the central and state governments introduced various development schemes/programmes enabling SCs to actively participate in the emerging economy and new avenues of employment. Third, the Indian Constitution made provisions for the reservation of seats for SCs (along with Scheduled Tribes) in legislative bodies and other representational institutions as per their proportion in the total population.

Notwithstanding these proactive measures initiated by the Indian state, the middle class that inherited power from the British colonial rulers shared the view that caste was essentially a mode of traditional life and would gradually decline and eventually disappear on its own as India moved on the path of development and modernisation. The engine of progress was to be the process of economic growth: industrialisation, modern technology and urbanisation.

Caste Today: Decline and Persistence

Despite the success of Indian democracy, the increasing participation of the historically marginalised groups and communities in the electoral process, and decades of development or modernisation and quotas for SCs, caste-based disparities have not disappeared. In other words, caste continues to be an important indicator of deprivation and marginality, both at the macro level, as reflected in the national-level data sets (see Thorat 2009) as also at the micro level (see Jodhka 2002, 2015; Shah et al. 2006; also see Mosse 2018 for a review of writings on caste and development). Caste continues to play an important role in the modern urban economy. For example, ownership of industry in India has historically been concentrated in the hands of a few social/cultural groups and the top jobs were always kept within the family (Munshi and Rosenzweig 2006; Rutten 2003). Recruitments to other jobs were opened to outsiders only when the required personnel were not available within the community or the wider kin group. Caste is almost always a negative social identity for Dalits when they wish to enter the modern/urban labour market and business (Jodhka and Newman 2007; Jodhka 2015; Deshpande 2011; Mosse 2018).

These emerging, often contradictory, trends have completely altered the discourse on caste. As mentioned before, since the early 1990s, the caste question has increasingly been raised by those who have historically been on the margins, that is, at the receiving end of the hierarchical system. Viewed from the point of view of those on margins, caste needs to be talked about not because of any love for a dying tradition or as an important marker of 'cultural tradition' or 'cultural difference' but because it continues to be a source of deprivation and discrimination for them. Caste influences development outcomes and reproduces older forms of exclusion in the emerging economic order. Therefore, from the perspective of the marginalised, there is a need to recognise the continued presence of caste as a reality of Indian society, as a system of power and domination. This kind of articulation of caste has opened up spaces for its engagement with state policy.

In the emerging narrative, the focus moves from culture and tradition to power and exclusion. Such a frame thus underlines three core features of caste. For those at the lower end of the traditional hierarchy, caste has always been a medium or source of their domination. It has always been an institutionalised form of authority, supported by a set of values, norms and institutions, some of which continue to be present even today while others have weakened or disintegrated. However, there has been no radical change. In the absence of a comprehensive structural change and its weakening ideological hold, caste tends to assert itself as coercive power, perhaps more often than before. Increase in the incidence of caste-based atrocities, brutal violence, often collective, or even suicides by young Dalit students are instances and evidence of this reality.

The second related dimension of caste is that it signifies disparities. The presence of caste does not simply imply power in the cultural sense of the term. It is also a structural reality where inequality is institutionalised in terms of unequal distribution of resources. Inequality, seen in terms of disparities, implies a different set of attributes when compared with the Dumontian notion of inequality, which refers to a cultural notion of hierarchy, something that exists only as an ideological category. Disparities, on the other hand, refer to inequalities in terms of entitlements, ownership and access to resources, material, social and cultural. However, the nature of disparities and inequalities in a caste society is different. Ambedkar describes them as 'graded inequalities' (Ambedkar 1936). Unlike class, castes do not face each other as opponents in an antagonistic relationship. The hierarchical nature of caste implies each group is both below and above or lesser and greater than another group, except for those at the two extremes of the hierarchical structure.

The third and the most important feature of caste is that it is an institutionalised system of discrimination and denials, socially and culturally. It produces a pattern of disadvantages, which in turn produce deprivations and poverty among certain groups. Denial is culturally institutionalised in the sense that it has had legitimacy and has produced long-term implications for the social and economic status of caste groups/communities. For example, in some regions of the country, the ex-untouchable communities were not allowed to own and cultivate land and become peasants. Such customary practices cannot be explained away by simply referring to the dialectics of pure and impure. These practices defined and limited the rights of different groups of people. More importantly, the effects of such a past tradition are felt even today by a large majority of Dalits. The absence of assets, such as agricultural land, makes Dalits much more vulnerable, economically as well as socially, when compared to other sections of rural society.

Beyond Orientialist Essentialisms

This chapter shows how the mainstream textbook view of caste has been largely shaped by the orientalist view of Indian society, reinforced by 'colonial forms of knowledge', to use Bernard Cohn's expression (Cohn 1996), and the administrative and enumerative practices of the colonial state. The orientalist and colonial view of caste, in a way, was further strengthened by the popular theories of modernisation and development. The influence of this view has been so far-reaching that it has come to be widely accepted as the past 'native tradition', which has indeed remained stable over time immemorial. For example, when economists began to study caste in the recent past through quantitative methods and statistical data, they have almost always tended to operationalise it through the varna model of hierarchy, treating the two (varna and/as caste) as being unproblematic empirical facts (see Munshi and Rosenzweig 2006). The varna model of describing and explaining caste is also pervasive in social science textbooks and in popular middle-class discourses on the subject. Even popular anti-caste social movements tend to invoke the idea of varna hierarchy quite uncritically.

This view of caste almost universally looks at it as a religious value, inscribed in certain classic Hindu texts. By implication, the practice of caste is seen as an outcome of the religious ideology of Hindus and hence a purely ideological phenomenon. This view also underlines the ancient and unchanging nature of caste, which could be challenged only by modern/Western technologies of economic organisation and colonial/Western modernisation of India. Another simplistic, but very widely shared, assumption in this framework is that India's modernisation ought to end caste over time through an evolutionary process, without requiring any political action. I describe this as the 'disappearance imperative'.

Indian society has indeed been undergoing a process of 'modernisation' for more than a century now. Modern cities like Mumbai, Kolkata and Bengaluru have been growing both in size and influence. Even though the proportion of the urban population in India today is only around 30 per cent, the influence of modern urban life goes far beyond. The decline of the old agrarian economy is clearly evident from the fact that its contribution to the national income came down from more than half in the early 1950s to merely 13 or 14 per cent by the second decade of the twenty-first century. A majority of Indians today are educated and mobile. The influence of urban middle classes and their lifestyles has been growing across regions and communities of the subcontinent, particularly in the post-1990s period.

Many among the middle class in urban India are likely to emphatically argue that indeed caste would and should have disappeared from public life by now had it not been kept alive by the wily actors in India's electoral politics. Its institutionalisation through the reservation policy is also cited as the reason for its continued survival in India today. Even when its presence is recognised as a substantive reality in mainstream academic circles, it is generally viewed as a typical case of 'change and continuity', the underlying assumption being that its continued presence is a result of incomplete modernisation of India's economy and its cultural values. As the process of development matures under the neoliberal market regime, caste is bound to disappear on its own, provided it is allowed to be forgotten by the political entrepreneurs of Indian democracy.

As is evident from the preceding discussion and from the large volume of empirical literature, caste continues to overlap with and articulate through newer forms of inequalities. While the older modes of social and economic life have changed, it has not meant an end of caste. Even when the ritual order is desacralised, it survives as a system of social inequality and as a value that ranks people on a scale of honour and humiliation. Viewed from this perspective, caste may not appear to be a uniquely Indian or Hindu social institution, and this is worth considering.

Note

1. A good example of this is the response of mainstream sociologists of the time to the introduction of the Mandal Commission recommendations by the Central government in 1990, which extended a regime of caste-based reservations to the Other Backward Classes (OBCs). Some of the leading practitioners of the discipline vehemently opposed this recognition of caste shaping economic opportunities and the need for direct state action in the form of affirmative action policies.

References

Ambedkar, B. R. 1936. *Annihilation of Caste*. Available at http://ccnmtl.columbia.edu/projects/mmt/ambedkar/web/readings/aoc_print_2004.pdf, accessed on 14 June 2019.

Bailey, F. G. 1960. *Tribe, Caste and Nation*. Bombay: Oxford University Press.

Beidelman, T. O. 1959. *A Comparative Analysis of the Jajmani System*. Association for Asian Studies, Monograph Series VIII.

Berreman, G. 1991. 'The Brahamanical View of Caste', in D. Gupta (ed.), *Social Stratification*, pp. 84–92. Delhi: Oxford University Press.

Béteille, A. 1980. 'The Indian Village: Past and Present', in E. J. Hobsbawm, W. Kula, A. Mitra, K. N. Raj and I. Sachs (eds), *Peasants in History: Essays in Honour of Daniel Thorner*, pp. 107–20. Calcutta: Oxford University Press.

Béteille, A. 1986. 'Individualism and Equality', *Current Anthropology*, 27 (2): 121–34.

Bouglé, C. 1971. *Essays on the Caste System*. Cambridge: Cambridge University Press.

Cohn, B. S. 1968. 'Notes on the History of the Study of Indian Society and Culture', in M. Singer and B. S. Cohn (eds), *Structure and Change in Indian Society*, pp. 3–28. New York: Aldine Publishing Company.

———. 1996. *Colonialism and Its Forms of Knowledge: The British in India*. Princeton: Princeton University Press.

Das, V. and J. P. S. Uberoi. 1971. 'The Elementary Structures of Caste', *Contributions to Indian Sociology*, 5: 33–43.

Deshpande, A. 2011. *The Grammar of Caste: Economic Discrimination in Contemporary India*. Delhi: Oxford University Press.

Dirks, N. B. 2001. *Castes of Mind: Colonialism and the Making of Modern India*. Princeton: Princeton University Press.

Dube S. C. 1955. *Indian Village*. London: Routledge and Kegan Paul.

Dumont, L. 1971 [1970]. *Homo Hierarchicus: The Caste System and Its Implications*. Delhi: Oxford University Press.

Fuller, C. J. 1977. 'British India or Traditional India? An Anthropological Problem', *Ethnos*, 42 (3–4): 95–121.

Frykenberg, R. 1989. 'The Emergence of Modern "Hinduism" as a Concept and as an Institution: A Reappraisal with Special Reference to South India', in G. D. Sontheimer and H. Kulke (eds), *Hinduism Reconsidered*, pp. 29–49. Manohar: Delhi.

Gupta, D. 1984. 'Continuous Hierarchies and Discrete Castes', *Economic and Political Weekly*, 19 (46): 1955–2053.

———. 2000. *Interrogating Caste: Understanding Hierarchy and Difference in Indian Society*. Delhi: Penguin Books.

Inden, R. 1990. *Imagining India*. Oxford: Blackwell.

Jodhka, S. S. 2002. 'Caste and Untouchability in Rural Punjab', *Economic and Political Weekly*, 37 (19): 1813–23.

———. 2015. *Caste in Contemporary India*. New Delhi: Routledge.

Jodhka, S. S. and A. Prakash. 2016. *The Indian Middle Class*. New Delhi: Oxford University Press.

Jodhka, S. S. and K. Newman 2007. 'In the Name of Globalisation: Meritocracy, Productivity and the Hidden Language of Caste', *Economic and Political Weekly*, 42 (41): 4125–32.

Kothari, R. (ed.). 1970. *Caste in Indian Politics*. Hyderabad: Orient Longman.

Marx, K. 1853. 'The British Rule in India', *New York Daily Tribune*, 25 June 1853. Available at http://www.marxists.org/archive/marx/works/1853/06/25.htm, accessed on 12 February 2013.

Mencher, J. P. 1978. *Agriculture and Social Structure in Tamil Nadu: Past Origins, Present Transformations and Future Prospects*. Delhi: Allied Publishers.

Mosse, D. 2018. 'Caste and Development: Contemporary Perspectives on a Structure of Discrimination and Advantage', *World Development*, 110: 422–36.

Munshi, K. and M. Rosenzweig. 2006. 'Traditional Institutions Meet the Modern World: Caste, Gender, and Schooling Choice in a Globalizing Economy', *American Economic Review*, 96 (4): 1225–52.

Oberoi, H. 1994. *The Construction of Religious Boundaries: Culture, Identity and Diversity in the Sikh Tradition*. Delhi: Oxford University Press.

Raheja, G. G. 1988. 'Caste, Kingship, and Dominance Reconsidered', *Annual Review of Anthropology*, 17: 497–522.

———. 1989. 'Centrality, Mutuality and Hierarchy: Shifting Aspects of Inter-caste Relationships in North India', *Contributions to Indian Sociology* (n.s.), 23 (1): 79–101.

Rudolph, L. I. and S. H. Rudolph. 1967. *The Modernity of Tradition: Political Development in India*. Hyderabad: Orient Longman.

Rutten, M. 2003. *Rural Capitalists in Asia: A Comparative Analysis on India, Indonesia, and Malaysia*. London: Routledge.

Said, E. 1985. *Orientalism*. Harmondsworth: Penguin

Shah, G., H. Mander and S. Thorat. 2006. *Untouchability in Rural India*, New Delhi: Sage Publications.

Smith, B. K. 1989. *Reflections on Resemblance, Ritual and Religion*. New York: Oxford University Press.

Srinivas, M. N. (ed.). 1955. *India's Villages*. London: Asia Publishing House.

Thapar, R. 1989. 'Imagined Religious Communities? Ancient History and the Modern Search for a Hindu Identity', *Modern Asian Studies*, 23: 209–31.

Thorat, S. 2009. *Dalits in India: Search for a Common Destiny*. New Delhi: Sage Publications.

Thorat, S. and K. S. Newman (eds). 2010. *Blocked by Caste: Economic Discrimination and Social Exclusion in Modern India*. New Delhi: Oxford University Press.

Weber, Max. 1946. *From Max Weber: Essays in Sociology*. Edited, translated and with an introduction by H. H. Gerth and C. Wright Mills. Oxford: Oxford University Press.

Wiser, W. H. 1936. *The Hindu Jajmani System*. Lucknow: Lucknow Publishing House.

5 Beyond State and Nation

Anthropology of Muslims in South Asia

FARHANA IBRAHIM

The initial years of Indian sociology, as the discipline was crafted within various institutional contexts of postcolonial India, were marked by a relative absence of ethnographic studies of Muslims and the lived experience of Islam in India. This lacuna was commented upon in 1972 by Imtiaz Ahmad in *Contributions to Indian Sociology*, which ran an annual feature titled 'For a Sociology of India'. Ahmad's point was that it was not the volume of work on Hindus compared to non-Hindus that was the issue; the question to ask was whether 'the available literature tells us as much about the structure of non-Hindu groups, and the socio-cultural processes that have been operating amongst them, as it does about Hindus' (1972: 172). On this count, he pointed out, 'the poverty of Indian sociology is clearly evinced' (ibid.). Not only did the first two decades of the institutionalisation of the discipline in India contribute very little to an understanding of India's Muslims, but the sociology/anthropology of Islam in Indian contexts hardly generated the kind of conceptual tools for the discipline that were produced by in-depth ethnographic studies, for instance, of the caste system. These studies ended up generating concepts that provided a strong analytic framework for subsequent generations of sociologists, e.g., sanskritisation, hierarchy, social stratification and dominant caste—all conceptual offshoots from ethnographic studies of Hindu social organisation.[1]

The lack of contemporary ethnographies on Muslims was in contrast to the relatively rich body of literature on Muslims in

South Asia by historians like Richard Eaton (1978), David Lelyveld (1978) and Barbara Metcalf (1982, 1984). This body of literature focused on Islamic reform in the colonial period and provided theoretical insights into aspects of social and bodily discipline such as *adab*. Ahmad then led a series of initiatives to address the lack of ethnographic work on Islam in India to put together what we now recognise as a classic series of edited volumes: *Caste and Social Stratification among Muslims in India* (1973), *Family, Kinship and Marriage among Muslims in India* (1976), *Ritual and Religion among Muslims in India* (1981) and *Modernization and Social Change among Muslims in India* (1983). These studies were welcome additions to the ethnographic study of Muslim communities in India, and they emphasised the manner in which the ritual, kinship and everyday social organisation of Muslims in India were deeply embedded in structures shared with their Hindu neighbours. This was also in tune with the political exigencies of post-Partition India: sociologists emphasising the fabric of everyday life that was shared by Hindus and Muslims in a particular region were perhaps calling into question the 'two-nation theory' that had culminated in the violent Partition of 1947. This so-called continuum between Hindu and Muslim lifeworlds provided the early context for sociological debates on 'Islamisation', once again in the pages of *Contributions* in the 1980s (Robinson 1983, 1986; Das 1984; Minault 1984). Much of this debate hinged on the so-called 'Indianness' of Islam as it was practised in the subcontinent (a view favoured by sociologists), while historians had for long emphasised aspects of Islamic universalism at the normative level, especially as it had played out during the colonial period, through debates on what has variously been termed 'Islamic reform', 'revival' or 'Islamisation' across Muslim societies globally (Robinson 1983; Lelyveld 1978; Sanyal 1996; Metcalf 1982). Veena Das' (1984) intervention in the debate pointed to the futility of thinking of text and practice as watertight terms, proposing instead the mediating categories of 'folk theology' and 'theological anthropology'.

In 2008, a special two-volume set of the journal *Modern Asian Studies* was dedicated to Islamic reform in South Asia. Articles examined the question of reform ethnographically to further nuance the anthropological understanding of Islam in South Asia, specifically pointing out the problems associated with attributing an exceptionalism to Indian Islam, which foreclosed the possibility of radical movements internal to it. Today, we are at a juncture where the breadth of anthropological work on Muslim communities in India has successfully moved the terms of academic debate away from a singular understanding of Muslims in India. It is now accepted, in academic discourse if not in the realm of policy, that Muslims in India—as indeed elsewhere—do not constitute a singularly defined community. Not only are there a range of formally identified 'sects' under the umbrella denominations of 'Shi'a' and 'Sunni' but also a series of *maslaks* or 'interpretive communities' (Alam 2008: 607n5) that may be deeply antagonistic to each other.

Taking this broad overview of the anthropological study of Islam in India as a point of departure, this chapter attempts to make two related arguments. First, what must distinguish an anthropological approach to Islam in India—or as I will argue, more broadly, in South Asia—ought to be a commitment to move the study of Muslims beyond terms naturalised by the framework of the nation state (territorial and ideological). In other words, it should be premised on a repudiation of methodological nationalism. Second, it must take seriously categories of belief and practice *as articulated by Muslims themselves*. In other words, what must distinguish an anthropological approach is an engagement with 'emic' categories, i.e., how do Muslims of various persuasions *see themselves* even when they challenge the normative views held by the researcher. As a series of ethnographic accounts have demonstrated, shared lifeworlds and ideas of 'syncretism' may often belie the ideological predispositions of the researcher rather than the group that is being studied, some members of which may vehemently deride the idea of a lifeworld that overlaps with members of other religions or even with groups within their own religion.

Rethinking 'Syncretism'

Richard Eaton (2003), a historian of medieval India, posed the question 'Who Are the Bengal Muslims' in an essay with the same title. He proceeded to offer a finely textured account of the embedding of Islam within the local agrarian and riverine economy of the Bengal delta. The rise of Islam in the deltaic regions of Bengal, he argued, was closely linked to the spread of rice cultivation and the work of charismatic forest pioneers who cleared the land for agrarian settlement. Eaton's work is useful to keep in mind today, because it reminds us that Islam does not spread in a modular fashion, regardless of the singular trajectory implied by the term 'Islamisation'. An emphasis on a shared agrarian lifeworld also indicates the limits of how far we might be able to take the 'syncretism' strand of debate that was once fashionable in the study of Islam in the South Asian context. The so-called syncretic elements of South Asian Islam were typically located at the site of the dargah, in the person of the pir and so on (Roy 2014). However, if we privilege the emic view, it becomes possible to identify the imposition of such heuristic categories (such as 'syncretism' or the 'folk') as a consequence of the ideological dispositions of the researcher rather than as categories holding merit with practitioners themselves. As Peter van der Veer (1994) points out, the attribution of 'syncretic' to a set of religious practices is premised on the certification of a religious 'truth' from which the 'syncretic' is a form of deviation. From the perspective of believers, 'syncretism' typically does not carry the moral or ideologically positive valence that it has had for a generation of scholars writing about Islam in India, just as the attribution of 'folk' does not usually find much positive purchase with those who follow practices deemed as such. As pointed out in a recent PhD thesis on the Barelvis, 'for believers the Barelwi interpretation of Islam is not a particular brand of Islam but Islam itself' (Farah 2016: 7). The advocacy of 'syncretism' by scholars is an ideological position that may not necessarily be reflected in the practice of religion as we encounter it in the field.

The well-known dargah of Haji Pir, nestled deep in the Rann of Kutch in the area known as Banni (in Gujarat state), hosts an annual *'urs* that draws devotees from far and wide among diasporic Kutchi communities in Mumbai and beyond—Hindus, Muslims and Jains—many of whom travel several kilometres on foot, a sign of their devotion to the pir. The pilgrimage is only undertaken when the *bulawa* (call) comes from the pir himself. During the season of the 'urs, in the dry hot summer period corresponding to the Hindu calendar's month of Chaitra, roadside kiosks come up to serve water and sherbet to passing pilgrims as a way of acquiring religious merit. As discussed elsewhere (Ibrahim 2009), the 'urs is routinely prefaced in Kutch with the phrase 'Hindu–Mussalman ekta na prateek' (a symbol of Hindu–Muslim unity) in all textual references to it carried in the local print media as well as on billboards and pamphlets. My initial fieldwork took place immediately on the heels of a pogrom against Gujarat's Muslims. In 2003, more pilgrims were expected to attend the 'urs after two consecutive years of disruptions—a massive earthquake in 2001 and the pogrom in 2002. I have argued (ibid.) that the Haji Pir dargah carries a great deal of symbolic value for the Indian state and civil society, which is somewhat disproportionate to the attention given to it by Muslims in Kutch. Its location on the border and attraction to non-Muslim devotees helps bolster the state's 'secular' credentials in contrast to neighbouring Pakistan, even as local pastoralists who have adopted the Ahl-e-Hadith maslak since the 1960s are steadfast about not worshipping at the shrine. The dargah's significance, in other words, is reinscribed into a very different framework that has little to do with Islam or the debates among Muslims regarding the propriety of saint worship. A website for the dargah describes it in the following terms:

> The shrine of Haji Pir in Kutch has many Hindu followers. 'Low' caste Kolis offer free service and keep the shrine clean, and a rich Jain industrialist has paid for constructing its boundary walls. These are the picture's [sic] of the mazaar of Haji Pir (R.A.) of Kutch Bhuj, India. It is about 2 km's [sic] from the Pakistan border, from the Mazaar boundary wall one can see the army post between these two country [sic].[2]

This short description is a good reflection of the key concerns that animate both the shrine and its annual festival—its location along the Pakistan border and its ability to draw participation from a cross-caste and -religious demographic. Haji Pir is advertised as 'Banni ka badshah' or 'Kutch ka shahenshah', but Muslim pastoralists of the Banni grasslands who live in the vicinity of the shrine have little to do with it. For some decades, they have been favouring the Ahl-e-Hadith maslak, which stigmatises shrine visitations and views them as deviations from 'properly' Islamic practices. The attribution of Hindu–Muslim amity to the shrine and the availability of popular audio CDs at the dargah, which clearly cater to a religiously plural audience, thus shore up ideological positions that do not necessarily reflect the way Muslims of the region see themselves. 'Communal harmony' and the supposedly syncretic leanings of certain Muslim shrines are more appropriately terms of discourse that reflect 'governmental strategy' (Menon 2015: 395) more accurately than the field itself. As Menon (ibid.) argues, 'the state's endorsement of *dargah*-centred Islamic piety ... as an exemplary site of communal harmony and particular ideas of the Indian nation legitimized by communal harmony "problematizes" the national belonging of certain kinds of pious Muslims'. In other words, those who shun 'dargah-centred' piety in favour of what they variously define as 'rational' and more 'literate' forms of Islamic practice are then singled out as 'hardliners' or 'fundamentalists', who are believed to threaten the presumably a priori syncretic nature of 'Indian' Islam, which is viewed in contrast to the Islam that is practised in Pakistan or Bangladesh. The dargah becomes key to the ongoing problem of representation of Islam and Muslims in the public sphere in India where broadly 'Hindu' cultural and religious symbolism is the unmarked category, the default normative identity of the 'Indian' citizen. The Sufi and the dargah then become components of the archetype of the 'good Muslim'. The dargah, however, as most scholars of Islam find out in the field, does not represent the effusive mingling of Hindus and Muslims as much as it is a flashpoint for competing interpretations of Islam.

Borders and Boundaries: Beyond Nationalist Frames of Reference

As argued in the preceding section, categories such as 'communal harmony' or 'syncretism' must be rigorously interrogated at the conceptual level, and anthropologists must, in particular, ask what meaning these concepts have on the ground. At a time when the political rhetoric of indigeneity has become a mode of political mobilisation and a means of reiterating citizenship claims—for instance, the relative evaluation of immigrants from Bangladesh as 'refugees' or 'infiltrators' depending upon their religious affiliation[3]—our scholarly task is to counter these claims without necessarily falling back into the very nationalist frame that takes recourse to either indigeneity or Indian exceptionalism. In other words, political rhetoric ought to be countered, without letting it set the terms of academic debate. What this also means is that studies on Islam and Muslims in India should not have to be apologetic about 'transnational' connections— every transnational religious connection does not necessarily counteract 'local' roots or confirm the 'separatist' tendencies of India's Muslims. This is excellently demonstrated in ethnographic studies of Kerala's Mujahids (members of the Kerala Nadvathul Mujahideen or KNM) (Osella and Osella 2008) and the Twelver Shi'ites of Kargil (Gupta 2014). The Osellas have argued that aspirations of pan-Islamism—or the desire to approximate globally recognisable forms of Islam—does not preclude the fact that idioms of reform in Kerala have been produced in local terms since at least the nineteenth century onwards. Reformist tendencies in Islam, they argue, are not without exception 'external' to the nation state. On the other hand, the Twelver Shi'as, who live along a contested national border in Kargil district of the Indian state of Jammu and Kashmir, are deeply invested in maintaining religious networks of learning that have historically linked the region to West Asia rather than the Indian mainland. These networks persist in the present and are crucial to the manner in which local political factions and religious schisms are managed. The existence of such networks per se can hardly be taken as proof of a lack of investment in the nation state; on the contrary, these transnational religious connections may often co-exist with a deep attachment to the Indian state. For Kargil's Shi'as, it is important to cultivate the role of loyal citizens, in marked contrast to the Sunnis of the Kashmir Valley (Gupta 2013). Borders and boundaries persist at multiple levels; to naturalise those of the nation state is to render a disservice to the particularities of different field sites.

For Muslims who literally live in national borderlands, that is, in areas that constitute the borders of the nation state, the border is not merely a heuristic device—it is performed on an everyday basis through encounters with various forms of state or military personnel, bureaucracy, religious leaders and others. But this is not a feature of the external border alone. During the decade of the 2000s and beyond, the state (in Gujarat and subsequently also at the Centre) has been identified with a particularly strident form of Hindu nationalist discourse that discursively produces Islam, Muslims, terrorism and cross-border infiltration within a dominant narrative of national insecurity, the onus of which is mapped to a considerable extent onto the figure of the Muslim. The state and the Muslim citizen are seemingly locked into a cycle of distrust and suspicion; this has often produced on the part of many Muslims a general sense of unease or 'unhomeliness', embedded within what has been referred to as the 'political economy of hopelessness' (Jeffery et al. 2008: 541). The casting of the Muslim as the 'outsider' or the 'internal enemy' is spatially instantiated by areas within cities being referred to as 'mini-Pakistans', demarcated by social and physical 'borders' (Subramaniam 1999; Ghassem-Fachandi 2012). The nation state's external political borders are transposed onto internal spatial, socio-political and cultural borders within the territorial heart of the nation.

When we move to the territorial 'national' border, we find again that the 'border' actualises itself in multiple and shifting ways. Through a decade and a half of ethnographic fieldwork in Gujarat's Kutch district, which forms a part of India's western border with Pakistan, among Muslim *maldharis* (pastoralists and cattle breeders) in the Banni grasslands, my research has revealed that for these borderland Muslims, the state is not always the chief antagonist. To be sure, the state is sedentarising and spatialising in nature, and as James Scott (1998) reminds us, it has a particular optic through which it organises and categorises. Within this framework, the cattle herder is not the normative settled peasant proprietor engaged in a revenue-generating relationship with the state. The maldhari is a far more fluid category and—if they are Muslims living on a border with Pakistan—then the postcolonial state's anxiety vis-à-vis border maintenance plays out in very particular ways in terms of how it reads, tracks and deploys particular modes of surveillance over them. For the state, these maldharis are incomplete citizens—their habitation on a national border with ties of kinship and religion that transcend the border (whether this is transcendence is something they desire or not; not all of them do) makes their loyalty suspect even as they are an important support base to shore up the state's bureaucratic outreach in remote and inhospitable areas through informer networks.

Even as the state sees them in terms of the unitary entity of 'Muslims', the maldharis are caught up in straddling several distinct boundaries of which the national border is only one. They are divided into fairly distinct endogamous groups that are locally referred to as *qaum* (contextually translated as community, people, nation), and while they share certain common attributes such as marriage practices and are united by an overarching pastoral ethos, there are subtle differences between each in terms of their relationship to mobility and animals. While the Jatts are unanimously decreed to be the most nomadic, travelling from place to place with their *mal* (in this case, animals) and packing up their households in search of better pastures, the Mutwas have always been more sedentary, outsourcing the grazing of their animals to others while focusing on trading in milk and ghee. Yet other communities are acknowledged as the custodians of the best secrets to good buffalo breeding. There is a hierarchy of status in the Banni region, with the Jatts occupying the lower echelons and the Mutwas in closer alliance with the state and in an earlier period with kings. Apart from distinct qaums, there is also the vexed question of maslak affiliation, with maldharis identifying themselves as Sunni (Ahl-e-Sunnat wa'l Jama'at) or Ahl-e-Hadith. I have discussed the production of Islamic identity in Kutch vis-à-vis these groups elsewhere (Ibrahim 2009, 2011), drawing attention to the inadequacy of viewing 'Muslims' as producing themselves in opposition to 'Hindus' or the 'state', all seen as homogeneous entities.

Much like the Shi'as in Kargil, who also live on a national border—and thus are useful for the state to cultivate as loyal citizens—the maldharis of Banni have produced themselves vis-à-vis a broad range of 'others' over time. In the early years after Partition, some Muslims of Banni and the neighbouring region of Khawda presented the chief commissioner with a 'declaration of loyalty', pledging their lives to the nation in the event of an 'attack' from Pakistan. The declaration opened with the statement, 'We the Muslims of Banni and Khawda', and demanded that it be forwarded to the prime ministers of both India and Pakistan, making an unambiguous statement of 'allegiance'. Here, they produced themselves as a unified bloc, yet at other moments, the production of a unified religious identity is fraught and deeply undercut with debates internal to the community about the nature of their engagement with not only the state and political power but also religious leaders and multiple maslak affiliations. At other times, the boundaries of religious belief and practice are drawn firmly around Kutch as a distinct regional entity uniting those within from 'outsiders'. One of my fieldwork encounters records the frustration of a village elder at not being able to recruit a suitable maulana for the madrassa in the village. 'I want a local man; not from Rajasthan, not from Arabistan, he must be *local*', he shouted emphatically. The tensions hinted at here have to do with not only maslak orientations (as the somewhat pejorative reference to Saudi Arabia connotes) but also linguistic abilities and the adab of the Kutchi-speaking person, something that the elder wanted transmitted to the children in the madrasa. These anxieties were articulated at a moment when, following the earthquake of 2001, the rapid urbanisation and 'development' of Bhuj provoked a number of anxieties related to the continuity of regional cultural identity in the face of 'external' challenges, both metropolitan urban planners and transnational religious aid organisations (Simpson 2013).

Contingent and shifting boundaries do not merely demarcate the so-called Indian Muslim from those who are outside national borders; these boundaries can also identify other splits and cleavages within, and these too are contingent divides. An ethnographic commitment to bring to light the diversity of Islam as it is practised—even as believers insist on the normative superiority of their own practice—must thus reject the dichotomy of an 'indigenous' or 'Indian' Islam versus a 'reformist' Islam that is attributed to 'external' influences (typically identified as Wahabism or Salafism, assumed to have been exported from Saudi Arabia). Islamic 'reform'—what I will loosely characterise for the moment as a set of practices that seek to distance the practice of Islam from what are perceived to be 'dilutions' or interpretive excesses—aspires towards what is deemed to be a more 'pure' form of the religion. These practices retain an element of aspiration—a state that is seen as desirable by its adherents but is ultimately a work in progress. Further, it is a state of being that is contested from maslak to maslak. Aspirations to reform, moreover, are neither 'external' to Indian Muslims nor threatening to cleave apart communities that shared some original coherence. They are an integral part of the historical development within various schools of Islamic thought, practice and jurisprudence 'within' South Asia. Similarly, maslak affiliation is not cast in stone and often varies within families or individuals as it becomes a mode of strategising individual choice in an ideologically varied marketplace (e.g., Jasani 2008) or within individual lifetimes as people move between and across ideological stances, rendering it almost impossible, if not misleading, to make broad generalisations about shifts in religiosity or maslak dominance in any given place (Simpson 2008). The anthropological shift from 'Muslims'—or at most 'Shi'a' and 'Sunni' Islam—to a serious examination of maslak affiliation is a welcome addition to the study of Islam in South Asia. As scholars have pointed out, the 'other' for many practising Muslims in India is not the 'Hindu' or the 'state' per se but those who do not share the ideological universe of a maslak identity. Arshad Alam (2008), in his study of madrasas in Azamgarh district of Uttar Pradesh, demonstrates that the madrasa is a site for making students more aware of their own ideological orientations, sharpening their sense of identity through the rigorous practice of learning, including debates and public discussions, by means of which non-maslaki Muslims are produced as the 'internal enemy' of Islam. He argues that the madrasa is not necessarily engaged in the production of anti-Hindu or anti-state rhetoric as is commonly thought, but it seeks to sharpen the awareness of identity 'within' maslaks, making it redundant to talk about any unified 'Islamic' identity as such (see also van der Veer 1992). It is thus difficult if not impossible to make sweeping generalisations, for instance, those that posit causality between Gulf migration and growing Islamic orthodoxy. Such shifts are often not as teleological as is assumed and may be more productively linked with processes such as middle class aspirations. In any case, such broad and unilateral shifts would be difficult to support ethnographically.

Towards an Anthropology of Muslims

This chapter has called into question the appropriateness of methodological nationalism implied in the designation 'sociology of India' still taught as such in university departments. This approach also extends to the sociology and anthropology of Islam in India. If our focus is to be the anthropology of Islam *in* India rather than the anthropology of 'Indian' Islam, we must necessarily be sceptical of the degree to which the nation state constitutes an adequate delimitation of the field. I have suggested in this chapter that the 'sociology of India' cannot remain impervious to the transnational, regional or global, and this is also true for the study of religion. In an age of globalisation and transnational networks and flows, what is the utility of the national border to circumscribe scholarly work? Historians have given us a great deal of remarkable scholarship on Islam in the subcontinent inflected by mobility and transnational flows through an exploration of networks both maritime and inland (Alexander et al. 2016; Ho 2006; Green 2011; Ricci 2011). In my recent research, I look at nineteenth-century mercantile networks between Bombay, Kutch, Zanzibar and Muscat in order to understand the constitution of the family and marriage networks in the context of mobility among merchant communities of western India. Anthropologists of Islam must therefore take seriously the conceptual turns in the study of borders, migration and mobility. While the implications of South Asia's various partitions—in 1947 and 1971—are explored in studies of migration and displacement, these histories and their implications for the present also need to be worked out by anthropologists of religion in South Asia.

I will then conclude by underscoring the need to be ever more nuanced in our studies by asking *who* are the Muslims of the subcontinent, *what* are their religious affiliations, *how* do they view their interactions within and across a domain of sociality and of belief that they deem to be Islamic and *who* are the 'others' against whom they identify themselves? Here, I would like to underscore the importance of not only how we—as academics, policymakers and others—identify India's Muslim communities, whether in terms of singular or plural identifications, but also how they identify themselves. While the democratic state is in the business of enumeration and identification, and may choose to apprehend a community as a singular and homogeneous bloc, how do various communities choose to self-identify? Who are the 'others' against whom they define themselves? To answer this, one must also be aware of the fact that this definition is contextual to geographical and historical specificities. Finally, the territorial limits of the nation state may no longer be the most useful conceptual delimiter of an academic study. To this extent, the study of Islam in India must engage with ethnographic work done in the broader region as well as take seriously the existing historical literature on South Asia's Muslim communities.

Notes

1. Non-Hindu communities were not the only ones neglected in the early years; women and Dalits also remained underrepresented (Kumar 2016).
2. Available at http://www.aulia-e-hind.com/dargah/Kutch.htm, accessed on 18 December 2016.
3. See http://indianexpress.com/article/india/politics/bangladeshi-infiltrators-must-go-back-refugees-welcome-say-narendra-modi/, accessed on 20 April 2017.

References

Ahmad, I. 1972. 'For a Sociology of India', *Contributions to Indian Sociology* (n.s.), 6 (1): 172–78.

———. (ed.). 1973. *Caste and Social Stratification among Muslims in India*. New Delhi: Manohar.

———. (ed.). 1976. *Family, Kinship and Marriage among Muslims in India*. New Delhi: South Asia Books.

———. (ed.). 1981. *Ritual and Religion among Muslims in India*. New Delhi: Manohar.

———. (ed.). 1983. *Modernization and Social Change among Muslims in India*. New Delhi: Manohar.

Alam, A. 2008. 'The Enemy Within: Madrasa and Muslim Identity in North India', *Modern Asian Studies*, 42 (2–3): 605–27.

Alexander, C., J. Chatterji and A. Jalais. 2016. *The Bengal Diaspora: Rethinking Muslim Migration*. London: Routledge.

Das, Veena. 1984. 'For a Folk-Theology and Theological Anthropology of Islam'. *Contributions to Indian Sociology* (n.s.): 18 (2): 239–305.

Eaton, R. M. 1978. *Sufis of Bijapur 1300–1700: Social Roles of Sufis in Medieval India*. Princeton: Princeton University Press.

———. 2003. 'Who Are the Bengal Muslims? Conversion and Islamization in Bengal', in R. Robinson and S. Clarke (eds), *Religious Conversion in India: Modes, Motivations, and Meanings*, pp. 75–97. New Delhi: Oxford University Press.

Farah, S. 2016. 'Piety and Politics in Local Level Islam: A Case Study of Barelwi Khanqahs', unpublished PhD dissertation submitted to the Department of Sociology, University of Delhi.

Ghassem-Fachandi, P. 2012. *Pogrom in Gujarat: Hindu Nationalism and Anti-Muslim Violence in India*. Princeton: Princeton University Press.

Green, N. 2011. *Bombay Islam: The Religious Economy of the West Indian Ocean, 1840–1915*. Cambridge: Cambridge University Press.

Gupta, R. 2013. 'Allegiance and Alienation: Border Dynamics in Kargil', in David Gellner (ed.), *Borderland Lives in Northern South Asia*, pp. 47–71. Durham: Duke University Press.

———. 2014. 'Experiments with Khomeini's Revolution in Kargil: Contemporary Shi'a Networks between India and West Asia', *Modern Asian Studies*, 48 (02): 370–98.

Ho, E. 2006. *The Graves of Tarim: Genealogy and Mobility across the Indian Ocean*. Berkeley: University of California Press.

Ibrahim, F. 2009. *Settlers, Saints and Sovereigns: An Ethnography of State Formation in Western India*. New Delhi: Routledge.

———. 2011. 'Border Transgressions and the Frontiers of Faith in Kachchh, Gujarat', in V. K. Jairath (ed.), *Frontiers of Embedded Muslim Communities in India*, pp. 29–48. New Delhi: Routledge.

Jasani, Rubina. 2008. 'Violence, Reconstruction and Islamic Reform: Stories from the Muslim "Ghetto"', *Modern Asian Studies*, 42 (2–3): 431–56.

Jeffery, Patricia, Roger Jeffery and Craig Jeffrey. 2008. 'Disputing Contraception: Muslim Reform, Secular Change and Fertility', *Modern Asian Studies*, 42 (2–3): 519–48.

Kumar, Vivek. 2016. 'How Egalitarian Is Indian Sociology?'*Economic and Political Weekly*, 51 (25): 33–39.

Lelyveld, D. 1978. *Aligarh's First Generation: Muslim Solidarity in British India*. Princeton: Princeton University Press.

Menon, N. R. 2015. 'Communal Harmony as Governmentality: Reciprocity, Peace-Keeping, State Legitimacy, and Citizenship in Contemporary India', *Modern Asian Studies*, 49 (2): 393–429.

Metcalf, B. D. 1982. *Islamic Revival in British India: Deoband, 1860–1900*. Princeton: Princeton University Press.

———. 1984. *Moral Conduct and Authority: The Place of Adab in South Asian Islam*. Berkeley: University of California Press.

Minault, G. 1984. 'Some Reflections on Islamic Revivalism vs. Assimilation among Muslims in India', *Contributions to Indian Sociology* (n.s.), 18 (2): 301–05.

Osella, F. and C. Osella. 2008. 'Islamism and Social Reform in Kerala, South India', *Modern Asian Studies*, 42 (2–3): 317–46.

Ricci, R. 2011. *Islam Translated: Literature, Conversion, and the Arabic Cosmopolis of South and Southeast Asia*. Chicago: University of Chicago Press.

Robinson, F. 1983. 'Islam and Muslim Society in South Asia', *Contributions to Indian Sociology* (n.s.), 17 (2): 185–203.

———. 1986. 'Islam and Muslim Society in South Asia: A Reply to Das and Minault', *Contributions to Indian Sociology* (n.s.), 20 (1): 97–104.

Roy, A. 2014. *The Islamic Syncretistic Tradition in Bengal*. Princeton: Princeton University Press.

Sanyal, U. 1996. *Devotional Islam and Politics in British India: Ahmad Riza Khan Barelwi and His Movement, 1870–1920*. New Delhi: Oxford University Press.

Scott, James C. 1998. *Seeing like a State: How Certain Schemes to Improve the Human Condition Have Failed*. New Haven: Yale University Press.

Simpson, E. 2008. 'The Changing Perspectives of Three Muslim Men on the Question of Saint Worship over a 10-Year Period in Gujarat, Western India', *Modern Asian Studies*, 42 (2–3): 377–403.

———. 2013. *The Political Biography of an Earthquake: Aftermath and Amnesia in Gujarat, India*. New Delhi: Oxford University Press.

Subramaniam, R.1999. 'Culture of Suspicion: Riots and Rumor in Bombay, 1992–1993', *Transforming Anthropology*, 8 (1–2): 97–110.

van der Veer, P. 1992. 'Playing or Praying: A Sufi Saint's Day in Surat', *The Journal of Asian Studies*, 51 (03): 545–64.

———. 1994. 'Syncretism, Multiculturalism and the Discourse of Tolerance', in C. Stewart and R. Shaw (eds), *Syncretism/Anti-syncretism: The Politics of Religious Synthesis*, pp. 196–211. London: Routledge.

SECTION TWO

Family, Marriage, Caste and Religiosities in Contemporary India

6 The Rebellious Woman and the Violence of Consensus

Contemporary Contestations of the Domestic Space

KAMALA GANESH*

Aftermath of a Gutsy Film

On 29 April 2016, a Marathi film called *Sairat* was released all over Maharashtra. It immediately created a huge buzz among the public and in the film industry, including Mumbai's Hindi film industry. When I watched it two weeks later, it was running to full houses, with a noisy audience whistling and endorsing every scene, dancing to the cracking music and then falling to pindrop silence in the last 15 minutes of the denouement. Along with slick craftsmanship influenced by Bollywood, the director forthrightly tackled a taboo topic in popular cinema. The first three-day weekend collection was over 12 crore rupees, the highest ever for a Marathi film. Eventually the film made box office history as the highest-grossing Marathi film ever. Despite its regional rootedness—even native Marathi speakers strained to follow the dialogues in the thick Solapur dialect—it was dubbed and screened all over India and won widespread critical acclaim as well as some criticism about its gender politics.[1]

Set in rural Maharashtra, *Sairat* is about the romance between an upper caste, wealthy, Patil (Maratha) girl Archi and a Dalit boy

* I would like to thank Ashish Upadhyay for research assistance.

Parshya from a fishing community. The idyllic village life and love and pampering that Archi receives from her family are turned upside down when the inter-caste love affair becomes known. She is beaten, shut off in her home and her marriage within the community is arranged. Parshya too is beaten up violently and threatened with murder. Archi, a high-spirited girl, rebels against the family norms and strictures. She runs away with Parshya to another city in another state. The two of them struggle with many difficulties, marry, eventually manage to find jobs, have a child and live in contentment. In a few years, they are tracked down by Archi's male kinsmen and murdered in revenge for defying the family and marrying out of caste.

The film is unusual because the romance is explicitly shown as inter-caste, with all its ramifications and consequences. Also unusual is the young woman's determination to marry the partner of her choice, fiercely opposing her family and outright rejecting the alternative alliance. Feisty and aggressive, in the romance too, she takes the initiative, demanding love, on the one hand, and loyally standing by her lover, on the other. She is certainly not a helpless victim. Her rebellion leads to loss of family and community support. Her own natal family, which had sent her to college and protected her in every way, eventually kills her for rebelling. The murder is a consensual act by the males in her natal family.

The film captures three current trends in marriage in India. First, assertion by young women to pursue their desires and make their own choices, thereby claiming agency over their lives. Second, the significance of choice or 'love' in marriage even though the preference for arranged, intra-caste marriage continues to be very high. Third, and this in some senses negates the first two, the intricate link between the immediate family, the extended clan and the caste community in the matter of women's sexuality and marriage. Caste honour is predicated on the honour of women, which has to be defended with violence if necessary. A marriage that violates caste rules is a major threat to 'honour'.

The third point is exemplified in not merely the storyline of *Sairat* but also the hostile reception to the film by Marathas. In a sense, the film catalysed the nascent ethno-political ambitions of the Marathas, a dominant caste in Maharashtra, comprising nearly one-third of the population. A full-fledged movement for the recognition of Marathas as a backward-caste (the official category of Other Backward Class or OBC) emerged in the year following *Sairat*, and it fructified partially with the Maharashtra assembly passing a bill proposing 16 per cent quota for Marathas on 29 November 2018 (*Times of India* 2018).

The anger of Marathas stemmed from the depiction of their community as casteist towards Dalits and violent towards their own women. In the backdrop of rising caste violence in Maharashtra, and specifically recent cases of young Dalit men being murdered, allegedly by Marathas,[2] the topic of inter-caste marriage was a contentious and volatile one. The recent right-wing campaigns against love, elopement and marriage between Hindu women and Muslim men had also tried intimidation and violence by mobilising the religious community. While inter-caste marriages have always been met with family opposition, such a widespread mobilisation of identity politics over marriage is a contemporary development.

There was widespread condemnation in the Maratha community of what was considered to be its demonisation by the film's director Nagaraj Manjule, himself a Dalit. A case[3] was filed in the lower court at Aurangabad complaining against the targeting of the community. A legal notice was sent to Manjule to remove objectionable dialogues from the film, which they alleged promoted animosity between different communities. In July 2016, a 14-year-old girl from a poor Maratha family was raped and brutally murdered in Kopardi village in Ahmednagar district. The alleged perpetrators were three Dalit youths, who were later arrested (Sonawane and Pagar 2016).[4] The incident stunned and then galvanised the Marathas into organising community-wide protests under the banner of Maratha Kranti Morcha. The protests were remarkable for their huge turnout, for the visible participation of women and girls, and for being peaceful and silent. Referred to as *muk morcha* (literally, silent rally), these protests had no sloganeering or speeches, only placards and lakh-strong protestors marching. The larger issue of reservation for Marathas in the OBC category was also raised. It had been first raised in 1997 and had been simmering on a low fire. It now assumed serious proportions, in the backdrop of recent mobilisations of dominant castes like Gujjars, Jats and Patels for similar demands (*Economic and Political Weekly* 2016: 9; Teltumbde 2016). Additionally, the Maratha Kranti Morcha was campaigning for the repeal of the Scheduled Castes and Scheduled Tribes (Prevention of Atrocities) Act, 1989.

The Maratha community is considered to have a conservative approach to women's education, employment, mobility and, in particular, participation in public life. In some self-definitions, the community describes Maratha women as 'those who do not cross the threshold of the home' (Gawali 2017).

The debate that raged about the status of Maratha women in the year following the release of *Sairat* also perhaps resulted in the defensive move of conspicuously including women and young girls, even small children, in the Maratha Kranti Morcha. The women are apparently tutored on their conduct in the morchas but not included in the planning of its activities. They speak about justice for the Kopardi victim but not about atrocities against women within the community. They are exhorted to follow the Maratha Hindu nationalist model attributed to Shivaji's mother Jijabai.[5] This harkens to a hypernationalist mode. The route to the contemporary politics of Maratha identity has been through the caste and gender nexus. Family is the proximate institution that socialises members into caste, sexual and marital norms, and enforces, polices and punishes violations. The Marathas have an elaborate clan network. With their associations with royalty, concomitantly the linkages among individual families, the extended clan and the caste are strongly preserved. The issue of and the mobilisation around Maratha identity is, however, not an isolated phenomenon. From the Khap panchayats in Haryana and western Uttar Pradesh to the Mukhtar Mai case in Pakistan and honour killings in the Punjabi diaspora in Canada and the UK, the onus of preserving group identity, whether that of caste, ethnicity or religion, is unsurprisingly put on the behaviour, especially sexual behaviour, of women.

Contemporary developments such as these gesture to the fraught atmosphere in the domain of marriage and family. The rebellion of young women inevitably seems to lead to the closing in of ranks by the family against them and violent reprisals against any show of agency. These visible and volatile contestations fly in the face of the cherished image of the Indian family as a united, cohesive and harmonious unit. Such is the power of this image that even the sociology of family in India has not been impervious to it (Ganesh 2013).

Let us now turn to the established field of the sociology of family and kinship to see if it has the conceptual and theoretical wherewithal to comprehend these developments.

A New Category in the Sociology of Family

The sociology of family and kinship is as old as the discipline of sociology itself. Changing family forms and structures since the Industrial Revolution have been the discipline's staple preoccupation. Globalisation processes in India over the last few decades have undeniably impacted the domestic domain—family structures and dynamics, household size and composition, the salience of extended kinship, relations between generations, between consanguines and between affines, and gender dynamics. The contours and meanings of these changes are complex, and a comprehensive analysis of these changes and the way sociology has responded to these is beyond the scope of this chapter.

This chapter focuses on an emerging category that sociology in India needs not only to recognise but also document quantitatively—the young, unmarried, working woman in the urbanised new middle class, with a relatively higher income compared to that of her parents. Her aspirations and assertions, and her negotiations with and responses from the family and community demand our attention. In a society whose demographic dividend is at a high point, this is a significant category. This chapter identifies the category and analyses its role in the dynamics of the domestic domain, rather than estimating its size and detailed demographic profile.

Recognising this category helps us move from an excessive focus on the marital family to the natal family as a potent source of control over women. On the one hand, new research such as Alice Clark's (2016) reveals that presently young women across social segments within the middle class get family encouragement for education and permission for employment at least until marriage. At the same time, the domestic space is implicated in the politics of caste, community, state and market. This is not new, but in recent decades, the sharper assertions of ethnic identities are tightly interlinked with the domestic arena. Controls and constraints on women regarding their personal behaviour, notably marriage, continue to be intense even as new openings for employment and mobility become available to them. How do we understand these contradictions? In recent times, many instances have been reported in the media of young couples defying norms of endogamy and meeting with violent reprisals at the hands of the family and community. This phenomenon requires a rethinking of the traditional sociological perspective on the family as a sealed, private, harmonious space. The newer approaches to kinship as interlinked with community—caring and nurturing in its benign form but patriarchal and violent when challenged—contain insights brought in by feminism since the 1970s, which were integrated within the sociology of family and kinship in India.[6]

The 'Domestic' in Sociology

The domestic domain has been long valorised in functionalist sociology as a privileged zone, based on consensus, a cushion against the outside world, providing succor to its own in times of need. This conceptualisation presumed a rational division of labour, with the breadwinner–father playing the instrumental role and the homemaker–wife–mother playing the expressive role. Such a nuclear family household, according to the dominant Parsonian paradigm, was best suited for emerging societies of the West after the Industrial Revolution. Kinship studies, on the other hand, have typically been absorbed in documenting the diverse kinship systems and fitting them into what Malinowski (1930: 19) termed the 'algebra' of descent and alliance. The material and psychological implications of kinship for human actors, the nature and quality of intra- and inter-familial relations, the place of gender, and the link between the intimate domain and macro social institutions were rarely emphasised.[7]

The evolution of sociology in India was undeniably influenced by colonial and nationalist discourses. Within the field of family and kinship studies, we can see this at work in the weight of the joint family model, derived from Indology and buttressed by colonial scholarship. This created a confusing picture, mixing up ideal types with practices. This is why sociologists in the 1950s and 1960s were preoccupied with clearing the ground, clarifying the distinction between family and household, and empirically demonstrating that joint and nuclear family types were neither polar opposites nor did they exhaust the wide gamut of actual living arrangements.[8] However, despite some fine ethnographic and conceptual work, gender and power were rarely problematised in the field.

Gender and Kinship

From the end of the 1970s, the field of family and kinship studies started transforming. Feminist insights made an important contribution in this. Although the discipline of sociology had included the topic of women and gender in its curriculum, giving cognitive space to feminism was a slow process. But the popularity of the topic with students writing assignments and dissertations, and its entry into policy and media successfully put pressure on the discipline to take feminism seriously. The articles in the special issue of *Contributions to Indian Sociology* in 2016, edited by Gita Chadha, document and analyse the long history of mutual engagement between feminism and sociology. The articles by Chaudhuri and

Patel in particular identify family and kinship as an area greatly influenced by feminist interventions; Patel notes that feminism has been especially significant in laying bare the nature of power in the private domain of family (Chaudhuri 2016: 344, 346–47; Patel 2016: 331). Germane to the present volume's theme of rethinking sociological traditions in India, this chapter will now briefly analyse the impact of feminism on the sociology of family and kinship and use the insights to look at the implications of the contemporary assertions made by the category of young, single women.

Much before Collier and Yanagisako's comprehensive charter in 1987 for a feminist approach to gender and kinship, Irawati Karve had flagged the idea of the material implications of kinship in India for women's lives.[9] From the late 1970s, significant contributions came from Leela Dube (1997, 2001) and later several others.[10] Through this lens, the family and household came to be seen not only in formalist terms of structure and composition but also through intra- and inter-familial networks and relations. Kinship and gender intersect with class, caste, ethnicity and religion. Intersectionality, power relations and hierarchy are part of the domestic domain too. The much-lauded consensus and harmony of the family is achieved through naturalising the authority of the *paterfamilias* and through the obedience of women and children by means of socialisation. At the same time, in a country like India where state benefits are meagre, it is significant to note that the family also provides irreplaceable material and emotional support.

Descent systems determine entitlements of individuals to crucial material resources and to social and symbolic capital. Yet, the practice and performance of kinship entails constant interpretations and negotiations, and all actors are imbued with some agency. Women are structurally disadvantaged in patrilineal systems but are not helpless victims. They actively comply or negotiate with, protest against or silently resist norms.[11] Moreover, patrilineal systems are neither universal nor monolithic, and we cannot assume that norms are immutable while only practices vary. For more than a century now, demographic changes like growing longevity, decrease in women's fertility, increasing migration and education of women have catalysed normative changes. Women's entitlements and life trajectories have also been impacted by the emancipation–liberation–empowerment discourses starting with various social reform movements. New reproductive technologies and the queer movement are posing serious challenges to the idea of the biological, heterosexual family being the unit of society.

Although significant, these changes are embedded in India within the dominant framework of patrilineal kinship and pervasive patriarchy, with its fundamental son preference and practice of dowry. Ethnographic evidence suggests that the past had more diversified norms and practices. Patrilineality coexisted with pockets of matrilineality along with the bilateral ethos of Dravidian cross-cousin marriage and the tribal custom of bride price. These diversities are increasingly being erased and the shift is towards mainstream patrilineality.

In 1974, the landmark report *Towards Equality* by the Committee on the Status of Women in India documented the deteriorating position of women. From the late 1970s, the autonomous women's movement campaigned on various issues related to the intimate sphere of the family, such as dowry, domestic violence, marital rape, incest and unfavourable sex ratio. Along with the folk constructions of a woman's marital home as the source of potential violence, there was, in these campaigns, a terrible indictment of the natal home as the primary source of son preference and daughter discrimination, from where started the female disadvantages in health, nutrition, education and other indices of well-being.

Feminist approaches have thus revised conventional sociological frameworks on family and kinship, rendering them nimble and sharp to comprehend the changing ground realities, by inserting ideas of power, location, reflexivity and micro–macro linkages. They have provided tools to identify what has changed, what has remained intact and what has been reinforced or newly created. What is the overall import and how does it translate into violence against young women are relevant questions to probe. Against this backdrop, let us now return to the category of young, single women in the new middle class, the nature of their rebellion and the implications of their agency.

Young, Single Women in the New Middle Class

An important source for the ongoing recasting of the domestic space is the changing economic dynamics of education and employment for young, single women. These women are beneficiaries of changes, which they are trying to leverage to actively shape their own lives, often in opposition to family opinion. Some are vocal in doing so, while for most, it is a silent rebellion.

But let us start with a few caveats.

First, the assertion by young, single women inevitably entails friction, conflicts and negotiations within and about the domestic space. Issues include education, work, leisure, personal mobility, accessing public spaces, modes of dressing, consumption patterns, friendships, falling in love and choosing a marriage partner. Second, this category, by and large, does not recognise systemic patriarchy and its cross-linkages with class, ethnicity and caste. Some women are explicitly anti-feminist, while others are indifferent to or ignorant about the enabling role of the women's movement in contesting societal norms. Often, they seek personal mobility and choice but implicitly they accept patriarchy within a framework of class–caste hierarchies as benign. Third, violent manifestations of patriarchy are increasing, both in the public arena and in the domestic arena. Crimes are more often than not perpetrated by family members, from incest to dowry harassment, wife beating and honour killing. Given the silence of the majority of women, the assertive minority is unable to overturn the structural reality of patriarchy. Patriarchy's collusion with the community has taken new forms and has in fact increased conflicts in the domestic sphere.

The creation and phenomenal expansion of a new middle class since the 1990s is a key development in which we locate the emergence of the new category of young women.

There are at least three distinct vantage points in the literature on the new Indian middle class (Jodhka and Prakash 2016). In the first perspective, the new middle class is seen an agent of change, comprising educated, hard-working, motivated, creative and upwardly mobile individuals who are transforming India into a modern developed nation. In the second, it is viewed in terms of its relationship to the market, i.e., as an exponentially growing class that is sustaining the globalised economy through its purchasing power and consumption desires.[12] The third perspective is a more critical appraisal of this class, viewing it as reflecting the structures of inequality in society, both in terms of its exclusionary relationship with other classes and its internal differentiation whereby the benefits accruing from class position are unevenly distributed.[13]

Although estimates on its size vary, all agree that the new middle class is large and heterogeneous and that it is not entirely comprehensible through the criteria of occupation, income and education, which defined the traditional middle class. Earlier values of austerity and simplicity are being replaced with the celebration of a culture of consumption and an ease with the novel facets of globalisation and technology. Kapur et al. (2016) argue that self-identification is a valid and a useful metric for the new middle class. It is a cognitive identity that includes some feeling of belonging. In the large, national-level sample used in the study, almost half the respondents self-identify as middle class, across income and education. The response is consistently positive in terms of economic optimism and social aspirations, characteristics defining the new middle class. This new class is elastic enough to accommodate members moving from the working class, and it provides for mobility within.

Of course, there is internal differentiation on income, caste, rural–urban and other axes. But we could argue that with high occupational and professional intermingling and media exposure among youth in this class, small vanguard sections wield a disproportionate influence on others. The demonstration effect and the effect of relative deprivation are powerful in shaping the character of the class as a whole. Young women from the lower-income segments of the new middle class spend differently from the elite segments; they shoulder family financial responsibilities and save up for their marriages. But as Donner (2012) points out, the identity of the middle class lies not so much in common consumption patterns as in common consumption desires, aspirations and hope.

Structural Variables: Education, Employment and Migration

The key tangible variables in the life trajectories of young, single women that have potential for self-reliance and self-expression are education, employment as well as migration for employment. Let us briefly look at the overall contemporary trends on these parameters for women in India as a whole, against which we will assess the impact of our small segment of young, single women in the new middle class. To anticipate an important trend, the rising female literacy and educational levels across segments is striking. Paradoxically, there is an overall decline in the labour force participation rate of women. It is a truism that decision making on these areas is largely guided and controlled by the family, especially for young women.

Education as Resource

The rise in female literacy and educational levels over the last few decades is a significant development in the country as a whole notwithstanding the caveats of regional, class- and caste-related variations. For the population as a whole, at Independence, women started out with an extremely low educational status. Since then, there have been substantial improvements. The gender gap has narrowed as women's literacy has increased at a higher rate than men's, even though it is nowhere near equal. The time series statistics on literacy and primary, secondary and higher education from the 1950s and more significantly from the 1990s show how the gender gap is decreasing in enrolment and dropout rates, performance levels and the proportion of female teachers.[14]

Up to the high-school level, the academic performance of girls is generally better than that of boys. It is now not unusual that when the Secondary School Certificate (SSC) or the Central Board of Secondary Examination (CBSE) results are reported in the media, the headlines are about girls outperforming boys.

The modest increases in percentages translate into large absolute numbers. The change can be attributed to the efforts of the women's movement to highlight *inter alia* the gender disparity and discrimination in education. This has triggered media, policy and civil society attention and state- and NGO-sponsored programmes for education of the girl child. Of course, there are multiple motivations for educating daughters. Educated women fare better in the marriage market; they are able to find spouses who are equally or more educated than them and, hence, have good earnings. Families of bridegrooms may forgo dowries and compromise on caste endogamy to find brides with educational qualifications that enhance earning potential (Mishra 2011).[15]

Declining Female Labour Force Participation

In contrast to the improvements in the literacy and educational levels of women, paradoxically, there have been clear trends of decline in women's labour force participation rate (LFPR) between the early 1990s and 2015. The same period has also seen a rise in household incomes and educational levels.[16] How does one explain this paradox? The declining LFPR is considered to be an alarming development that negates efforts to empower women and is also detrimental to the economy as a whole.

Reasons for the decline have been sought in a variety of factors, both 'cultural' and 'structural'. The globalised labour market with its emphasis on flexibility and the inferior nature of its proliferating informal sector with part-time, non-standard jobs is an important factor. Women who work outside homes are mostly in the informal sector, which explains their weak economic status globally (Crompton and Harris 1998: 132). In India, non-farm jobs in rural areas are sparse, and there is a lack of adequate training and skilling for jobs in the new economy.[17] The rising educational level of girls, apart from delaying their employment, makes them reluctant to take up manual labour. Rise in household income has led to social mobility, which, at least in India, seems to precipitate the withdrawal of working-class women from manual labour outside the home.

Opportunity Cost of Women's Employment

Before we proceed to disaggregate the LFPR decline, let us look at the broad relationship between women's work and family control. Papanek's (1979) insightful analysis of the role of women in family 'status production' provides us with some leads to pursue the reasons for the declining presence of women in the labour market in India. Beyond the level of sheer survival, where women have no choice but to work for very low wages, their labour is deployed to enhance the status and mobility of the family as a whole. This consists of a basket of tasks and roles including not only income generation (no longer a taboo in itself) but also child care, housework, networking with extended kin and community, meeting obligations, nurturing relationships and preserving cultural notions of honour and prestige. In situations of social churning like the present, mobility for the family can be achieved in a variety of ways. Women's role is significant in raising children with training and qualifications that will propel the family as a whole into a higher social class. Thus, teaching children; helping with homework; ferrying them to various tuitions, sports and hobby classes; being active in parent–teacher meetings and so on are fairly new tasks in this basket.

Within this range of responsibilities, the opportunity cost of employment is a critical factor in the decision on how a woman's labour is deployed. Afridi et al. (2016: 29–30) argue that the relative returns from an educated woman working in home production versus the market is weighed before a family-level decision is taken on the same. Within this dynamic, married women have a greater engagement in family status production work than unmarried women, who are freer to seek outside employment.

This argument explains the U curve that contemporary studies have noted, that is, with rising education, the LFPR decreases (for those who have finished school).[18] After this, there is a U turn, since higher education means better jobs and the monetary returns bring in family support. Sonalde Desai's (2019) disaggregation of the declining work participation rate (WPR) for women from 2004–05 to 2017–18 provides insights on the rural–urban divide. We can extrapolate from this how the new category of unmarried working women in towns and cities is emerging. The decline in the presence of women in the labour force is steep in rural areas, and within that, among poorer households and among women with low levels of education. The decline is mostly through reduced participation in agriculture and allied activities. The decline in urban areas, despite a gender gap, is much milder. The very factors behind rural women's decreasing labour force participation are pushing young unmarried women, with some skills or training, to migrate to urban areas for new economy jobs. Married women are unable to follow this path, unless it involves marriage migration. Even so, when children are born, they tend to drop out of the workforce.[19]

While the declining LFPR needs correction, we cannot underestimate the effect of social change, both planned and unintended, post Independence and of the new opportunities in the post-1990s globalised economy in loosening attitudes of the family towards women's employment. These attitudes are no longer hostile *per se* for unmarried daughters, with much depending on the nature and conditions of employment and its opportunity cost. However, when it comes to matters of love and marriage, 'honour' continues to have currency.

The secondary position of women as a whole in the occupationally segregated and gendered labour market is undeniable. Whether women make a 'choice' to work part-time or for lower wages in jobs that are compatible with their existential situation of being naturalised care givers, whether it is the labour market structure that marginalises them or whether they are lodged in an interactive continuum of both situations is a matter of considerable debate.[20] Either way, there is a tacit assumption that women act as individual agents, which is a fallacy. In the Indian context, ethnographic data has repeatedly averred that the family, whether natal or affinal, plays a key role in arriving at both educational and employment-related decisions for women. Individual women may negotiate, but they rarely act as autonomous agents who can bypass the family.

There are significant exceptions to the declining female LFPR. Suitably skilled and trained young women who are willing to migrate get relatively high-paying jobs in the new economy. Women from traditional middle class families have already inherited a culture of education. Post Independence, they started making inroads into employment, first in genteel professions like teaching and often in part-time jobs. Later generations of women have entered lucrative and competitive professions, with family support.

Young women moving up from the working classes—where women's education has traditionally been weak and employment has been in low-paid unskilled and semi-skilled jobs—have also benefited from positive changes in popular attitudes towards girls' education. The notion of a desirable education has changed in the globalised economy, with a preference for short-term training for specific skills and an emphasis on employability. Women are preferred for certain sectors. Typically, the requirements for these jobs are completion of higher secondary schooling, a minimum working knowledge of English and a technical skill set. Women being employed as beauty parlour assistants, embroiderers or sales assistants has become even more widespread and better paying, while new jobs have opened up for professionals at the lower end of the information technology chain, business process outsourcing (BPO), the hospitality industry and the like. Occupational taboos for women regarding late working hours, travelling on the job, taking up out of town jobs have loosened, although families, in collaboration with employers, devise methods for ensuring safety and for policing to ensure that conventional canons of morality are maintained. There are also new, unconventional occupations—from surrogacy services to bar tending—that clearly violate family norms. Though few, these occupations have media visibility and send a message to aspiring young women. Overall, the attitude of parents towards education and employment for daughters has become more supportive, more in the case of mothers compared to fathers. Alice Clark's recent research (2016) painstakingly and convincingly documents this phenomenon among the middle and lower middle classes.

Migration and New Economy Jobs

Jobs in the new economy often entail migration. For women, migration by itself increases employment opportunities. Being mostly in the informal sector, these jobs are not well paid. But for those with relevant training, the scenario is brighter. Among young, single women, independent employment–related migration has been increasing since the late 1990s. It provides women an opportunity to live away from the close supervision of the family and a chance to earn and spend on themselves. K. Shanthi's (2006) research makes extensive use of the National Sample Survey Office (NSSO) data and estimates the autonomous migration of unmarried women as a tenth of all migration. Among the semi-literate, the phenomena of young girls migrating to cities to work in export processing units, the garment industry, electronic assembling and food processing units is continuously on the increase in recent years. How male and female migrants reformulate their work and life arrangements is of course influenced by preexisting gender stereotypes. In more traditional set-ups, especially if the woman is married, migration and income generation may not substantially alter unequal domestic power relations. But evidence is that younger women migrants, educated beyond a certain threshold, are moving away from these stereotypes. On the other hand, an analysis of interstate variations indicates that attitudes of the family, especially male members, towards women vary enormously (Banerjee and Raju 2009: 122). We can infer that where young women reject old gender stereotypes, they may meet with opposition and hostility.

There is a lag between young women's real or aspired lifestyles and what their families, in particular male kin, expect. This often results in young women leading a double life, concealing from their families the full range of their activities and plans. Yet this does not mean that they forsake their families. Young, single women with income often support their families financially.

Among the issues that young, single women negotiate with their families is the right to extend their spatial mobility beyond the domestic and access public spaces for not only functional purposes but also leisure and pleasure. Campaigns in 2009 that protested against right-wing attacks on women in pubs and in 2016 against the ban on women entering certain temples have impacted a larger and more heterogeneous constituency than anticipated.

Constraints and Agency

How do education, employment and migration actually affect the ability of women to take charge of their lives? An experiment that provided three years of recruiting services to help young women in randomly selected Indian villages migrate and get jobs in the BPO industry has provided instructive insights.

Initially, there was almost no awareness of these jobs among the women. But, during the three-year period, they were spurred to take charge of their professional and personal lives. They were significantly less likely to get married or have children and more likely to enter the labour market or obtain more schooling or training. They also reported wanting to have fewer children and pursue a career rather than take stopgap jobs (Jensen 2012: 753).

A painstaking piece of research conducted for the *New York Times* in rural Odisha and Bangalore city by Ellen Barry in 2016 tracks the process by which young, single girls from remote villages are mobilised for urban employment through Gram Tarang, a private agency to whom the state government has outsourced recruitment. Barry follows a batch of 37 girls journeying to Bangalore to a garments production factory. It is a journey of many firsts—train travel, going to the city, earning, adapting to strange city ways. The arduous process of persuading parents to let them go, long hours of back-breaking, eye-watering work, crowded dormitory living and policing of their free time by the employers notwithstanding, the girls savour their freedom and are unwilling to return to the village. There is a lurking fear that the family may call them back. They share with each other plans and devices for avoiding marriage fixed by their respective families. In the joy of opening a bank account, getting an ATM card or buying a smartphone, we see an unmistakable kindling of aspirations. Love letters from male co-workers, WhatsApp messages from boyfriends, persuading the family for marriage with a partner of choice—all these speak of a boldness that is not possible in the village. Most women send money home. They do not often question parents' authority openly but instead pursue their desires through negotiation, wiles, deceit and remarkable resourcefulness. Occasionally, there is open rebellion and elopement.

A similar picture emerges from the many studies on the call centre industry. A sizeable section of its workforce, just less than half, comprises young, single, often migrant women. The families of these women are supportive but also apprehensive about night shifts and intermingling with male colleagues. Employers take on board these concerns, devise strategies and provide facilities to allay them. The call centre industry is an instructive example of new economy employment supported by the natal family, employer and state alike to harvest opportunities for extra income, cheap, docile labour and improved GDP respectively. All three parties collaborate to keep the traditional gender paradigm intact by providing or supporting legal cover and a policed working and travel environment. But the young women have themselves moved away from normative control in their new setting. Their income is a key factor in increasing the bargaining power in the domestic domain.[21] When it comes to romance and marriage, the family is more strict, and in this, the fear of or pressure from community plays a role. The domestic space is thus at once a battle ground, a zone of negotiation and a haven of security.

Community, Family and Gender

In India, community is interpreted as a group of primordial affiliation, and it includes caste, religion and ethnicity. Region and language too sometimes take on primordial hues. The family–household, the smallest unit of kinship, which in turn is closely linked to the larger community, is the domain for socialisation of members into community values. It polices the activities and behaviour of its members, punishing transgressions. Even when families may desire to adopt pragmatic changes, the hold of the community can pressurise individual families. In the case of caste as community, the very structure of exogamy and endogamy creates a network of blood and marital ties which when extended beyond the household, lineage and clan, reaches to the boundaries of the sub-caste.

The linkage between women's conduct and community honour is fundamental to patrilineal societies with elaborate hierarchies. In caste society, this is articulated in the language of ritual purity, wherein upper castes maintain their ritual purity through multiple devices but especially through control over women's sexual purity, which is equated with chastity and fidelity.[22] But this is not an exclusive feature of caste society.

Women are crucial symbols of group differentiation in non-caste societies as well. Violation of and violence on women of the 'other' group becomes a way of humiliating that group itself, as is evident in Mediterranean notions of honour and shame, honour killings in the northwest parts of the subcontinent, civil wars between ethnic groups and wars between nations where a group's subjugation is symbolically validated by the subjugation of its women.

Issue of Marriage

In this scenario, the appropriate marriage of daughters is deemed to be of great importance to the family and the community. Given the fundamental patrilineal premise of daughters as temporary members of the natal family, rights on their labour, sexuality and fertility are, during the marriage ceremony, ritually transferred to the affinal family. In fact, this is the central ritual in patrilineal marriage. Unmarried daughters are therefore treated by the natal family as a vulnerable category that needs to be under constant surveillance, control and protection until marriage. This premise, explored and commented upon extensively in feminist scholarship, continues to be the basis for contemporary marriages in India. Education and employment for daughters, though not taboo, have to be accommodated within a larger paradigm in which their potential to make socially appropriate marriage choices is not compromised.

At another level, marriage, as it prevails in contemporary India, is a means of pursuing social mobility and establishing social status. The consumerist economy has reinforced this old function. While caste-based hypergamy or 'marrying up' was the earlier norm, new opportunities have forced families to replace it with economic 'marrying up'. As Donner (2012) puts it, 'In a rapidly changing world, marriage becomes one of the main institutions to ensure the reproduction of class, which explains why arranged marriages are still very much the norm.'

In India, marriage was never a matter solely between the conjugal couple. Currently, marriages of choice are more frequent, but even in these cases, the need for parental consent, parental financing of the daughters' wedding and dowry, and residence with husband's family are not uncommon features.

Choice-Making in Arranged Marriage

The most vexatious issue for young, single women is marriage, on which even the most liberal families can turn violent. In the light of the fury unleashed when daughters, and sometimes sons too, choose their marital partners, we need to evaluate the current pattern of 'choice' exertion in mainstream arranged marriage as a reference point. Are young women part of the decision-making process in their own (arranged) marriages? Why are certain modes of choice exertion fraught with tension and violence. To answer this, we need to engage with the popular vocabulary of arranged vs love marriage and inter-caste marriage vs endogamous marriage.[23] The two sets overlap but are not identical.

Arranged marriage and love marriage are often pitted as polar opposites. In the former, the initiative is taken by family elders. In the latter, the couple meet, fall in love and decide to get married, with or without the consent of their families. Such a classification is dichotomous and does not accommodate the diversity of and recent changes in marriage practices. Arranged marriages are almost always endogamous, i.e., the couple belong to the same caste, religion and/or ethnicity. The converse is not necessarily true. Love marriages could also be within the same caste cluster, broad caste group or the same sub-caste.

It is a truism that a large majority of marriages in contemporary India are still within one's birth ascribed group. There are signs of some limited change. State policy encourages the change, and from 2006 onwards, it has started offering cash incentives to inter-caste couples. Several estimates put inter-caste marriage at between 5 and 10 per cent of all marriages in India.[24] Analysing and extrapolating from the India Human Development Survey of 2010, Goli et al. (2013: 7–8), while reiterating the low figures for inter-caste and inter-religious marriages, emphasise that the figures have doubled during 1981–2005.[25] They also point out that inter-caste marriages are more frequent in urban families with some education and economic status and where the women are not very young, i.e., over 21 years of age, and are able to have a say in decision making on their marriages. This in fact is the demographic of the category that we are focusing on.

The percentage of inter-caste marriage is indeed quite small, but it translates into fairly large absolute numbers—enough to be visible and constitute a threat to the established caste order. Ambedkar had made a perceptive point that it is only by breaking the rule of endogamy that caste can be annihilated. The obverse is that the very basis of traditional caste hierarchies is threatened by such marriages. I would argue that the incredible violence surrounding inter-caste marriages is not because they are so few but because they are occurring in enough numbers to threaten the sense of social order. Yet, the numbers have not yet reached a critical mass to be able to sway public opinion. When these grow large enough to be undeniable, they will become part of the mosaic of the cultural diversity characteristic of India.

Arranged marriage is indeed the preference of the vast majority as repeatedly iterated by surveys and reports, but love marriages have also increased. Banerjee et al. (2009) used matrimonial ads and interviews for advanced statistical analysis and estimated that 20 per cent opted to marry for 'love', of which most were inter-caste marriages. Of course their sample is specific, comprising educated, middle class, Kolkata residents, all readers of the Bengali newspaper *Anandabazar Patrika*. But the whole point is that assertions and rebellions are occurring in a not insignificant group of visible dissenters, who are challenging the majority norm. Due to the impact of the entertainment content of globalised media, the idea of 'love marriage' is very much a part of contemporary youth narratives. It influences the way 'arranged' marriages are actually arranged. Contemporary arranged marriages in the new middle class have moved away from earlier forms where the prospective couple had little opportunity to interact before marrying and young women hardly had any say on who and how they should marry. Now, there is some scope for young women to negotiate and pursue their partner preferences under the umbrella of the natal family. Marriages are also arranged through matrimonial bureaus and websites, where the initiative and subsequent steps are taken by the couple, with the collaboration of relatives or the other way round. In either case, the prospective couple has opportunities to interact over a period and then arrive at a decision. Mukta Sharangpani's study (2010) of marriage bureaus in Mumbai vividly describes how the traditional practice of arranged marriage is invoked, appropriated and reproduced for very contemporary purposes. Specifically, young women in urban India, lodged within the patriarchal structure of arranged marriage, strategically exercise choice and work towards achieving their dreams and desires for the good life as defined by the consumerist culture of a liberalising economy. Even orthodox groups, which till recently were rigid about sub-caste endogamy, have changed their priorities. With urbanisation and education, they have democratised the process of finding partners. Both prospective grooms and brides are active participants in the search.[26]

The acceptance and rejection of proposals by young women may not always be as civil a process as suggested by the two aforementioned examples, which are from relatively secure and monitored environments. Frequent news reports of violence, particularly acid-throwing incidents on young women by men whose proposals have been spurned, show the inability of the 'macho' personality to accept defeat and its power to extract revenge. They also show the presence of active and often lengthy interactions between unrelated young men and women and the exertion of choice by the latter—a rare scenario even one generation ago.

In the category that is the focus of this chapter, the age of marriage is rising. Desai and Andrist (2010: 682) argue that Indian families are increasingly torn in two directions: status attainment through gender performance or status attainment through the performance of modernity. The latter motivates parents to educate their daughters, thus delaying marriage. This is further strengthened by the changing political culture. But even with the rising age at marriage, parents still take it upon themselves to be closely involved in arranging the marriage of their children.

Politics of Identity

It is in this minefield, with a complicated interweaving of education, income, migration, love and marriage that the new politics of identity is playing out. Public and private assertions of young women are resented and opposed by men from several class positions. Young women's quest for education and employment and, to an extent, choice in life style is supported by their natal families, across several class segments, provided it does not violate the 'honour' code. Families are intricately connected to community networks—in fact, the family acts as enforcer of community norms. This was so in the traditional social order, where the connection was organic. In the era of globalised postmodernity, the community has been shorn of its earlier structural moorings and is paradoxically in resurgence in new deterritorialised forms. Its engagements are at the intersections of family, state and market—what is now known as identity politics. Its power over families to discipline daughters is especially evident when love affairs, elopements or marriages are between families separated by great social distance—for instance, between Dalits and non-Dalits or between Hindus and Muslims. The community then deploys the vocabulary and arsenal of identity politics. On the other hand, caste-based Khap panchayat organisations take punitive action against families whose children violate the traditional rule of *gotra* or clan exogamy. Strangely, this rule does not have to do with inter-caste marriage but with ensuring that endogamous marriages are not 'too endogamous'. The diminishing clout of such locality and region-based community organisations in the new economic and legal regimes has impelled them to deploy social power to assert their presence.

Families may set store by traditional notions of 'honour' or relax them in the dialogue with modernity. Individual women may push for more decision-making power within and more autonomy from the family. Ultimately, these are trivialised and turned into grist to the mill of the much larger self-interests at stake in the murky politics of identity.

Notes

1. The typical newspaper or magazine review of the film is short and breezy, or breathless in its appreciation (Shivakumar 2016), while some are politically inflected and applaud the film from an Ambedkarian perspective (Waghule 2016). Others, for instance, Soni (2016) question the film's effectiveness in challenging caste and patriarchy.
2. Teltumbde (2016: 10) specifically refers to three murder cases of Dalits in the course of 18 months—at Kharda in Jamkhed tehsil in April 2014; in Sonai village in January 2013; and at Javkheda in October 2014.

3. 'Case Filed against Marathi Film "Sairat" Producer', 16 May 2016. Available at https://news.webindia123.com/news/articles/india/20160516/2861557.html, accessed on 18 January 2019.
4. Sonawane and Pagar's (2016) fact-finding report was published in *Satyashodhak*, the online journal of the Maratha Seva Sangh, within a fortnight of the incident. It minutely details the course of the crime and its aftermath, and also raises larger questions about the partisan role of the media and the caste hostilities between Marathas and Dalits.
5. Gawali's 2017 article profiles the Maratha Kranti Morcha, providing a historical and ethnographic context and highlighting the multiple and contested meanings of being Maratha.
6. In India, unlike the West, sociology and social anthropology are treated as a unified cluster, and the separation of family studies from kinship studies is not sharp.
7. See, for instance, Dube (1997) and Ganesh and Risseeuw (1998: 11–12) for the limitations of the conventional approach in family and kinship studies.
8. For a succinct summaries of the issues in this debate on Indological constructs of the family and on joint versus nuclear households, see Ganesh (1998: 118–19, 2013); Shah (1998); Shah and Patel (2011: 47–51); Uberoi (2003).
9. Karve's scholarly writing on women is brief but path-breaking. Her analysis of kinship as not an abstract, neutral system but rather as having material consequences for the people who are part of it was taken up by feminist anthropology much later. She brilliantly contrasts the Indo-Aryan and Dravidian kinship and marriage practices and their implications for women (Karve 1953: 129–30, 134–35, 163, 219–20, 229).
10. Leela Dube mentored several younger scholars, who have cumulatively created a substantial body of interventions in the field of gender and kinship. My own work (Ganesh 1998, 1999, 2001, 2005, 2013; Ganesh and Risseeuw 1998) is part of this tradition along with the work of scholars like Karuna Chanana, Prem Chowdhry, Ravinder Kaur, Tiplut Nongbri, Rajni Palriwala, Tulsi Patel, Susan Viswanathan and Patricia Uberoi.
11. See Ganesh (1999). The issue of agency entered somewhat late into feminist analysis, following the early phase that emphasised the victimhood of women.
12. The celebratory report by Beinhocker et al. (2007) about the contribution of the new middle class to economic growth and the prediction by Singhi and Jain (2016) of its further rise are typical of this genre.
13. See, for instance, the survey by Sircar and Reed (2015) and the argument by Scrase (2006).

14. There are of course state-wise and urban–rural variations, as well as for Scheduled Castes and Scheduled Tribes. For recent statistics on women's education, see Government of India (2011, 2014); 'Education for All in India (n.d.); Im4change (n.d.).
15. Mishra's (2011) data suggests that education has become a value in itself, part of the 'status' requirements for an educated groom. While earning potential of a woman is important, but whether or not she will actually work depends on her husband and his family.
16. These trends and the reasons and solutions have been widely discussed. See, for instance, the data and arguments in Verick (2014), Sanghi et al. (2015), Afridi et al. (2016); Chatterjee et al. (2014).
17. Broadly defined as an economy created by the digital age, which has supplanted the industrial and agricultural age.
18. See, for instance Chatterjee et al. (2014: 1); Afridi et al. (2016: 3); Jensen (2012: 755).
19. For a nuanced and disaggregated reading of the data on LFPR, see Afridi et al. (2016: 5–7, 24–28); Sanghi et al. (2015: 260–65); Surie (2016).
20. Crompton and Harris (1998: 131–33), who have elaborated on the various positions in the debate on women's 'orientations to work', argue that employment structures are the outcome of both choice and constraint.
21. For the contradictory nature of family support to women working in call centres, see Tara and Ilavarasan (2009); Ganguly-Scrase and Vandenbroek (2005); Forey (2013); Clarke and Sekher (2007).
22. Yalman (1963) and Ganesh (1982) have developed this argument. It has been elaborated later with specific reference to Dalit women by Uma Chakravarti (2003) and others.
23. Inter-caste here subsumes inter-religious and inter-ethnic in the context of endogamy.
24. This is a subject on which reliable statistics are hard to come by. The most cited source is the India Human Development Survey (IHDS) 2010 covering 42,000 households conducted by the National Council for Applied Economic Research and the University of Maryland, where the figure is put at 5.4 per cent (*The Hindu* 2014). Another estimate is almost double—10 per cent—based on data from 43,102 couples of the National Family Health Survey of 2005–06 (Das et al. 2011). The urban figure is higher than the rural. Of course, there are state-wise variations.
25. Inter-caste marriages rose from 3.5 per cent in 1981 to 6.1 per cent in 2005. Inter-religious marriages also rose, from 1.6 per cent in 1981 to 2.7 per cent in 2005 (Goli et al. 2013: 7).

26. The Eighteen-Village Vattimas, a Tamil Brahmin sub-caste, illustrate this transition vividly. Formerly rural landlords and socially conservative, they now mostly comprise educated, urban middle class and have adapted to modernity. Child marriage has disappeared and the age of marriage has risen further. Close-kin marriage is no longer preferred. Sub-caste endogamy remains the norm, with some adaptations among the diaspora. What is most striking is that education, employment and personal compatibility are the criteria for fixing matrimonial alliances, and both young men and women are involved in arranging their own marriages. Such endogamous companionate marriages, now commonplace in many communities, play a role in reproducing both caste and the middle class in contemporary India (Fuller and Narasimhan 2008: 745–46, 751–52).

References

Afridi, F., T. Dinkelman and K. Mahajan. 2016. 'Why Are Fewer Married Women Joining the Work force in India: A Decomposition Analysis over Two Decades', Discussion Paper Series, No. 9722, Institute for the Study of Labor (IZA), Bonn. Available at http://ftp.iza.org/dp9722.pdf, accessed on 18 January 2019.

Banerjee, A., E. Duo, M. Ghatak and J. Lafortune. 2009. 'Marry for What? Caste and Mate Selection in Modern India', NBER Working Paper Series, No. 14958, National Bureau of Economic Research (NBER), Cambridge, MA. Available at http://www.nber.org/papers/w14958.pdf, accessed on 19 January 2019.

Banerjee, A. and S. Raju. 2009. 'Gendered Mobility: Women Migrants and Work in Urban India', *Economic and Political Weekly,* 44 (28), 115–23.

Barry, E. 2016. 'Young Rural Women in India Chase Big-City Dreams', *The New York Times*. Available at https://www.nytimes.com/2016/09/25/world/asia/bangalore-india-women-factories.html, accessed on 19 January 2019.

Beinhocker, E. D., D. Farrell and A. S. Zainulbhai. 2007. 'Tracking the Growth of India's Middle Class', *The McKinsey Quarterly*, 3 (3): 51–61. Available at https://ecell.in/eureka13/resources/tracking%20the%20growth%20of%20indian%20middle%20class.pdf,accessed on 17 January 2019.

Chakravarti, U. 2003. *Gendering Caste through a Feminist Lens.* Calcutta: Stree.

Chatterjee, E., S. Desai and R. Vanneman. 2014. 'Growing Economy and Declining Female Employment: An Indian Paradox'. Available at http://paa2014.princeton.edu/papers/142718, accessed on 19 January 2019.

Chaudhuri, M. 2016. 'Feminism and Sociologies: Locations and Intersections in a Global Context', *Contribution to Indian Sociology*, 50 (3): 343–67.

Clark, A. W. 2016. *Valued Daughters: First-Generation Career Women*. New Delhi: Sage Publications.

Clarke, A. W. and T. V. Sekher. 2007. 'Can Career-Minded Young Women Reverse Gender Discrimination? A View from Bangalore's High-Tech Sector', *Gender, Technology and Development*, 11 (3): 285–319.

Collier, J. and S. J. Yanagisako. 1987. 'Introduction', in J. Collier and S. J. Yanagisako (eds), *Gender and Kinship: Essays Toward a Unified Analysis*, pp. 1–13. Stanford: Stanford University Press.

Committee on the Status of Women in India. 1974. *Towards Equality*. New Delhi: Government of India.

Crompton, R. and F. Harris. 1998. 'Explaining Women's Employment Patterns: "Orientations to Work" Revisited', *The British Journal of Sociology*, 49 (1): 118–36.

Das, K., K. C. Das, T. K. Roy and P. K. Tripathy. 2011. 'Dynamics of Inter-religious and Inter-caste Marriages in India'. Available at http://paa2011.princeton.edu/papers/111281, accessed on 14 January 2019.

Desai, S. 2019. 'Squandering the Gender Dividend', *The Hindu*, 12 June. Available at https://www.thehindu.com/opinion/lead/squandering-the-gender-dividend/article27819805.ece, accessed on 16 June 2019.

Desai, S. and L. Andrist. 2010. 'Gender Scripts and Age at Marriage in India', *Demography*, 47 (3): 667–87.

Donner, H. 2012. 'Marriage in Modern India: The Middle-Class Ideal of an Indian Marriage Has Not Changed', The London School of Economics and Political Science (LSE) Blog, South Asia @ LSE. Available at http://blogs.lse.ac.uk/southasia/2012/10/01/marriage-in-modern-india-the-middle-class-ideal-of-an-indian-marriage-has-not-changed-henrike-donner/, accessed on 20 January 2019.

Dube, L. 1997. *Women and Kinship: Comparative Perspectives on Gender in South and South-East Asia*. Tokyo: United University Press and New Delhi: Vistaar Publications.

———. 2001. *Anthropological Explorations in Gender: Intersecting Fields*. New Delhi: Sage Publications.

Economic and Political Weekly. 2016. 'Silence of the Marathas', Editorial, *Economic and Political Weekly*, 51 (39): 9.

'Education for All in India'. n.d. *Time Series Data*. Available at http://www.educationforallinindia.com/SESall-india-time-series-2005-06.pdf, accessed on 18 January 2019.

Forey, G. 2013. 'The Impact of Call Centre Employment on Women in India', *World Englishes*, 32 (4): 503–20.

Fuller, C. J. and H. Narasimhan. 2008. 'Companionate Marriage in India: The Changing Marriage System in a Middle-Class Brahman Sub-caste', *Journal of the Royal Anthropological Institute*, 14: 734–54.

Ganesh, K. 1982. 'The Kottai Pillaimar of Srivaikutam: A Socio-historical Study', PhD thesis, Department of Sociology, University of Bombay.

———. 1998. 'Gender and Kinship: Indian Materials and Context', in C. Risseeuw and K. Ganesh (eds), *Negotiation and Social Space: A Gendered Analysis of Changing Kin and Security Networks in South Asia and Sub-Saharan Africa*, pp. 113–36. New Delhi: Sage Publications.

———. 1999. 'Patrilineal Structure and Agency of Women: Issues in Gendered Socialization', in T. S. Saraswathi (ed.), *Culture, Socialization and Human Development: Theory, Research and Applications*, pp. 235–54. New Delhi: Sage Publications.

———. 2000. 'Households and Families: South Asia', in C. Kramarae and D. Spender (eds), *Routledge International Encyclopedia of Women: Global Women's Issues and Knowledge*, Vol. 2, pp. 1049–51. London: Routledge.

———. 2001. 'Maps for a Different Journey: Introduction to the Themes in the Work of Leela Dube', in L. Dube, *Anthropological Explorations in Gender: Intersecting Fields*, pp. 13–32. New Delhi: Sage Publications.

———. 2005. 'Made to Measure: Dutch Elder Care at the Intersections of Policy and Culture', in C. Risseeuw, R. Palriwala and K. Ganesh, *Care, Culture and Citizenship: Revisiting the Politics of the Dutch Welfare State*, pp. 116–58. Amsterdam: HetSpinhuis.

———. 2013. 'New Wine in Old Bottles? Family and Kinship Studies in the Bombay School', *Sociological Bulletin*, 62 (2): 101–23.

Ganesh, K. and C. Risseeuw. 1998. 'Introduction—Gendered Change in Marriage and Family: A Policy Concern', in C. Risseeuw and K. Ganesh (eds), *Negotiation and Social Space: A Gendered Analysis of Changing Kin and Security Networks in South Asia and Sub-Saharan Africa*, pp. 11–43. New Delhi: Sage Publications.

Ganguly-Scrase, R. and D. Vandenbroek. 2005. 'Globalisation, Liberalisation and the Transformation of Women's Work in India', in R. Julian, R. Rottier and R. White (eds), *Community, Place, Change: TASA 2005 Conference Proceedings*, 6–8 December 2005. Australia: The Sociological Association of Australia (TASA). Available at http://ro.uow.edu.au/cgi/viewcontent.cgi?article=1664&context=artspapers, 17 January 2019.

Gawali, S. 2017. 'Maratha Kranti (Muk) Morcha: When Will Maratha Women Cross the Threshold?' *Roundtable India*. Available at https://roundtableindia.co.in/index.php?option=com_content&view=article&id=8945:maratha-kranti-muk-morcha-when-maratha-women-cross-the-threshold&catid=119&Itemid=132, accessed on 19 January 2019.

Goli, S., D. Singh and T. V. Sekher. 2013. 'Exploring the Myth of Mixed Marriages in India: Evidence from a Nation-wide Survey', International Union for the Scientific Study of Population (IUSSP), XXVII International Population Conference, Busan, Republic of Korea, 26–31 August 2013. Available at https://iussp.org/sites/default/files/event_call_for_papers/Final%20revised%20Edited%20Mixed%20Marriage%20Paper%5B1%5D.pdf, accessed on 18 January 2019.

Government of India. n.d. *Selected Educational Statistics 2000–2001*. New Delhi: Ministry of Human Resources Development, Government of India. Available at http://www.educationforallinindia.com/selected-educational-statistics-2000-2001.pdf, accessed on 19 January 2019.

———. 2011. *Educational Statistics at a Glance*. New Delhi: Ministry of Human Resources Development, Government of India.

———. 2014. *Educational Statistics at a Glance*. New Delhi: Ministry of Human Resources Development, Government of India. Available at http://mhrd.gov.in/sites/upload_files/mhrd/files/statistics/EAG2014_0.pdf, accessed on 19 January 2019.

The Hindu. 2014. 'Just 5% of Indian Marriages are Intercaste: Survey', 13 November 2014.

Im4change. n.d. 'Literacy and Education'. Available at http://www.im4change.org/siteadmin/tinymce//uploaded/Chapter%203_1.pdf, accessed on 5 January 2019.

Jensen, R. 2012. 'Do Labour Market Opportunities Affect Young Women's Work and Family Decisions? Experimental Evidence from India', *The Quarterly Journal of Economics*, 127: 753–92.

Jodhka, S. and A. Prakash. 2016. 'Who Are Middle Class in India?' 15 July 2016, OUP Blog. Available at https://blog.oup.com/2016/07/india-middle-class/, accessed on 17 January 2019.

Kapur, D., N. Sircar and M. Vaishnav. 2016. 'The Importance of Being Middle Class in India', Vaishnavmilan Blog, Available at https://carnegieendowment.org/2017/11/03/importance-of-being-middle-class-in-india-pub-74615, accessed on 12 January 2019.

Karve, I. 1953. *Kinship Organisation in India*. Poona: Deccan College Post Graduate and Research Institute.

Malinowski, B. 1930. 'Kinship', *Man*, 30 (2): 19–29.

Mishra, A. 2011. 'India: Degrees Replace Dowries for Educated Classes', *University World News*, 27 November 2011. Available at http://www.universityworldnews.com/article.php?story=20111125211736183, accessed on 6 January 2019.

Papanek, H. 1979. 'Family Status Production: The "Work" and "Non-Work" of Women, *Signs*, 4 (4): 775–81.

Patel, S. 2016. 'Feminist Challenges to Sociology in India: An Essay in Disciplinary History', *Contributions to Indian Sociology*, 50 (3): 320–42.

Sanghi, S., A. Srija and S. S. Vijay. 2015. 'Decline in Rural Labour Force Participation in India: A Relook into the Causes', *Vikalpa*, 40 (3): 255–68.

Scrase, T. J. 2006. 'The New Middle Class in India: A Reassessment', University of Wollongong, Australia, Research Online. Available at http://ro.uow.edu.au/artspapers/722/, accessed on 7 January 2019.

Shah, A. M. 1998. 'Introduction', in A. M. Shah (ed.), *The Family in India: Critical Essays*, pp. 1–13. New Delhi: Orient Longman Limited.

Shah, A. M. and T. Patel. 2011. 'Family', in K. A. Jacobsen (ed.), *Brill's Encyclopedia of Hinduism,*Vol. III, pp. 46–59. Leiden: Brill Publications.

Shanthi, K. 2006. 'Female Labour Migration in India: Insights from NSSO Data', Working Paper 4/2006, Madras School of Economics, Chennai. Available at www.mse.ac.in/wp-content/uploads/2016/09/santhi_wp.pdf, accessed on 6 January 2019.

Sharangpani, M. 2010. 'Browsing for Bridegrooms: Matchmaking and Modernity in Mumbai', *Indian Journal of Gender Studies*, 17 (2): 249–76.

Shivakumar, S. 2016, 12 May). 'Old Story New Twist', *The Hindu*, 12 May 2016. Available at http://www.thehindu.com/features/friday-review/old-story-new-twist/article8590448.ece, accessed on 6 January 2019.

Singhi, A. and N. Jain. 2016. 'The Rise of India's Neo Middle Class', *Mint*, 4 October 2016. Available at http://www.livemint.com/Politics/HY9TzjQzljCZNRHb2ejC2H/The-rise-of-Indias-neo-middle-class.html, accessed on 7 January 2019.

Sircar, N. and M. Reed. 2015. 'Choosing Thy Neighbour', *The Hindu*, 10 January 2105. Available at www.thehindu.com/opinion/op-ed/comment-article-choosing-thy-neighbour/article6772534.ece, accessed on 6 January 2019.

Sonawane, J. and M. Pagar. 2016. 'Once Again, a Blackout—A Fact Finding Report on Kopardi Rape and Murder', *Satyasodhak*, 25 July 2016. Retrieved from https://satyashodhak.com/once-again-a-blackout-a-fact-finding-report-on-kopardi-rape-and-murder/, accessed on 18 January 2019.

Soni, F. 2016. 'Questioning Sairat's Politics', *Himal Southasian*, 25 July 2016. Available at http://himalmag.com/sairat-caste-gender-politics/, accessed on 20 January 2019.

Surie, M. D. 2016. 'Where Are India's Working Women?' Asia Foundation. Available at http://asiafoundation.org/2016/03/09/where-are-indias-working-women/, accessed on 9 January 2019.

Tara, S. and P. V. Ilavarasan. 2009. '"I Would Not Have Been Working Here!" Parental Support to Unmarried Daughters as Call Center Agents in India', *Gender, Technology and Development*, 13 (3): 385–406.

Teltumbde, A. 2016. 'Behind the Ire of the Marathas', *Economic and Political Weekly*, 51 (40): 10–11.

Times of India. 2018. 'Maharashtra Assembly Passes Bill Proposing 16% Quota for Marathas', 29 November. Available at https://timesofindia.indiatimes.com/india/maharashtra-govt-proposes-16-reservation-for-maratha-community/articleshow/66861960.cms, accessed on 19 January 2019.

Uberoi, P. 2003. 'The Family in India: Beyond the Joint versus Nuclear Debate', in Veena Das (ed.), *Oxford India Companion to Sociology and Social Anthropology*, Vol. 2, pp. 1061–103. New Delhi: Oxford University Press.

Verick, S. 2014. 'Women's Labour Force Participation in India: Why Is It So Low?' International Labour Organization (ILO). Available at http://www.ilo.org/wcmsp5/groups/public/---asia/---ro-bangkok/---sro-new_delhi/documents/genericdocument/wcms_342357.pdf, accessed on 20 January 2019.

Waghule, P. 2016. 'The Big House', *Economic and Political Weekly,* 51 (20): 71–72.

Yalman, N. 1963. 'On the Purity of the Women in the Castes of Ceylon and Malabar', *Journal of Royal Anthropology Institute of Great Britain and Ireland*, 93 (1): 25–58.

7 Deterritorialising Heteronormative Family and Kinship

Hybrid Existence and Queer Intimacies in Contemporary India

PUSHPESH KUMAR

I wish to begin this chapter by underscoring the evocative submission of Patricia Uberoi (1994), an acclaimed sociologist with noteworthy contributions to family and kinship studies, regarding certain unaddressed areas in the sociological reflections on family and kinship. In her introduction to *Family, Kinship and Marriage in India* (1994), Uberoi expressed her concern over the indifference of kinship and family sociologists towards the qualitative dimensions of love, sex, marriage and aspects of domestic violence in India. Uberoi (ibid.) did, however, mention the efforts of some feminist scholars in taking the lead in subjecting these intimate areas to qualitative inquiry. She appears to be alluding to Leela Dube who has been a catalyst in the development of kinship and gender studies in India (see Ganesh 2001). As early as the 1970s, Dube had begun to scrutinise kinship from a gender perspective, and through her subsequent works, she sharpened her feminist gaze on those structural and ideological dimensions of kinship that bear material and constraining implications on women's 'daily business of living'. Following Dube, and also in her collaborations (see Dube and Palriwala 1990), many feminist sociologists during the 1990s intensified their investigation of the domain of kinship and family to demonstrate how these institutions organise sexual division of labour and property inheritance along gender lines, how different types of households affect women's well being, how kinship ideologies translate into control over women's body and sexuality, and how gendered socialisation within family and kin contexts serve to naturalise women's differential access to resources and the subsequent denial of public spaces to them. The interaction of the political economy of the state with a given kinship structure and ideology, resulting in the alteration and modification of customs and practices associated with the latter, and its effects on the lives of men and women were further brought into the discourse (see Palriwala and Risseeuw 1996). Thus, feminist interventions tremendously invigorated the sub-field of gender and kinship as global processes, diasporas, mass media, the Internet, and technologies influencing and shaping marriage, migration and intimate relations went on to capture feminist attention (see Kaur and Palriwala 2014). While this progress in the area of gender and kinship in Indian and South Asian sociologies is noteworthy and deserves to be applauded, I must submit that the sub-field of gender and kinship has yet to expand its horizons to include alternative and transgressive aspirations to kinship and family beyond the heteronormative structures despite the challenges emergent from the queer constituencies in India and South Asia over the past two decades (see Kumar 2017).

To my mind, the broader agenda of feminist scholarship within the sub-field of gender and kinship or any other sub-field within gender studies for that matter has been to highlight and contest the impediments posed by patriarchy in working out democratic gender relations. In view of this common concern of feminist emancipatory aspiration across disciplinary fields, I posit the need for each of these sub-fields to engage with arrangements that can potentially throw the gender binary of masculine and feminine out of gear. By waging the battle of gender emancipation within the existing binary of male and female, feminist politics risks the creation of an enclosure where other modes of doing gender (Butler 1997) are precluded and the latter's creative role in remapping social structures remains unforeseen and unutilised. Therefore, feminist scholarship including that on kinship and gender needs to be aware of this unconscious erasure and must pay heed to the queer constituency's potential in disturbing the dominant mode of organising gender.

This chapter, as the title suggests, constitutes a rather small attempt in interrupting a territorialised understanding of kinship and gender that deems kinship, first, as constituted exclusively of only men and women tracing descent from certain ancestors and in a procreative relationship to perpetuate a family line, and, second, as an arrangement wherein women as objects of exchange circulate between and among different families and or groups. Since sociologists and social anthropologists in India and South Asia have yet to attempt any study exploring alternative family and kinship patterns, unlike their counterparts in the Western academia, which has witnessed the growth of queer sociology (Plummer 2012) and queer anthropology (Boellstorff 2007), an endeavour such as this has to rely on scholarship emerging from the West such as the critique of heterosexism within kinship studies offered by Gayle Rubin (1975) and Judith Butler (1997), or the concept of 'families of choice' for gays and lesbians, supposedly an alternative to 'mainstream' hetero-gendered families that Kath Weston (1997) proposes in her ethnography of Bay area in San Francisco. I, however, wish to draw upon Elizabeth Freeman (2007) who has used Bourdieu's ideas of practical kinship in my analysis of queer kinship in India.

Bourdieu (1977) imagined practical kinship as embedded in everydayness and in considerable ways different from 'official kinship'. The latter is static, based on highly abstract formal rules and principles of social structure explicitly codified in quasi-juridical formalism (Peletz 1996). Practical kinship, on the other hand, denotes the usages and representations of kinship in everyday practical situations that are more oriented towards 'getting things done' than formal representations of kinship and social structure (ibid.). With this hindsight, I submit that non-heterosexual sexual desire can create possibilities for deviations from procreative heterosexist kinship without necessarily and openly questioning the dominant heterosexual family and kinship arrangement. While elite gay couples have been part of the elite gay subculture in

India, the decriminalisation of homosexuality in September 2018 encouraged a few same-sex couples to publicly assert their right to live together as partners. But legal reforms would not dramatically institute alternative forms of family and kinship as a way of life for the majority of queer persons given the fact that exercising 'choice' and autonomy against the dominant morality are also contingent upon the class position of those queer who have disposable income, credit cards and inviting homes (Duggan 2004). In such situations, the formation of alternative families, a 'family of choice' to use Kath Weston's phrase, parallel to the heteronormative, procreative family is not so unchallenging given the economic and other dependencies of majority queer on heteronormative families. The latter are not so willing and accepting of queer persons settling into alternative family lives, which would compromise the honour of the respective heteronormative families.

It is rather too early in contemporary India to visualise a radical shift in terms of instituting 'families of choice' in opposition to heteronormative families. I reiterate here the points raised by Jin Haritaworn (2015: 4) to foreground the majority of underclass queer beyond the experiences of white, middle class, 'innocent and respectable queer subjects' who are worthy of intimacy, protection and safe spaces and are born in 'topographies of cruelty'. Moreover, there are many queer persons who are heterosexually married and do not find it easy to give up or severe their ties from such marital bonds as existing networks of family and kin exert greater influence in terms of compelling the former to remain within these contexts. So, a large number of queer persons establish homoerotic relations and lead dual lives, without overtly challenging the heteronormative family and kinship arrangement. Even many hijra women lead dual lives and perform dual gender roles to maintain the prestige and honour of their natal families.[1] In other words, this practical negotiation is carried out without rejecting the heteronormative family, kinship and community arrangements, with queer lives simultaneously associating and splitting from the heteronormative family and kinship structures. This situation seems somewhat similar to Jose Quiroga's (2000) description of Latin American lesbian and gay men who use invisibility as a tactical tool in opposition to the imperative to 'come out'. Silence about sexual identity in this understanding is *strategic* (see Kumar 2017). A gay participant in my interview, who belongs to city H in southern India and works with a corporate group, normalises clandestine homosexual encounters on the part of middle-class heterosexual men from the corporate sector. He says,

> It is not so unusual to see men experimenting with erotic possibilities even when they are married. Travel provides this possibility; the spa, gym and access to gay apps like Grindr just make it possible; travel and tour are very integral to the corporate world and it is easier to access a male body than a female body.[2] So, many married men are comfy with same-sex encounters when they are away from family and home.

This narrative points to the fact that for middle-class men who wish to experiment with sexual choices and are mobile, the affirmation of heterosexuality coexists with the possibility of homoerotic encounters. On the other hand, working-class men cruise around public spaces like parks, public toilets and certain identified areas in the city, spaces which non-governmental organisations (NGOs) refer to as 'hot spots'. Many of these men are married with wives, children and dependent parents and kin.[3]

'Families of choice' as a cultural alternative to mainstream heterosexual kinship, which Kath Weston (1997) speaks of in the Western context, might be a reality for only a small segment of the queer population in India that is privileged in terms of class and cultural capital (see Shahani 2008). My arguments here will be limited in scope and I do not claim to exhaust the entire spectrum of queer possibilities within the realm of family and kinship. I substantiate my arguments with qualitative data collected from some provincial cities in western and southern India as well as in the metropolitan city H on how transgender familial arrangements are mediated by one's connection to the heteronormative family and kin world. The hijra community and kinship, which remain visible sites where alternative structures of family and kinship have been ethnographically mapped (Reddy 2005), may not constitute what Weston has termed 'families of choice' since hijras strictly abide by cultural practices that subsume their lives within community norms and render them without 'individual status' in the modern sense. I submit here that queer life in India and South Asia, except for a few exceptions, does not entirely constitute an alternative to heterosexual kinship but reflects a 'hybridity' wherein these lives keep oscillating between the dialectics of heteronomative and homoerotic. The term hybridity also refers to the fact that the majority of queer lives, though primarily located within a wider heteronormative context, also circulates on a number of other sites through their association with the lesbian, gay, bisexual and transgendered (LGBT) community, NGOs that work around sexuality as well as in online alternative communities and online cruising sites for homoerotically oriented persons across the globe.

Deterritorialising Kinship

In this section, I try to discuss the term deteritorialisation, which is borrowed from Deleuze and Guattari (1972).[4] Deterritorialisation here stands for de-Oedipalisation of Oedipus as this Freudian concept not only restricts and territorialises (sexual) desire but also universalises heterosexist family and kinship (the mummy, daddy and me triangle). A deterritorialising of Oedipus would amount to acknowledging and validating the multiple directionality of desire, indicating alternative possibilities of erotic relations and a logical extension of the family and kinship bond beyond monogamous heterosexuality. The myth of Oedipus centres around the incest taboo, and the latter, in turn, creates what Judith Butler calls 'exogamous heterosexuality' where women are exchanged in marriage between different kin groups (read male).

The project of deterritorialising, which this chapter aims to achieve, thereby stands at the cusp of psychoanalysis (Oedipus) and anthropology (kinship). Both the Freudian concept of Oedipus and Levi-Strauss's understanding of the elementary structure of kinship (1969) provide academic justification to the so-called naturalness of heterosexuality (Rubin 1975) and hence reaffirm and territorialise the radical play of (erotic) desire, which can otherwise flow in many directions, creating possibilities of alternative arrangements of family and kinship beyond heteronormative imaginings. Gilles Deleuze and Felix Guattari are exponents of the term 'deterritorialising' in their book *Anti-Oedipus: Capitalism and Schizophrenia* published in 1972. But before I engage with how anti-Oedipus serves as an analytical tool in denaturalising 'normalised adult heterosexuality' produced through Oedipus and the incest taboo, which in turn are 'scientifically' dressed as an inevitable civilisational imperative,[5] I wish to nudge the readers in the direction of some of the hijra narratives that potentially deterritorialise the hegemonic understanding of the politics, power, gender and sexuality of kinship. The hijras from Madhya Pradesh who entered into the state-level electoral battle in the late 1990s parodied the mainstream understanding of gender, sexuality, family and politics, thereby falsifying heteronormative institutions as the only way to organise human existence. The following are some of the de-gendering expositions that emerged in the course of the electoral campaigning, which also mocked at genealogical kinship (Khan 2014):

> *Kinnar ko jitao, vamswad se chutkara pao.*
> (Elect a 'eunuch' and get rid of nepotism.)
>
> *Nikamme netaon ka ek ilaz; hijron ke sar par rakh do taj.*
> (Teach a lesson to the worthless politicians by crowning the 'eunuchs'.)
>
> *Rajniti ling se nahin, dimag aur imandari se ki jati hai.*
> (You don't need genitals for politics, one needs brain and integrity.)
>
> *Kuwaron ko lao, bharat bachao.*
> (Elect the bachelors to save India).

These speech acts represent not only a radical redoing of gender but also point to the fact that bodies that are not engaged in heterosexual procreation stand in opposition to the primacy of genealogical kinship and the nepotism in which power politics in India is embedded. What seems implicit in these expositions is that non-reproducing bodies with no interest in perpetuating the family line and preserving caste and class status would serve the interests of the nation better than those who procreate and perpetuate the family line and therefore have a greater likelihood of losing interest in working for the nation. This resonates with Indrani Chatterjee's (2002) historical accounts of what she calls 'eunuchism in Nizamat polity of Bengal', where she portrays these non-procreating entities as embodiments of commercial, political and intellectual agencies. The divinisation of the emperor's body and the ritualisation of those inner spaces of the Nizamat where the emperor's body would move around were mediated by the proximity of hijra bodies, which were considered neither male nor female, neither infant nor adult, neither fully human nor fully divine. Hijras held strategic official positions including the controlling of finance and trade and were conferred special titles by the Nizams. They constituted 'non-blood kin' who were preferred over and above the 'blood kin' due to the latter's inclination towards inheritance and property issues, which resulted in tensions and conflicts within the Nizamat polity. The transphobia of the East India Company resulted in dismissal of hijra officials from the Nizamat polity, subsequently rendering all those trans-persons who held visible and strategic positions within the polity helpless and unemployed. The Company and later the British Raj were instrumental in heterogendering middle-class consciousness in India during its long colonial history (see Gupta 2001; Chandra 2012).

Kinship, family, love and desire are territorialised through what Deleuze and Guattari (1972) call Oedipalisation,[6] which reinstitutes the 'normalised gender' and privileges heterosexuality as ahistorical, universal and timeless. David E. Eng (2003: 302) poses an interesting question, 'Why do we have numerous accounts of language but few post-structuralist accounts of kinship?' He argues,

> The structuralist account burdened us with traditional kinship relation underwritten by Oedipal—a structuralist legacy establishing

> certain forms of kinship as the only intelligible and livable ones . . . to imagine a post-structuralist account of kinship not predicated on subordination of women and normative forms of Oedipalization, what would such a post-structuralist project look like? (ibid.)

Deleuze and Guattari (1972) propose a philosophical perspective against the Oedipal and Oedipalised territorialities (family, church, school, nation and party). Their idea of deconstructing Oedipus seeks to deterritorialise the flow of (sexual) desire. Deleuze and Guattari pose a fundamental question as to whether the Oedipal is a requirement or a consequence of social reproduction. In their perception, Oedipalising stands for linearising the productive unconscious that is unterritorialised within the individual. They use the term 'desiring production of unconscious', which hints at the polyvocality of the psyche. The heteronormativity of kinship based on the politics of reproduction preempts any possibility of articulating the 'productive polyvocal psyche' within the individual. The un-Oedipal nature of desiring production remains, which is interpreted as 'preoedipal, paraoedipal and quasi oedipal' by Deleuze and Guattari (ibid.: 11). The existence of the pre-Oedipal itself denaturalises heterosexuality and social institutions based on non-incestuous heterosexual bonding. The institutionalised non-incestuous heterosexual reproductive sexuality then constitutes a person's entry into the symbolic—the sphere of laws and norms of kinship that governs speech and speakability according to Butler (2001). Butler (ibid.) points out that kinship and family cannot be derived from any naturalistic cause and even the incest taboo is not biologically motivated. From where then, asks Butler, does the 'elementary structure of kinship' proposed by Levi-Strauss (1969) emerge? Therefore, the puzzle here is whether kinship creates Oedipalisation or Oedipalisation creates kinship. Gayle Rubin (1975) significantly points out that the pre-Oedipal female who sexually desires her mother challenges the very idea of primordial heterosexuality.[7] When the girl's desire for her mother is active and aggressive, her ultimate accession to femininity needs exploration. Freud attempts to explain it through penis envy,[8] which orchestrates in the girl's psyche. But Rubin (ibid.: 198) asks, 'If the pre-oedipal lesbian is not confronted with the heterosexuality of mother she might draw different conclusion about the relative status of genitals.' In Lacan's scheme (quoted in Rubin 1975), the Oedipal crisis occurs when a child learns the sexual rules embedded in kinship terminology. Before the Oedipal phase, a child's sexuality contains all sexual possibilities available to human expression. For Lacan (ibid.), by the time a child leaves the Oedipal phase, its libido and gender identity have been organised in conformity with the existing rules.

'Chosen Families and Kin' versus 'Practical Kinship'

The idea of lesbian and gay families as 'chosen families' emerges from Kath Weston's ethnography of the Bay Area in San Francisco during the 1980s. During the 1970s, the gay and lesbian discourse emphasised a diffused, substitute 'kinship' of shared homosexual identity (Strathern 1993). In this understanding, the homosexual community itself constitutes an extended kinship network. But during the late 1980s, there was a shift wherein members of the culturally recognisable lesbian and gay families would negotiate their shared and differentiated responsibilities by appealing to the family's foundational choice (ibid.). In this sense, the alternative chosen family was not so much a diffused kinship of homosexuals but a reflection of the tendencies inherent in existing kinship structures (i.e., to reproduce) while simultaneously representing a contrast to the 'reproductive families' (ibid.). These 'chosen families' displace the centrality of the biological symbolism of reproduction without fully disputing it, although the element of biogenic substance in forging family and kinship ties is made possible through reproductive technology (ibid.). So, the diffuseness of the 1970s homosexual kinship was replaced by more concentric family bonds selectively appropriating biogenic substance through reproductive technology while simultaneously rejecting the centrality of heterosexual procreation (Weston 1997). As Cori Hayden (1995: 44) writes, 'Although these "chosen families" bring up crucial questions about kinship without biological connection (or without expectation of creating biological kin through procreation), quite different questions arise in the creation of lesbian and gay parenting families in which biology, via procreation, reenters the picture.' Citing instances from lesbian motherhood and how biology reenters lesbian families, Hayden submits that in the face of the cultural logic through which gay and lesbian relationships are deemed illegitimate because of their figurative impotence/sterility, procreative ideologies are negotiated without replicating the heterosexual genealogical connections based on biology (see ibid.). In pregnancy through artificial insemination, the lesbian 'biological' mother assumes and/or appropriates the same generative power that places her in the realm of (male) authorship in reproduction (ibid.). American cultural conceptions of procreation based on symbolic asymmetry emphasise female receptivity and attribute primacy to male contribution in imparting identity (see ibid.: 50).[9] For Hayden (ibid.: 51), the 'lesbian co-mother', who takes a generative role in the conception of her children, claims space for female creativity. In so doing, the co-mother does not attempt to become male but rather carves out a distinctive but recognisable place in the birth of her child. Hayden surmises that this might constitute a powerful reworking of the idea of genetic authorship, as such claims to female creativity can remove the sperm donor's genetic contributions from the picture. Hence, the generative power of the lesbian mother becomes more *kinetic* than *genetic* in the understanding of Hayden. Biology here is abstracted and dispersed in a way that challenges the cultural assumption of primacy of the male seed (Delany, quoted in Hayden 1995: 53). Hayden reiterates that lesbians may take great care in choosing a donor; and the act of insemination by eliminating direct physical contact is often seen as minimising the man's role as a *gendered individual in conception*. Drawing on Kath Weston, Hayden mentions that the lesbian's link to the donor in this instance is partially non-sexual. Sometimes, the donor is also incorporated in the lesbian family arrangement to legitimise the birth, and the latter might constitute an extended kin but may not symbolically reproduce heteronormative kinship on account of the presence of the lesbian co-parent as well as the lack of physical and sexual contact between the biological mother and the donor.

As it appears from the discussion in the preceding sections, alternative families and kinship may not discount but extract, appropriate and rework biology to dismantle the heterosexist claim of sterility of queer bodies while also not representing or replicating heterosexual kinship. As Freeman (2007) mentions, gay kinship *transforms* rather than merely derives from its heterosexual corollaries. In the Indian and South Asian contexts, however, instances of donor insemination and surrogacy among gay and lesbian persons are very rare, primarily due to illegality[10] and also because queer persons in these social and cultural contexts are yet to open themselves up to such a possibility. Gay and lesbian couples are not so unheard of in India and South Asia (see Rao and Sharma 2009), but a public performance of coupling and articulation of the desire for adoption[11] and inheritance are not so conspicuous despite the presence of an elite gay constituency across metropolitan cities of South Asia (see Shahani 2008). For Elizabeth Freeman (2007), 'choice' in this context is the product of a liberal discourse that views it as remaining unfettered by various forms of difference and dependency. Freeman (ibid.: 304) writes, '"Chosen family" is a peculiarly queer unfriendly model, however, friendly it may be to bourgeois lesbians and gays. For it presumes a range of economic, racial, gender and national privileges to which many sexual dissidents do not have access'. For example, many foreign gay couples over the past few years have visited Mumbai and other cities in India to access surrogacy, but lower middle and working class queer in India and elsewhere would certainly find it too difficult to do so even if it were made legal (see *Times of India* 2010). Taking a cue from Hayden's concept of 'kinetic kinship' in lesbian co-parenting where the impregnation through artificial insemination positions the woman in authorship, Freeman reproduces Butler's (2001) and David Schneider's (1984) idea of kinship as 'doing' rather than 'being'. In the context of queer kinship then, Freeman finds Pierre Bourdieu's idea of 'practical kinship', embedded in strategies of everydayness and temporalities as opposed to formal and official genealogical kinship, which may not serve everyday practical purposes, to be more relevant. Thus, Freeman (2007: 308) writes,

> What Bourdieu calls practical kinship consists of the 'utilization of connections', or we can surmise, the calling of various favour and debts, whether there be of a child to its mother or between a pair who have met once or twice. 'Practical kinship' is maintained and is oriented towards getting things done rather than official representations of genealogical connections.

Bourdieu (1977: 34) also characterises practical kinship as 'private' and 'hidden' and reigning in the realm of 'strategic choice'. I reiterate the adjectives 'private', 'hidden' and 'strategic choice' while trying to understand queer kinship in the Indian context.

As a prologue to the arguments I present in the following section, I wish to submit here that queer existence in India is marked by a hybridity that does not solely comprise alternative kinship and family arrangements that Kath Weston (1997) and Cori Hayden (1995) have observed in the privileged, white American context. Except in the case of a small group of hijras whose biological families have completely severed ties with them (Reddy 2005), the majority of queer persons occupy an 'intermediate position': they are either located within heteronormative families and kin group networks and negotiate their sexual life without questioning the existing structures or they are physically and spatially separated yet connected to their natal kin. Hijra and *kothi*[12] practices entail the formation of the alternative kinship of *guru–chela* (mentor and disciple), but many kothis continue to stay with their natal families while secretly maintaining their alternative kinship.[13] In the remainder of the chapter, I attempt to map out queer kinship and family arrangements in India on the basis of qualitative data generated through interviews with some transgender persons in the metropolitan city H and two provincial cities in southern and western India respectively. In some ways, these negotiations with homoerotic and heteronormative contexts come close to what Bourdieu terms as 'practical kinship', which is 'hidden', 'private' and 'strategic'.

Transgender Negotiations of Kinship and Family Arrangements

I use Deniz Kandiyoti's (1988) concept of 'patriarchal bargain' to understand the strategic negotiation of non-elite queer transgender women with heteronormative family and kinship through how they traverse both heteronormative and queer connections. Kandiyoti questions the idea of universal patriarchy as well as a common programme of overtly resisting patriarchal privileges and oppressions. Instead, she introduces the term 'patriarchal bargain' to designate the strategic negotiations within concrete constrains posed in a patriarchal context, which reveal and define the blueprint of resistance in a given society and may exhibit variations according to class, caste and ethnicity. Different concrete constrains of patriarchies present women with distinct 'rules of the game' and call for different strategies to maximise security and optimise life options, with varying potential for active and passive resistance in the face of oppression (ibid.). Moreover, 'patriarchal bargains' are not timeless or immutable entities but are susceptible to historical transformations that open up new areas of struggle and renegotiations of the relation between genders (ibid.). I try to explicate the transgender negotiations of family and kinship in the context of a few cities in India within the framework of 'patriarchal bargain' and 'strategic negotiation', in which I find Bourdieu's idea of practical kinship, appropriated by Elizabeth Freeman (2007), useful in explaining queer kinship beyond gay ghettos. The latter might resonate with 'families of choice', which constitute an individualistic and bourgeoisie notion that focuses on the subjective power of 'I' to relate to people providing the ground for transcending social conflict and stratification (ibid.). The queer people who live beyond this Western bourgeois race and class privileges and who cannot afford to escape their embeddedness in social stratification find it difficult to create a complete alternative to heteronormative families and kinship. Their patriarchal bargain betrays a kind of hybrid and intermediate existence between the heteronormative and homoerotic contexts without creating alternative families of 'choice'. This does not, however, mean that the content of the heteronormative is uncontaminated by the homoerotic and vice versa as there seems to be an interaction between the two as the narratives that follow illustrate. This rather indeterminate and non-linear interaction would indicate a culturally generative improvisation in a temporal sense if not a structural transformation and creation of a parallel queer kinship and family.

While explicating the 'intermediate position' and practical kinship of queer persons in India, we need to focus on their everyday temporality and spatiality (see Reddy 2005). From my interviews with kothi men in a provincial city in western India, it appears that kothis who generally belong to the lower socio-economic strata stay connected to their natal families while managing to mingle with their co-kothis, kothi sisters and *panthi*s (sexual partners) in their secret subcultural spaces within the city.[14] In their heteronormative kin world, they retain their male names, while in their kothi world, they have feminine names. Thus, they are Ramesh, Suresh, Sanjay and Ismail in their heteronormative kin world, while they are Rekha, Babli, Priya and Sowmya in their kothi world. Kothis have their respective mentors, and each kothi can in turn be a mentor to her chelas (disciples). All the chelas of a particular kothi are sisters to one another. The 'masculine partner' of a kothi is treated as a brother-in-law by the 'sisters' of that particular kothi. Kothi–panthi relations are generally not everlasting and the partners keep changing. Kothis feel that they cannot produce children for their panthis, and they allow the panthis to marry women to resolve this practical issue. Some of them carry on with the sexual relationship even after the heterosexual marriage of their panthis. As they say in Hindi, 'Panthi ko hamari aadat lag gayi hai' ('The panthis have gotten used to us and can't live without us'). Many a time a kothi visits 'her' panthi's conjugal home situated in the same city as a male friend and develops a close relationship with her panthi's (female) wife. A kothi sometimes imagines that the panthi has two wives—'a biological woman' and a male who is close to yet not a biological woman. The negotiations involved in allowing a panthi to marry heterosexually without affecting the kothi–panthi relationship subsequently correspond to what Bourdieu calls 'private' and 'strategic'.

In the provincial city N in Maharashtra, I came across two men who are married to women and have children. They belong to the Banjara community and have completed their school education. They are also kothis and are well known in their local kothi circle in the city N. They confide in me that they are also caring husbands and responsible fathers and that they take care of the economic and other needs of the family including the education of their children. Despite their location within heteronormative families and kinship structures, they feel burdened with feminine desires and feel the need to cater to their feminine selves. As married men in a provincial city, they find it very difficult to perform femininity in their homes. Therefore, for seven to eight months they migrate to Mumbai, where they live the hijra life, decking up in saris and jewellery of their choice and sometimes donning Western (feminine) robes. They earn money through sex work and send remittances to their families and kin who stay in the provincial city N. They tell their families and kin that they work in factories in Mumbai. I was told that the wives know that these men cross-dress and dance in the orchestra, and hence they ignore the men's attempts at feminising their bodies through practices such as plucking eyebrows. The remittances, the gifts, the care and concern for their families along with claims of their 'flawless' sexual performance in heterosexual encounters with their respective female spouses make up for what subtle femininity surfaces on their bodies. When I met the two men in the market, they were on bikes and claimed that they look like panthis and not kothis. But back home in the city N, both of these gender-fluid interlocutors—the kothis performing dual gender—are secretly 'married' to panthis who they regard as their respective husbands. They have sex with their wives and perform masculinity and simultaneously engage in anal intercourse with their panthis or 'secret husbands'. The latter in turn keep visiting Mumbai to see their 'hijra wives' and have sex, fun and picnics. These secret husbands are, in turn, heterosexually married and have children but maintain relations with their respective hijra wives as well. The 'secret husbands' are aware of the marital status and families of their hijra wives. They visit each other's homes as 'male friends' in the provincial city N. The hijra wives have warned their respective 'secret straight husbands' or panthis to not engage in extra-marital liaisons. So these men can either have sex with their female wives or their hijra wives; if found to engage in sex with any other person, the hijra wives would take this matter seriously and expose the panthis' inner sexual lives to their respective wives. The hijra wives sustain themselves on sex work in Mumbai, which is their sole source of income; they control their 'secret husbands' and try to ensure loyalty, at least in sexual matters. Both hijras and their 'secret husbands' belong to the middle economic stratum and are not poor by Indian standards.[15] The hijras here perform multiple sexual and gender identities: of a hijra—an indigenous transgender identity, of men and husbands to their female wives, of kothi men in the kothi subculture of the provincial city and of 'wives' to their 'secret husbands'. They engage in both 'homo' and 'hetero' sexual acts; they inhabit the heteronormative kinship and family order while also 'secretly' transcending it and negotiating kinship outside hetero-bonding. They love their children from their heterosexual marriages while feeling equally connected to their 'secret husbands'. They imagine themselves as co-wives to the female wives of their 'secret husbands'. These ethnographic encounters show the limitations of the heterosexist representation of family and kinship to diagrammatically capture the alternative ways in which 'sexual dissidents' negotiate lives and affects beyond the heteronormative order. Kinship diagrams consisting of triangles and circles cannot capture the complexities of the relationships discussed. The triangles and circles are imagined in terms of heterogender and the dominant heterosexuality perspective, and these symbols cannot account for diversities even within kinship arrangements based on reproduction.

I met a Muslim transgender person from the metropolitan city H. She works with an NGO involved in AIDS/HIV work. She has undergone 'nirvana' (castration surgery) but continues to stay with her natal kin as the eldest 'son' of the family. She has eight siblings of whom two sisters are married. The natal family knows that she is a transgender, but they hide this fact from the neighbours and other kin. Within her natal home, she wears male clothing, and the junior siblings address her as *bade bhai* (eldest brother). She does not talk much when she is with her family and kin and pretends to be disciplined, and she extracts deference and respect from 'her' junior siblings as the eldest brother of the family. This bodily comportment in observing discipline strategically distances the family and kin from coming very close to 'her', and the family continues to allow this arrangement to forestall the dishonour that a revelation of her transgender status would bring upon them and their extended kin in and around the city H. In her workplace, she articulates her hijra identity and also cross-dresses on her way to office by stopping at a hijra friend's place. On her way back home, she changes back into male robes. The anonymity of the city makes this compartmentalisation possible for her in everyday life. This transgender person is a firm believer and offers Friday prayers in the mosque in male attire as cross-dressers are not allowed within the mosque premises. 'She' is located in her natal family and kin world but she is also a hijra who is a disciple of another hijra guru and to a certain extent abides by hijra norms like supporting her guru with money and other forms of physical support if required. She sometimes hangs out with her hijra sisters and actively participates in AIDS/HIV-related activism. She definitely holds an intermediate position and inhabits a hybrid existence. She also feels more confident about herself as she has been working with an NGO for the past five years, which has exposed her to the issue of rights of sexual minorities.

Feminist engagements with kinship have foregrounded the fact that kinship is not only genealogical but also organises work, property, care, labour, ceremonial gift giving, remittances and many other aspects of life. Among the hijras who intake female hormones and develop feminine features, it is difficult to hide patches of femininity from their bodies, and thus visiting their natal homes becomes a problem. I meet Sobha and Rekha, the two hijras from the city H who have been taking female hormones and also have silicone implants in their breasts. When Rekha saw other hijra friends with silicon implants visiting their respective homes in provincial cities, she also wanted to give it a shot. Accordingly, she planned a trip two years back to meet her family and kin. Upon her visit, however, her brothers asked her to leave because it was difficult to hide the femininity of her silicon-stuffed body. Frustrated and hopeless, Rekha returned to the city where she has a rented accommodation along with her other hijra friends. She resumed her sex work and began to save money. However, she kept in touch with her mother and sister over phone. When her natal family ran into a financial crisis, she was approached for money; she not only extended financial support to her family from where she was once driven away but also helped her parents shift to the city by arranging for a separate rented accommodation for them. This helped Rekha to reconnect with her natal family, but she prefers to stay away from them in view of the stigma a transgender person can transmit to the 'straight' family by her sheer presence. The metropolitan city life, however, offers some opportunities to keep up the connection by virtue of the anonymity it offers in everyday life. The members of the natal family meet Rekha at certain places in the city where others do not know who they are and what the connection between them is.

On the other hand, Sobha and Rekha and their other hijra friends together constitute a kinship that is closer to Bourdieu's idea of practical kinship; these hijra friends earn their livelihood through sex work and begging. When other friends go for begging and sex work, one of them remains at home to cook for everyone. They equally share this responsibility in shifts. This practical kinship helps them manage their everyday cooking and cleaning duties in strategic ways. This further strengthens their friendship, which translates into an emotional bond, and many a time, they lend and borrow money from each other. Such an arrangement may be taken as an empirical unit quite akin to what A. M. Shah (2014) calls the 'household dimensions of family'. The 'straight household' conceptualised by A. M. Shah can be given a queer twist to accommodate alternative households since the tasks of pooling and sharing of resources, production and consumption configure as much as characteristics of hijra households arranged in terms of 'sisterhood' or 'friends and companions' as of 'straight' households. The qualities of affect, emotions, conflict, cooperation, the departure of old members and the arrival of new members, as those reconfigure in these household arrangements, constitute a hitherto unexplored area to which social anthropologists/sociologists in South Asia need to pay attention if these disciplines are committed to expanding their horizons (see Kumar 2018).

Sangeeta is another hijra with whom I had a conversation. Coming from a working class family from a provincial city in Andhra Pradesh, Sangeeta decided to migrate to the nearby metropolitan city H not only to fulfill her feminine desire away from 'her' kin and family but also because of the financial crisis that befell 'her' family some 25 years back. 'She'[16] got some work in a factory but fell ill badly due to the unsafe and hazardous working conditions. Her parents rushed to the city to take 'her' to the hospital. Due to her indebtedness, the parents also began to work in the same factory as labourers. As the family was in a severe financial crisis, Sangeeta began to do sex work to earn a living without the knowledge of her parents. As she was not cross-dressing at this time, the family could not suspect 'her'.[17] She helped the family to repay their debts and financially supported her elder brother to start a small business in the city. No one knew what she was doing in the night as she would say that she was working in another factory. After helping the parents repay their debt and the brother establish a small business, Sangeeta spoke about her gender dysphoria to her family, which was not violently opposed. The father decided to stay apart in the factory premises and the mother shifted to Sangeeta's rented house in proximity to her other hijra friends. The brother stayed with the father and later got married and set up his own household. The sister-in-law visits Sangeeta often. The latter has several chelas whom she addresses as daughters. Within the hijra kinship structure, chelas support the guru, who is also like a mother to them. A few transgender interlocutors from the metro city H have left their natal homes as their working hours are odd and they need to undergo a physical makeover in the night before engaging in sex work in the city. They have decided to move to rented rooms to conceal the fact that they are associated with trans-sex work. They confide that they have boyfriends with whom they are in 'living-in-relations'. The boyfriend lends money without charging any interest from his trans-girlfriend. Many trans-women, in turn, send money home to sustain the education of their junior siblings and also towards meeting the monthly household expenses.

Naz is another hijra from city H who is heterosexually married and has children out of this marriage. 'She' is a father during the day and a trans-sex worker in the evening. She cannot undergo the physical transformation her work requires her to in front of the wife and children. So she has rented a room in the same city, which offers a private space for her to deck up in fineries, sometimes in an Indian sari and at other times in skirts, with expensive lingerie showing through her backless top. I ask her, 'What about your family? Do they know?' She replies, 'Abhi tak to sab thik hai' ('Up until now, everything is okay'). She has a son who has appeared in the intermediate examination. She tells her family that she has 'night duty'. In the morning, she dresses up as a man and comes back to her conjugal and family life. The family survives on sex work without the other members knowing what exactly the 'earning member' of the family does. This compartmentalisation of everyday lives is made possible by the spatial enormity of the city where 'deviant subcultures' have always found an expression (see D'Emilio 1983; Aldrich 2004).

De-Oedipalising and Intermediate and Hybrid Existence

In this section, I try to explicate why this 'intermediate existence' configures as a viable and practical mode of being and becoming in India for the majority of people aspiring to an alternative erotic life without challenging the 'normative' family and kinship ties. These people negotiate their sexual lives without creating a parallel family and kinship arrangement akin to what Weston calls 'families of choice'. An 'individualistic' decision to create a parallel alternative family and kinship arrangement in the sense of Weston or a reworking of biology that Hayden points to as taking place in the case of lesbian families are rarely encountered in the Indian situation. Sanjay Srivastava (2013) aptly mentions that colonial anxieties and concerns about sexuality—both at the level of the state and non-state actors—have remained undiminished even in the postcolonial era. India has witnessed a pornographisation of culture with smart phones making pornography easily accessible to different classes and strata of the population. On the other hand, a restorative sexual culture, which condones 'honour killings' and censorships, is flourishing, and sex education remains still controversial. While the 2014 National Legal Services Authority of India (NALSA) judgment of the Supreme Court of India extends the rights of citizenship to the transgender population, the entry of women in reproductive age to Sabrimala is strongly opposed amidst the Supreme Court verdict allowing such entry and reaffirming the rights of religious communities. The reworking of the NALSA verdict in the recent Transgender Persons (Protection of Rights) Bill, 2016, passed by the Lok Sabha brings another setback to the empowerment of the sexually marginalised (Banerjie 2018). Sunil Khilnani (1999) explicates how it is the 'community' and not the 'individual' that configures as the reference point for people in India, with the result that the centrality of the 'individual' is not so ingrained in Indian modernity. The colonial 'shame culture' (Vanita and Kidwai 2007) continues to haunt even postcolonial articulations as the recent call for a ban on selling books on Khajuraho imageries by the right-wing suggests (Pateriya 2017). Queer life and its alternative aspirations have to be situated within the complex interplay of these contradictory pulls. Despite the emergence of global nodes of queer connections and what Altman (2001) terms as 'global gay identity', queer lives in India and South Asia do not yet constitute an 'alternative community' based on common interests in city spaces as has been made possible in the West through capitalist transformations that have displaced conventional family and kin networks to pave the way for alternative formations (D'Emilio 1983; Floyd 2009). Except for a tiny segment of the gay and lesbian population that is privileged in terms of class and transnational mobility, the majority of queer lives hinges on numerous possibilities and constrains within which they exercise agency to differing degrees. The need to negotiate their erotic life is, however, created by the fluidity and indeterminacy of their sexual psyche that refuses to be fully Oedipalised. Many of them, in an attempt to Odepalise, i.e., 'perform the normal' through association with heteronormative family and kinship structures also lead a de-Oedipalised existence as stories from transgender lives in the preceding sections show. Thus, in the Indian context, the Oedipal and the de-Oedipal combine and interact in complex ways to mediate sexual life in a manner quite different from what Weston (1997) and Hayden (1995) propose.

Notes

1. Despite the availability of hijra alternative kinship and family, many hijra women lead dual lives. Many hijras are married to women, and they also have children out of these marital unions. Such hijra women retain their masculine identity at their natal homes while playing out their hijra identity in the cities where they migrate. We need to see the spatiality and temporality involved in playing out a gendered self. There are hijra women who have wives and children in the same city. In such instances, many of them have to compartmentalise their lives and play dual gender. Many kothi men also play dual gender and traverse both the heteronormative and homoerotic domains in everyday life (see Kumar 2018). In other instances, families of transpersons and gay

persons maintain contact with them in case they are receiving financial support on a regular basis. In such cases also both the natal families and queer persons pretend and perform heteronormative selves in their social contexts. This will be brought in the later part of the chapter. Hijra persons who openly challenge heteronormative codes of honour find it very difficult to connect to their natal families. In case of working-class lesbian women, forming alternative familial arrangements have been not an easy choice. Sahyatrika, a voluntary organisation working among lesbian women, has recorded that many of these women want to establish homoerotic relations without challenging the heteronormative family and community contexts.

2. It emerged from the conversation that there are young gay men available on gay apps like Grindr that also show the exact location of the members. Men can ping, exchange photographs and share their erotic taste/s on the app. Members whose profiles match meet each other for sex in a hotel or any private space. A man who wears a heterosexual identity in public can simultaneously enjoy homoerotic intimacy during a trip/travel. Mankekar (2004) mentions how the Internet has created a possibility to reshape desire and reorganise sexual life. Trivedi (2011) mentions how gay men in metropolitan cities in India may chat through online cruising sites and that it takes no longer than 45 minutes to make love and return to one's own place!
3. See Gupta (2005) about class divisions among the queer community in India.
4. 'Deterritorialising' has been borrowed from Deleuze and Guattari (1972) who deconstruct the Freudian concept of Oedipus through which desire and sexuality get stabilised. Oedipus fixates and territorialises the polymorphous human (sexual) desire that can traverse multiple directions. As a result, heterosexuality reigns as the 'normal' and supreme and the 'mummy, daddy and me' triangle as the only institutionalised expression of family and kinship. Butler (1997) has also critiqued the universality of exogamous heterosexuality while attacking Levi-Strauss's *Elementary Structure of Kinship* (1969) premised on a territorialised understanding of desire, sexuality and masculine agency; the latter (masculine agency) is reinforced through Strauss's 'exchange of women argument' where men are the exchanging parties and women are exchanged as commodities by various groups of men through marriage, cementing the ties between exogamous unions. By dismantling the Oedipus myth as heterosexist, Deleuze and Guattari question the heterosexual family and kinship being regarded as 'normal'. Such normalising constitutes a pre-emptive ban on homosexual desire and hence on alternative forms of family and kinship bonds.

5. See Katz (2004) who suggests that the coinage of the word 'heterosexuality' with its existing connotation is not ahistorcal but has been arrived at during a certain specific period of Victorian modernity in the West.
6. Oedipalisation would refer to what Sigmund Freud understood as the process of resolving the Oedipal crisis during pre-Oedipal phase to attain hetrosexuality. Pre-Oedipal children of both sexes are psychically indistinguishable, bisexual and exhibit a full range of libidinal attitude, active and passive (Rubin 1975: 186). And, for children of both sexes, the mother is the object of desire (ibid.).
7. In Freudian understanding, pre-Oedipal children of both sexes are psychically indistinguishable, bisexual and exhibit a full range of libidinal attitude, active and passive. And, for children of both sexes, the mother is the object of desire (see Rubin 1975).
8. For explaining female sexuality, Freud employs the concept of 'penis envy'. The girl compares her tiny clitoris with the larger penis of the brother, and in face of its evident superior ability to satisfy the body of the mother, falls prey to penis envy and a sense of inferiority. She gives up her struggle for the mother and assumes a passive feminine stance vis-à-vis her brother (see Rubin 1975).
9. In South Asia, patrilineal societies uphold a similar stance where the (biological) mother's body is imagined as earth and the father's contribution in biological reproduction is compared with the act of sowing the seed. This is the reason why children's identity derives from the father and lineage, property and inheritance are transmitted along male lines. This also translates into control over the bodies and sexualities of women (see Dube 1986).
10. The recent surrogacy bill has made homosexual and commercial surrogacy illegal, and allows for altruistic surrogacy only.
11. There has been a controversy over the Union Cabinet approving the Surrogacy (Regulation) Bill, 2016, in India, which allows surrogacy only to married couples. Oversees Indians, foreigners, live-in couples and gay couples are barred from accessing these opportunities. For gay and lesbian couples in India, having a child through artificial insemination appears to be impossible at the moment (see Malhotra 2017).
12. Kothi is supposedly a South Asian 'feminine' homosexual identity taken up mostly by men from lower-middle and working-class backgrounds. Many kothis do not cross-dress and look like men, and they negotiate their existence within heteronormative family and kin contexts. They apparently conform to heteronormative structures and many of them get married to women. But every provincial city and town as well as metropolitan city has a kothi subculture that is hidden from the public.

In their secret subculture, kothis meet each other and socialise. In these subcultural moments and spaces, kothis assert their real selves and express their sisterhood. Kothis perform dual gender roles as men as well as kothis, wherein they cherish feminine values and imagine themselves as women (see Dutta 2012).

13. See notes 6 and 8.
14. Kothi subculture is very similar to hijra culture where there are kothis who are both mentors and disciples. A senior kothi is mentor to junior kothis, and the latter in turn have their disciples. The kothis know each other, and they meet at certain places in the city to socialise and talk about problems affecting their lives. Their masculine partners are called panthis, who are familiar with the kothi subculture. The panthis are sometimes married men.
15. The kothis earn through sex work in Mumbai and both have built their own houses in their native place in the provincial city. The material conditions of their houses reflect their middle-income status. Similarly, the panthis hold good jobs in a multinational bank in the same provincial city.
16. At that time, she did not wear a hijra identity; she migrated to the city as male.
17. See Khan (1999) on male sex work in South Asia.

References

Aldrich, R. 2004. 'Homosexuality and City: A Historical Overview', *Urban Studies*, 41 (9): 1719–37.

Altman, D. 2001. *Global Sex*. Chicago: University of Chicago Press.

Banerjie, A. 2018. 'Against the Mandate for Inclusion: The Transgender Person Bill 2018', *The Hindu*, 21 December. Available at https://www.thehindu.com/opinion/op-ed/against-the-mandate-for-inclusion/article25791080.ece, accessed on 29 June 2019.

Boellstorff, T. 2007. 'Queer Studies in the House of Anthropology', *Annual Review of Anthropology*, 36: 17–35.

Bourdieu, P. 1977. *Outline of a Theory of Practice*. Cambridge, UK, and New York: Cambridge University Press.

Butler, J. 1997. *Gender Trouble: Feminism and the Subversion of Identity*. New York: Routledge

———. 2001. *Antigone's Claim: Kinship between Life and Death*. New York: Columbia University Press.

Chandra, S. 2012. *The Sexual Life of English: Language of Caste and Desire in Colonial India*. Delhi: Zubaan.

Chatterjee, I. 2002. *Gender, Slavery and Law in Colonial India*. Delhi: Oxford University Press.

Deleuze, G. and F. Guattari. 1972. *Anti-Oedipus: Capitalism and Schizophrenia*. USA: Penguin.

D'Emilio, J. 1983. 'Capitalism and Gay Identity', in A. Snitow, C. Stansell and S. Thompson (eds), *Powers of Desire: The Politics of Sexuality*, pp. 100–13. New York: Monthly Review Press.

Dube, L. 1986. 'Seed and Earth: The Symbolism of Biological Reproduction and Sexual Relations of Production', in L. Dube, E. Leacock and S. Ardener (eds), *Visibility and Power: Essays on Women in Society and Development*, pp. 22–53. Delhi: Oxford University Press

Dube, L. and R. Palriwala (eds). 1990. *Structures and Strategies: Women, Work and Family*. New Delhi: Sage Publications.

Duggan, L. 2004. *The Twilight of Equality? Neoliberalism, Cultural Politics and the Attack on Democracy*. Boston: Beacon Press.

Dutta, A. 2012. 'An Epistemology of Collusion: Hijras, Kothis and Historical (Dis)continuity of Gender/Sexual Identities in Eastern India', *Gender and History*, 24 (3): 825–49

Eng, D. L. 'Transnational Adoption and Queer Diasporas', *Social Text*, 21 (3): 301–23.

Floyd, K. 2009. *The Reification of Desire: Toward a Queer Marxism*. Minneapolis: University of Minnesota Press.

Freeman, E. 2007. 'Queer Belongings: Kinship Theory and Queer Theory', in G. Haggerty and M. McGarry (eds), *A Companion to Lesbian, Gay, Bisexual, Transgender, and Queer Studies*, pp. 295–314. Madden, MA: Wiley-Blackwell.

Ganesh, K. 2001. 'Maps for a Different Journey: Themes in the Works of Leela Dube', introductory essay to Leela Dube, *Anthropological Explorations in Gender: Intersecting Fields*, pp.14–32. New Delhi: Sage Publications.

Gupta, A. 2005. 'Englishpur Ki Kothi: Class Dynamics in the Queer Movement in India', in A. Narrain and G. Bhan (eds), *Because I Have a Voice*, pp. 123–42. New Delhi: Yoda Press.

Gupta, C. 2001. *Sexuality, Obscenity, Community: Women, Muslims and the Hindu Public in Colonial India*. Delhi: Permanent Black.

Haritaworn, J. 2015. *Queer Lovers and Hateful Others: Regenerating Violent Times and Places*. London: Pluto Press

Hayden, C. P. 1995. 'Gender, Genetics, and Generation: Reformulating Biology in Lesbian Kinship', *Cultural Anthropology*, 10 (1): 41–63.

Kandiyoti, D. 1988. 'Bargaining with Patriarchy', *Gender and Society*, 2 (3): 274–90.

Katz, J. 2004. *The Invention of Heterosexuality*. Chicago: University of Chicago Press.

Kaur, R. and R. Palriwala. 2014. *Marrying in South Asia: Shifting Concepts, Changing Practices in a Globalizing World*. Hyderabad: Orient Blackswan.

Khan, S. 1999. 'Through a Window Darkly: Men who Sell Sex to Men in India and Bangladesh', in P. Aggleton (ed.), *Men Who Sell Sex: International Perspective on Male Prostitution and HIV/AIDS*, pp. 195–212. London: UCL Press.

Khan, A. 2014. *Eunuchs in Politics, Politics in Eunuchs*. Delhi: Concept Publishers.

Khilnani, S. 1999. *The Idea of India*. New York: Farrar, Straus and Giroux.

Kumar, P. 2017. 'Religion, Erotic Sensibilities, and Marginality', in S. Bandopadhyay and A. Sen (eds), *Religion and Modernity in India*, pp. 133–56. New Delhi: Oxford University Press.

———. 2018. 'Queering Indian Sociology: A Critical Engagement', *Explorations* (E-journal of Indian Sociological Society), 2 (1): 60–85.

Lévi-Strauss, C. 1969. *Elementary Structures of Kinship*. Boston: Beacon Press.

Malhotra, A. 2017. 'Draft Surrogacy Bill Violates Fundamental Rights of People to Choose Modes of Parenthood'. Available at http://indianexpress.com/article/opinion/columns/surrogacy-bill-ban-commercial-2998128/, accessed on 21 November 2018.

Mankekar, P. 2004. 'Dangerous Desires: Television and Erotics in Late Twentieth-Century India', *The Journal of Asian Studies*, 63 (2): 403–31.

Palriwala, R. and C. Risseeuw. 1996. *Shifting Circles of Support: Contextualizing Kinship and Gender in South Asia and Sub-Saharan Africa*. New Delhi: Sage Publications.

Pateriya, A. 2017. 'Kamasutra Books Can't Be Sold at Khajuraho Temple, Saffron Group Seeks Ban', *Hindustan Times*. Available at http://www.hindustantimes.com/india-news/bajrang-sena-says-sale-of-kamasutra-books-at-khajuraho-against-india-s-culture-wants-ban/story-u8C9rLEcd32i2ciFWlMIgM.html, accessed on 18 August 2017.

Peletz, M. G. 1996. *Reason and Passion: Representation of Gender in Malay Society*. Berkeley: University of California Press.

Plummer, K. 2012. 'Critical Sexualities Study', in G. Ritzer (ed.), *The Wiley-Blackwell Companion to Sociology*, pp. 243–68. West Sussex, UK: Blackwell Publishing Ltd.

Quiroga, J. 2000. *Tropics of Desire: Interventions from Queer Latino America*. New York: New York University Press.

Rao, R. and D. Sharma. 2009. *Whistling in the Dark: Twenty-One Queer Interviews*. New Delhi: Sage Publications.

Reddy, G. 2005. *With Respect to Sex: Negotiating Hijra Identity in South India*. Chicago: University of Chicago Press.

Rubin, G. 1975. 'The Traffic in Women: Notes on the Political Economy of Sex', in R. Reiter (ed.), *Toward an Anthropology of Women*, pp. 157–209. New York: Monthly Review Press.

Schneider, D. 1984. *American Kinship: A Cultural Account*. Chicago: University of Chicago Press.

Shah, A. M. 2014. *The Writings of A. M. Shah: The Household and Family in India*. New Delhi: Orient Blackswan.

Shahani, P. 2008. *Gay Bombay: Globalization, Love and Belonging in Contemporary India*. New Delhi: Sage Publications.

Srivastava, S. 2013. *Sexuality Studies*. New Delhi: Oxford University Press.

Strathern, M. 1993. 'Review: *Families We Choose: Lesbians, Gays, Kinship*. by Kath Weston', *Man*, 28 (1), 195–96.

Times of India. 2010. 'Surrogacy Still Not an Option for Indian Gay, Lesbian Couples', 27 May. Available at https://timesofindia.indiatimes.com/india/Surrogacy-still-not-an-option-for-Indian-gay-lesbian-couples/articleshow/5978164.cms, accessed on 21 January 2018.

Trivedi, I. 2011. *India in Love: Marriage and Sexuality in the 21st Century*. Delhi: Aleph.

Uberoi, P. 1994. 'Introduction', in P. Uberoi (ed.), *Family, Marriage and Kinship in India*, pp. 2–44. Delhi: Oxford University Press.

Vanita, R. and S. Kidwai, S. 2007. *Same-Sex Love in India: Readings in Indian Literature*. London: Palgrave Macmillan.

Weston, K. 1997. *Families We Choose: Lesbians, Gays, Kinship*. New York: Columbia University Press.

8 Modernity without Alterity

Deshastha Brahmins and Hindu Cosmopolitanism in Mumbai*

SURYAKANT WAGHMORE

Are caste and cosmopolitanism antithetical? They will seem antithetical indeed if approached from a liberal cosmopolitan point of view as caste distinctions result in social closure and are based on ideas of hierarchy. This chapter engages with the question of caste and cosmopolitanism by exploring the role of caste associations of the privileged in contested cosmopolitanisms of Mumbai, their worldview, the challenges they face and the opportunities they cultivate in contemporary cities, thus contributing to varieties of cosmopolitanisms and simultaneously consolidating Hindu cosmopolitanism. We begin by pondering over cosmopolitanism and its urban meanings beyond the liberal moorings of inclusiveness.

Urban Cosmopolitanism

A critical view of cosmopolitanism in contemporary times would broadly understand it as an elitist, Western, bourgeois and liberal project that provides moral and political meaning to the lives of the socially privileged who can cross national boundaries between the East and the West with ease. In this moment of mobility enhanced by the advance of capitalism, the mobile *global citizen* learns and

* This chapter draws from a larger project titled 'Withering Caste in Urban Locales' funded by the Indian Council of Social Science Research (ICSSR) (Grant Number SC-15/2014-15/ICSSR/RPS).

unlearns culture and politics across space and time. Truly global and cosmopolitan citizens thus lack 'rigid' local roots. However, despite increased mobility across classes and national boundaries such political and cultural life is limited to a select few.

Cosmopolitanism, however, has deeper historical roots, with moral meanings and implications. For Stoic philosophers, the lack of reason amongst humans was tantamount to slavery, and they believed that the use of reason alone would lead us into being citizens of the world. Neither status nor states could impinge upon our natural inclination towards cosmopolitanism (Long and Sedley 1987). Besides certain spontaneity of reason, the Stoic philosophers counterposed a challenge of civility as universal to the particular nature of city-states. Cosmopolitanism found deeper humanist and liberal roots in the Kantian project of perpetual peace (Kant 2006). The Kantian project was, however, far less dialogical and more prescriptive than Stoicism. Cosmopolitanism should not only be traced in Western history and philosophy (Pollock 2000) but also considered in the plural (cosmopolitanisms) to acknowledge the plurality of modes and histories not necessarily shared in degree or concept (Pollock et al. 2000). For socialist writers, likewise, cosmopolitanism was linked to the bourgeoisie and enlightenment ideas of humanism (Volland 2017). Cosmopolitanism therefore had to he brought down from the high horses of Western liberal imperialism to look at its multiple meanings, leading to discoveries of cosmopolitanism(s) in unlikely times and places (Volland 2017: 10).

One natural place to look for cosmopolitanism is in cities and urban spaces as sites of openness and accommodation where co-existence of varied cultures, races and classes was both possible and necessary. How did cosmopolitanism configure and consolidate in cities of the non-Western world? A major drawback of writings on cosmopolitanism and urbanism in India has been their inability to bring together sociological and postcolonial insights; hence questions such as this have remained unaddressed. This is best reflected in the way caste has been ignored or approached in the study of cities and urban cosmopolitanism. I draw here from

Hall (2002), Calhoun (2002), Pollock (2000) and Chatterjee (2016) to desist from the top-down modes of studying and understanding cosmopolitanism as an extension of liberal ideas of global citizenship (Appiah 2006). I contribute to the diverse version of cosmopolitanisms (Pollock et al. 2000) that is soaked in local ethics, politics and urbanisms of the East.

Urban Cosmopolitanism in India

Rural life in India is deeply segmented and simultaneously regulated through inter- and intra-caste intimacy. Due to the ethics and regulations of caste hierarchy, villages make a contra site for the possibilities of cosmopolitanism and genuine civility (Waghmore 2013). On the other hand, cities as prime movers of modernity are considered favourable spaces for dissolving status-based identities and hierarchies towards achieving a larger public based on spontaneity, dialogue and openness. Historically, urban spaces have also advanced individual liberty and an associational culture conducive for 'civil' society (Morris 1998). Due to their dynamic density, urban spaces are said to produce organic solidarity, taking individuals beyond solidarities of kinship ties (Durkheim 2014).

City life could be seen as an ideal space for practising the ethics of alterity based on the centrality of free-flowing dialogue, not guided by instrumental reasoning central to modernity or communal bonds tied to traditionalism, thus producing a sociability through spontaneity and impulse, which is artistic, free flowing and based on pure humanity (Simmel and Hughes 1949). Perhaps for this reason, B. R. Ambedkar called upon ex-untouchables to leave villages for cities, as caste construed a deep challenge to the possibilities of cosmopolitanism and civility in rural life. For subalterns, cities constitute spaces of emancipation from the tyranny of the rural social order. Urban margins could also construct subaltern cosmopolitanism as a politics from below (Gidwani 2006). Contrary to Durkheim, however, caste helps form organic solidarity where the cult of the individual is not void of the collective conscience of caste in contemporary cities. Further, cities have turned out to be a mixed blessing for deprived groups, as they may constitute sites of social emancipation coupled with economic hardships (Mendelsohn and Vicziany (2000).

To explore the multiple meanings and possibilities of urban cosmopolitanism, we may also need to look for cosmopolitanism beyond the compulsions and hard lives of poor and excluded populations. This chapter examines the meaning of city spaces for the communities considered 'higher' and 'pure' in contemporary times. I explore this through caste associations of these communities to understand how they negotiate cosmopolitan urbanism. Are these caste associations anti-cosmopolitan, or do they promote a different form of cosmopolitanism?

Bombay–Mumbai evokes the romance of cosmopolitanism due to its specific and spectacular commercial development and its impressive diversity stemming from colonial and postcolonial times. A rupture occurred in 1992, when the cosmopolitanism of Mumbai was said to have been undermined by the communal violence following the demolition of the Babri Masjid (Appadurai 2000). Such approaches, however, underplay the role of caste in Mumbai's social and associational life and may not realise that cosmopolitanism was long compromised in the landscapes of Bombay. It is here that we need to bring together critical postcolonial insights and sociological understandings of caste and urbanisation to grasp the rooted nature of urban cosmopolitanisms in India.

Caste in its plasticity took the form of guilds and trade unions with urbanisation and industrialisation (Mukerjee 1937). Caste in Bombay thrived under the British as the colonial government maintained its policy of non-interference in indigenous religion. Bombay saw a reorientation of primordial groups (castes and religious sects) as a response to ideological and political changes and a new form of urban leadership that had primordial linkages (Dobbin 1972). Caste groups that had better jobs used ties of caste and kinship to fill future job openings and solidify their respective group position. The flip side of this is that caste also influences economic inequalities and exclusion in labour markets (Thorat and Attewell 2007). Caste has also historically shaped the organisation of residential space, especially at the village level, and it appears to continue to do so in contemporary urban India (Vithayathil and Singh 2012).

In a recent study, Coffey et al. (2018) speak of 'explicit prejudice', but does the presence of caste in cities necessarily mean the end of urban cosmopolitanism? Could the presence of caste as community also point to 'traditional urbanism and structural continuity' (Rao 1991) between the rural and the urban? Does caste as community also provide a social and moral base for urban lifeworlds and cosmopolitanism in India? The intimate nature of caste sociality or regulation in rural spaces is difficult to find in urban areas but urban India is not uncongenial to caste, and caste constitutes a linkage between the city and the countryside (Conlon 1977). Caste interaction in the city, however, increasingly emphasises distinction and separation over hierarchy (Cort 2004). Is such an emphasis on separation and difference anti-cosmopolitan? Or, could this also point to the making of a non-Western ideal—of Hindu cosmopolitanism based on social closure and limited alterity?

Hindu Cosmopolitanism?

Cosmopolitanism may be a necessity of capitalist urban life, but its forms are varied. In its liberal form, cosmopolitanism emphasises the individual over community, which undermines the (continuing) imperial basis of liberal cosmopolitanism (Chatterjee 2016: 331). In India, 'laws of the state have limited jurisdiction and are more often subordinated to the rules of the right conduct prescribed by community practices' (ibid.). Chatterjee's doubts about cosmopolitanism and its liberal ills echo Hall's (2002) problems with cosmopolitanism and its implicit faith in liberal civic nationalism. Civic nationalism for Hall (ibid.: 29) cannot proceed without cultural embededness and identity cannot be constructed in relation to political systems alone. Thus neither liberal universalism nor segmented communities can possibly exist in a vacuum. A combination of equality and difference is central to understanding existential (not logical) political positions (ibid.: 30).

The crucial question for Hall therefore is to understand if the framework of difference and equality enables society to enhance life chances.

A similar critical cue is provided by Calhoun (2002) who reflects on the nature of cosmopolitanism and its implications for cosmopolitan democracy. Food, tourism, music, literature and clothes are all easy faces of consumerist cosmopolitanism; 'soft cosmopolitanism' can well be an elite project with an emphasis on the individual and on capital, but it may not lead to a 'cosmopolitan democracy' (ibid.: 889). Cosmopolitan democracy, on the other hand, depends on finding ways to relate diverse solidarities to each other rather than trying to overcome them (ibid.: 893). Cosmopolitan democracy for Calhoun, thus, is not exactly in contrast to the centrality that Chatterjee assigns to *community* and the postcolonial nation state in the making of the Indian ideal. Calhoun, however, makes a case for dialogue across communities in an agnostic form to achieve cosmopolitan democracy, and is thus closer to those emphasising alterity in everyday forms of sociality. Alterity enables experiencing oneself through unhindered encounters with the other. The individualism of modernity, on the other hand, produces a utilitarian individual who is guided by instrumental interests, thus affecting possibilities of a genuine dialogue. Alterity lies therefore 'in-between' the individual and the community and we need to look for possibilities of an ontology based on dialogue for achieving a dialogical community (Gardiner 1996).

If caste plays the role of community in cities, how does this dynamic of collective peaceful living via community identities translate as a social and political practice of cosmopolitan urbanism in contemporary times? Would this be similar to the civility of indifference that was suggested by Bailey (1996). Could this also result in some form of pragmatic indifference towards the 'other' and proximity towards the ones closer in status, purity, honour and culture? Would such forms of civility not be part of urban cosmopolitanism? McFarlane helps us further transcend the definitions of liberal cosmopolitanism that present cosmopolitanism as *only* inclusive: 'All forms of cosmopolitanism are to varying extents inclusive or exclusive, implying that one important role for the critic is to illuminate the politics, limits, and exclusions of different forms of cosmopolitan imaginary and practice' (2008: 497).

While Pollock et al. (2000) view cosmopolitanism in the plural, that is, *cosmopolitanisms*, a grounded understanding of cosmopolitanism will also require us to accommodate specific attitudes towards difference, including those that may seem anti-cosmopolitan from a liberal point of view. Chatterjee (2016: 332) rightly suggests that there is a certain anti-political impulse in the political ruminations of Appiah (2006). Accommodating non-inclusive cosmopolitanism also paves the way for a critical study of cosmopolitan enclaves and their role in constituting pragmatic urbanity (Bridge 2006).

Cosmopolitanism, or its diluted practice, is also a strategy of urban survival for both marginal and dominant groups. I do not term the cosmopolitanisms arising out of caste associations as 'vernacular' cosmopolitanism, since such an approach could unintentionally place the Western liberal cosmopolitanism as 'universal' and other forms as poor imitations. Instead, I use a broader canon of 'Hindu cosmopolitanism' to understand and elaborate the cosmos that caste associations of the pure and privileged work towards consolidating. Hindu cosmopolitanism also helps us conceptualise a new ideal type of cosmopolitanism that is void of alterity.

Does cosmopolitanism based on caste difference and closure enhance the 'life chances' (Hall 2002) of Hindus and others? Does it lead to a deepening of democracy as opposed to procedural democracy? In contemporary cities, Sennett (2002) suggests, the trend of highly flexibilised corporations constructing physical spaces produces a regime of non-interactive differences in which the city is managed by the principles of non-interaction: 'Non-interaction becomes the guarantor of public order and the alterity of the population is replaced by the marking of difference, and the result is that difference produces social relations of indifference' (ibid.: 46–47).

The problem, for Sennett, is how do you get the intensity of interactions on the streets of the city? This question remains critical and significant in our case as well—do caste associations and their Hindu cosmopolitanism produce such intensity? As I will suggest in the rest of the chapter, in celebrating and consolidating caste as community, Hindu cosmopolitanism faces the challenge of genuine alterity. Hindu cosmopolitanism encourages soft cosmopolitanism and is not completely antithetical to cosmopolitan democracy. An urban individual may be able to realise his/her 'self' only when he/she is rooted in the community. Such a realisation of the self in contemporary times and urban spaces values a degree of caste closure as an ideal ethic for urban cosmopolitanism and is partially based on the remnants of the ideology of caste hierarchy. Against alterity, spontaneity and genuine dialogue, Hindu cosmopolitanism has caste closure (with the materialist individual) as an ideal ethic to struggle for in the urban metropolis of Mumbai.

Through the study of caste associations, I argue that cosmopolitanism, while being a necessity of life in a metropolis, results from the compulsion as well as the seductions that accompany life in a megacity. The political and economic consequences of absolute segmentation are tremendous in modern times as they can freeze technical innovation and perpetuate the ritualised 'tyranny of cousins' (Gellner 1995: 33). Caste associations present 'caste as community' as a social solidarity, based on 'choice' rather than birth, that helps individuals negotiate urbanism and indulge in consumptive (soft) cosmopolitanism. Some interventions of caste associations may seem anti-cosmopolitan as they mostly encourage horizontal alterity. However, I suggest that cosmopolitanism should not necessarily be judged through parameters of inclusion alone since (some) exclusion may well be part of Hindu cosmopolitanism, which drives postcolonial urbanism in India.

In the section that follows, I examine one caste association that attempts to provide roots to freely moving individuality and alterity in a non-violent form. Such regulation is not absolute closure and is congruent with the idea of coexistence of diverse communities. In latent forms, however, caste associations try to dissuade those who may want to move beyond caste for love, sympathy and compassion. Caste associations are thus opposed to dialogue and alterity, as they affect the possibilities of reciprocity, spontaneity and free-flowing sociality in the city.

Strategies used by these caste associations encompass both material and cultural spheres. For the caste associations of the privileged, the city holds no promise of liberation and equality. The golden age of caste as community is lost or is seen as eroding radically. Caste associations work towards forming a new urban identity from within caste groups, thus working towards the difficult task of holding together the *inner* solidarity of very jati itself in ethical ways under the rubric of urban Hindu cosmopolitanism. They thus aid in constructing soft cosmopolitanism that downplays alterity and helps negotiate the moral density of urban spaces. As opposed to Durkheim's (2014) organic solidarity that privileges the solidarity among individuals, caste as community continues to provide a foundational basis for cosmopolitan urbanism and Hindu cosmopolitanism.

Caste Associations and Hindu Cosmopolitanism in Mumbai

Caste associations have helped caste groups negotiate modernity and democracy (Rudolph 1965), bridge social and ritual distance between sub-castes within a caste (Conlon 1974), initiate social reform within castes (Conlon 1977) and organise cooperatives for economic mobility (Rao 2013). These are formal civil associations of caste with a traditional ideological base that have dynamically evolved to suit changing contexts and institutions. Contemporary caste associations of high-caste Hindus have new roles and challenges to face. The reforms from within, increased education and independence of women, and the overall context of urbanism construct new challenges for these associations. Bairy's (2013) study of Brahmin caste associations framed them as modes of enunciation with the outside world. I complement such an effort by exploring the struggles of caste Hindu associations to hold together the inner worlds of caste in new ethical ways in keeping with the challenges posed by urbanism.

According to Sheth (1999), caste today signifies more of a kinship-based cultural community than status groups. Natarajan (2011), however, suggests that castes cannot exist without casteism. Following Natarajan may undermine any possibility of recovering cosmopolitanism amongst caste Hindus, whilst complimenting Sheth could provide insights into the new forms of civility in urban spaces as negotiated and practised by caste Hindus. How does this movement from status to kinship (ibid.) and from hierarchy to separation (Cort 2004) help in cosmopolitan urbanism? What happens to the ideas of hierarchy and purity in the context of a metropolis? Some of these questions could help us grasp the dynamics of caste and the making of cosmopolitan caste subjects in contemporary cities.

Urban contexts are plagued with high consumerism and dangers of fragmented individualism. With increasing urbanisation, kinship-based cultural communities face the challenge of rupture and the possible decentring of caste subjects. The modernity of alterity and the fear of strangers walking into one's own private family–caste space make caste associations a very important site of sociation and sociability. Caste associations, thus, become very important modes of keeping caste subjects culturally rooted and ordered as Hindu cosmopolitans, protecting caste as a community against the onslaught of strangers and the seduction of the adventures that city life may contain. How successful are they?

This chapter presents the case of Deshastha Rigvedi Brahmin Sangh (DRBS). Like several other associations in the city, DRBS is a registered organisation formed for the cultural, educational, economic and general welfare of Deshasthas. It has annual general body meetings, audited accounts, annual reports, and monthly and bi-monthly or bi-annual magazines. These activities are coupled with cultural events specific to Deshasthas and are targeted only towards this caste. Associations such as these are, thus, a variant of vibrant civil society associations run in a democratic and transparent manner without 'external' funding.

Deshastha Rigvedi Brahmin Sangh

Deshastha Brahmins are a caste mostly found in Maharashtra and Karnataka. They were a scribal caste in the pre-colonial times, which was mostly close to courts and kings, and they were highly urbanised in the colonial times. The Deshastha Brahmins are divided into two major caste groups: the Rigvedi Deshastha Brahmins and the Shukla Yajurvedi Brahmins. Deshastha Rigvedi Brahmin Sangh (DRBS, Vile Parle) was established in 1935.[1] Formed for Rigvedis living in the heart of colonial Bombay, DRBS, Vile Parle, currently has over a thousand members. It organises events like the *jayanti* of Shri Ram, Khande Navami, Rigvedi Shravani,[2] celebrations of 'national' importance such as Independence Day and Republic Day, health camps with the Inner Wheel Club, discussions with television stars from the community and felicitation ceremonies for public figures from the community. The main source of funding is the community hall[3] of DRBS in Vile Parle, which is rented out for social and private functions.

Beyond Deshastha Rigvedis, DRBS is open to involving other Brahmins, and the enrolment of non-Deshastha Brahmin members as well-wishers (*hita-chintak*) is allowed, though these members are discouraged from contesting elections or holding any positions. Members of other Brahmin castes can participate in the annual Rigvedi Shravani organised by DRBS. Beyond Brahmins, the association engages with non-sectarian organisations like the Inner Wheel Club of Mumbai.[4] Members of DRBS occasionally volunteered and made visits to tribal villages in Thane along with the Inner Wheel Club members. Some members who visited these villages shared their concern about the deprived and vulnerable status of tribals and the need to contribute voluntarily to such 'backward communities'. What we see in DRBS is a form of horizontal cosmopolitanism where the association, albeit in a limited form, allows other Brahmins to be members of the association and occasionally demonstrates concern towards other marginal groups. Though such concern may be limited and may seem like self-aggrandisement of Rigvedis, the element of (limited) sympathy beyond ones' own caste needs to be understood as a new form of sociality for privileged caste subjects.

Participation of the younger generation is however negligible in most of the aforementioned programmes. This does not mean that youth are caste-less, but for them, caste is limited to the family and personal spaces. Not all want to make caste a public identity or a mode of collective identity. Beyond this, a 'lack of time' is considered a major hurdle for youth to get involved or volunteer in DRBS.

The elderly members had varied and complex reactions to the changing nature of caste as a community in Mumbai and the resulting challenges for DRBS. While a few saw the *possible* erasure of caste as a positive development, this process was also seen as fraught with the danger of annihilating the institution of family, culture and ethical life in general. DRBS respondents did not emphasise their ritual purity or their high-caste status, unlike members of other Brahmin castes interviewed for this study. Some even suggested that the origin of caste consciousness among the Deshasthas lay in the Bhakti saint Dynaneshwar known for his inclusive preaching and critique of caste. Senior members considered DRBS as a progressive Brahmin association, while Deshasthas were generally seen to be a progressive caste, which is open to mingling as compared other castes. However, Deshasthas viewed caste as simultaneously community and culture. This maps on to the idea of caste as difference and informs the struggle of Deshasthas to retain their cultural difference in the context of Mumbai. Such difference could have elements of horizontal alterity extendable *only* to other Brahmins.

The DRBS is primarily run by elderly members(over 60 years of age), who volunteer to take up leadership and managerial tasks. Presently Dr Kulkarni is the chairman of the association. He retired as principal from a management college. In a group discussion, Dr Kulkarni and other members shared their concern about the declining interests of younger members in the affairs of the association. One member called DRBS an *organisation of senior citizens*. Most of the elderly active members are either retired or close to retirement. These members felt that people are going to 'forget caste', but their feelings towards such erasure of caste from memory were mixed. It was more a matter of worry that younger generations do not come to these associations. They viewed this problem as peculiar to the metropolis of Mumbai and not in interior parts of Maharashtra like Pune, Satara and Sangli. In the group discussion, the challenges facing the progressive Deshastha Rigvedis of Mumbai were seen to be peculiar but linked to the general decay of culture in cities:

> Kulkarni: Konkanashthas [Brahmins] are a closed community more likely to marry within and think of their caste first. Konkanasthas also look down upon the Deshasthas ...
>
> Kanvilkar:[5] But we can absorb [accommodate] you. For example, you do tend to take some non-veg.; for us it is not binding. It will not be that we would separate you from this [DRBS]. But they [Konkanastha] are very particular ...
>
> Kulkarni: We are that way liberal, broad minded, large hearted, you know because we don't mind. We are not strict. Here also we are saying that all Brahmins should come together. That is our feeling, basic feeling.
>
> (Group Discussion in English, November 2016)

> Dhotikar:[6] Marathas are very orthodox people. They feel that they have ruled this state for 300 years. Shivaji Maharaj! [Kulkarni smirks]. So they believe that they are the rulers. And all the other communities are second rate.
>
> Kanvilkar: [Comparatively] Brahmins are not orthodox; they are liberal. They marry Muslims also.
>
> Dhotikar: Earlier you could say Brahmins were orthodox. Earlier thinking has gone. Brahmins are no longer orthodox
>
> Kanvilkar: They are not orthodox.
>
> All: Not orthodox, not orthodox ... [in agreement]
>
> (Group Discussion in English, December 2016)

Amongst Brahmins, Konkanastha Brahmins were considered to be the most conservative and closed. However, Brahmins overall were seen to be more progressive, urbane and cosmopolitan than others, especially Marathas, as they were open to marrying 'even' Muslims. In other informal conversations, members of several [upper] caste associations saw this as a matter of compulsion and not choice. Though they recognise that movement beyond caste connotes cosmopolitanism and is progressive in nature, such openness towards other castes is not necessarily considered good for moral and cultured living that requires rootedness in caste and family, which the forces of urbanisation were seen as eroding.

DRBS had a marriage *mandal* that was closed down five years back as there was little response from the community and government regulations on running marriage bureaus was seen as disabling. It was also difficult for the bureau to compete with matrimonial websites that offer more profiles along with caste-specific choices. Mr Desai who is also the joint secretary of DRBS, explained the peculiar problem facing Deshasthas in marriage, and how this was eroding the very bond that holds the community together:

> A peculiar problem facing Brahmin girls, more particularly Deshastha girls is that they are more educated than the boys. They get good jobs. They don't get good match [within caste] and go outside caste.
>
> Girls have good salaries. They do not want to be dependent on husbands and follow men in US. The girls in the Brahmin community want boys from within India. They do not want to go to USA [and become housewife]. If they do not get boys from within caste, then they marry outside community.
>
> (Group Discussion in English, December 2017)

The problem of educated and/or economically independent girls seeking compatibility over caste in marriage alliances was not mentioned by Deshastha Rigvedis alone. Education and the new 'individual intellectualism' were seen as problems by most volunteers of such caste associations. This was a recurring theme in other Brahmin associations as well. Despite the progressive nature of Deshasthas, Desai felt that marriages outside caste point to a breakdown of the family system in particular and of social cohesion in general. Though undesirable, it was near *impossible* to regulate these new processes. The multiple choices of urban material and cultural life were seen to create a life of compulsion in which it was not possible to fully regulate the younger members, more particularly women.

> Desai: [Just assume] I am earning 75K. My wife is earning 75K. I have freedom of thought; my wife has freedom of thought. After one and a half years, I don't like you; you don't like me—finish get lost. Marriage system itself is breaking down in these times. The instances of divorces are more because of inter-caste marriages... Earlier the girl used to be in the control of the parents. Now it is not like that. When a girl is outside whole day, parents have no control.
>
> Kanvilkar: In the city nobody has time. I have no time to see where my son is going or my daughter is going.
>
> Desai: See, once you step outside your house, do you know the person sitting next to you is Mahar or Muslim? No. Brahmins believe that I am upper caste. Those things have gone now. It is only media that is propagating caste in a big way.
>
> (Group Discussion in English, December 2016)

The aforementioned members viewed the Mumbai metropolis as a site of compulsion-induced cosmopolitanism, whereby Deshasthas had turned progressive and liberal. Others, however, emphasised the moral challenges and the looming risk of self-annihilation that accompanies the 'progressive' life in cities. Mr Purandhare (52 years) is the son of one of the founder members of DRBS. He held similar views on marriage and other individualist transgressions but with a lot more clarity on ethics and culture. Such transgressions were seen as a failure of *sanskar* (values). Mr Purandhare was critical of Western influence on the youth, which he thought was against a cultured way of life. His concern was less animated by cosmopolitan patriotism than an anxiety over the erasure of caste vis-à-vis the erasure of a cultured self in the metropolis of Mumbai. His concerns ranged from the celebration of non-Hindu festivals like New Year to meat eating by Brahmins in cities:

> When do you marry outside [caste]? When you do not have sanskar, then you do not listen to your parents; you do not follow guidelines. In a short period, people fall in love and start hanging together; most have physical attraction and because of this they leave their own caste and go outside. Most of these love marriages result in divorce. Women are concerned that their figure [physical appearance] should not get spoiled and that is why they do not want issue [children]. How serious is this! This is *rakshasi pravritti* [evil nature].
>
> Since Brahmins have started eating [meat], the prices have gone up. If you eat meat, your body reacts that way; you get thoughts of that kind [violent]. Look at a Brahmin's face; you will not find negativity. But once you start eating meat, your way of being changes. You go on that track. You are cutting, killing and eating. People who eat such things are aggressive; they are a threat to society.
>
> (Personal interview in Hindi and Marathi, January 2018)

The caste self was not against modern or material life but against the erasure of self-identity rooted in caste and caste closure. The cultured way of being Brahmin if resorted to in a classical way could ensure that one stayed clear of the evils of urbanism in Mumbai. Meat eating, unregulated love and sexual urges beyond caste, and other adventures that the sociability of the city provided could best be mitigated through Brahmin sanskar. DRBS is not worried about the lack of financial resources in running the organisation—its main challenge is the younger generations' liking for fractured individualism and the possibilities of transgressing caste identity. Dr Kulkarni may not agree with the rather orthodox view of Purandhare, but he was positive and hopeful of attracting youth into the association:

> After some time, youngsters too will come. We are thinking of designing something that will attract youngsters. We need to programme it so as to suit the requirements of youngsters.
>
> (Group Discussion in English, December 2016)

That a 70-year-old caste association like DRBS with no lack of economic resources is struggling to stay relevant amongst its younger members tells us about the challenge of forcing caste as a long associational contact on city life or individuals. Market- and state-induced cosmopolitanism seems to have been seductive for the youth, which is increasingly disinterested in DRBS and its social function. This may have to do with DRBS being too specifically limited to Rigvedi Deshasthas. DRBS was working on 'new' plans to attract young members by consulting other successful caste associations, organising workshops on entrepreneurship and cultural festivals like *garba* celebrations, and creating a website.[7] Deshastha youth who participated in these events emphasised the feeling of community and how such events resembled family events or entailed giving back to your own community. To counter the blasé attitude amongst the younger generation, caste is being reworked to entice young minds so as to help them find their social roots and community membership as well as build greater trust between them and their co-caste members. DRBS seeks to constitute a new individual who takes pride in caste as community while being part of cosmopolitan urban life.

Maya Kulkarni (25 years) was advised by her parents to participate in DRBS activities. She was not sure of the difference between Deshastha Brahmins and other Brahmins. Her mother is a Kokanastha and father a Deshastha. She has also been part of Rotaract Society and is now active in DRBS. Maya shared:

> I like DRBS; it encourages me plus it was something for my community. I get [the] feeling that one should help their community. DRBS gives me a sense of unity and business opportunity [she had attended a workshop on business]. If it was going to help my community then it's not a bad idea definitely. I attended the meeting for new businessmen and firms. It was a networking opportunity with your own [community] for business. Instead of looking for ten other people to collaborate, you can have one person who you can trust. I also attended the *dandia* night they [DBRS] organised.

Regarding marriage, Yeshashree was uncomfortable about marrying a non-vegetarian, and had similar views on inter-religious marriages: 'Marrying the person [you like] is important and not caste. I would say no to inter-religious marriage; there is too much adjustment in inter-religious marriage'.

All self-representations and imaginaries of the city are bound to be in a state of flux, and the Deshashta Rigvedi identity is better subsumed within the larger Brahmin cosmos but not restricted to it. An individual (Brahmin) could thus simultaneously participate in the public (charity, politics, religion and nation), but the primary and parallel identity is one of caste. DRBS continues to mobilise caste sentiments from within the caste so as to produce modern materialist subjects and a Hindu cosmopolitan for whom caste as community continues to remain the primary cultural and associational affiliation along with other modular affiliations of city life.

Hindu Cosmopolitanism and the Challenge of Alterity

Would community (caste) be less relevant for Hindu cosmopolitans in New York or some other city of North America? This question is broadly answered in the negative by Chatterjee (2016), who emphasises 'community over individuals' as an Eastern ideal. The virtual world offers more clues, for instance, the website of the Brahman Samaj of North America (BSNA) refers to the BSNA as the largest Brahmin organisation, 'with sole objective of bringing Brahmans together and help[ing] *them seek their own cultural and social identity*.... BSNA strongly disapproves [of] the evils of the Hindu caste system' (emphasis original).[8]

Hindu cosmopolitanism and its civic engagement in cities across the world is largely filtered through caste. Urbanism in the megacity of Mumbai curtails the intimate nature of caste through the consistent seductions and stimulations that challenge hierarchical ideas of caste. Caste associations of the privileged and pure castes promote consumptive or soft cosmopolitanism without challenging caste hierarchy. Through the case of Deshasthas, I have suggested that caste associations continue to influence sociation and sociability in their attempt to govern and discipline individuals towards achieving Hindu cosmopolitanism. Committed caste subjects who act as volunteers of caste associations are anxious about rootless individualism and the possibilities of dialogical community that could 'destroy' cultured belonging in urban spaces.

Caste associations have the morals of a communal collective that can help individuals thrive economically in urban areas. Do they generate cosmopolitan values and practices for urban living that could help individuals move beyond caste for love, friendship, sympathy and greater civility? The Hindu cosmopolitanism of DRBS discussed in this chapter points to both the limits of liberal cosmopolitanism as an ideal and the lack of alterity as a necessity in urban publics that Hindu cosmopolitans seek to constitute. Hindu cosmopolitans claim to host critical cosmopolitanism in their moves, which challenge Westernised ways of individualism, to retain community at the heart of urban consumerism. They, however, obstruct spontaneity, sociability and genuine alterity that make a dialogical community possible.

Hindu cosmopolitanism proposes an alternative universal urbanism that values distinction and social closure along with material indulgence and mobility. It is identical to soft or consumptive cosmopolitanism but proposes an alternative ethical and moral positioning that celebrates closure as resistance against Western and other local/lower varieties of cosmopolitanisms. Hindu cosmopolitanism thus helps us develop a new ideal type of cosmopolitanism that is void of alterity.

Broadly, as hierarchy becomes distinction and difference, and caste becomes community, caste associations continue to provide roots to free-moving individuals in their respective communities by invoking community pride and history. Hindu cosmopolitanism does not seem to lack politeness, order, peace and other elements that are essential for urban cosmopolitanism. Paradoxically, these co-exist with elements of vulgarity, which affect the possibilities of individual self-realisation in the city by making the individual inward-looking for morals and sympathy. Hindu cosmopolitanism, in this sense, lacks the virtue of civility, and may produce an urban modernity void of alterity. It, however, constitutes an important and dominant form of cosmopolitanism in urban India.

Notes

1. There are other branches of DRBS in Thane, Mulund, Kalyan, Girgaum, Dombivili and Mahim. All the branches of DRBS are networked/parented by Akhil Deshastha Rigvedi Madyavarti Mandal (ADRMM) in Mahim.
2. Rigvedi Shravani is an annual thread-changing ceremony organised on the occasion of Shravani Purnima (the full moon day), in the holy month of Shravan (Hindu calendar).
3. Constructed through contributions and loans provided by members on a piece of land donated (secured for a nominal price).
4. Inner Wheel is an international women's organisation, aimed at creating friendship, service and understanding, originally comprising wives of Rotarians and now open to other women as well.
5. Kanvilkar is a retired banker who joined the association 20 years ago.
6. Dhotikar is the secretary of DRBS and a retired engineer. He joined the association 30 years ago. Both he and his wife are active members of the Sangha.
7. The newly elected president of ADRMM has made a similar agenda central 'in the interest of the community'. The plan includes starting Deshastha associations in all blocks so as to ensure active participation of women and youth in the association. The new constitution of ADRMM allows enrolment of Deshasthas who are based outside India and efforts are being made to enroll them as members (*Deshastha Rigvedi Brahmin Samachar*, September 2018).
8. See https://bsnaconvention.info, accessed 10 December 2017.

References

Appadurai, A. 2000. 'Spectral Housing and Urban Cleansing: Notes on Millennial Mumbai', *Public Culture*, 12 (3): 627–51.

Appiah, K. 2006. *Cosmopolitanism: Ethics in a World of Strangers*. New York: W. W. Norton & Company.

Bailey, F. G. 1996. *The Civility of Indifference: On Domesticating Ethnicity*. Ithaca: Cornell University Press.

Bairy, R. 2013. *Being Brahmin, Being Modern: Exploring the Lives of Caste Today*. New Delhi: Taylor & Francis.

Bridge, G. 2006. 'The Paradox of Cosmopolitan Urbanism: Rationality, Difference and the Circuits of Cultural Capital', in J. Binnie, J. Holloway, S. Millington and C. Young (eds), *Cosmopolitan Urbanism*, pp. 53–69. London: Routledge.

Calhoun, C. 2002. 'The Class Consciousness of Frequent Travelers: Toward a Critique of Actually Existing Cosmopolitanism', *The South Atlantic Quarterly*, 101 (4): 869–97.

Chatterjee, P. 2016. 'Nationalism, Internationalism, and Cosmopolitanism: Some Observations from Modern Indian History', *Comparative Studies of South Asia Africa and the Middle East*, 36 (2): 320–34.

Coffey, D., P. Hathi, N. Khurana and A. Thorat. 2018. 'Explicit Prejudice: Evidence from a New Survey', *Economic and Political Weekly*, 53 (1): 46–54.

Conlon, F. 1974.'Caste by Association: The Gauda Sarasvata Unification Movement', *Journal of Asian Studies*, 33 (3): 361–65.

———. 1977. *A Caste in a Changing World: The Chitrapur Saraswat Brahmans, 1700–1935*. Berkeley and Los Angeles: University of California Press.

Cort, J. 2004. 'Jains, Caste and Hierarchy in North Gujarat', in D. Gupta (ed.), *Caste in Question: Identity or Hierarchy*? pp. 73–112. New Delhi: Sage Publications.

Dobbin, C. 1972. *Urban Leadership in Western India: Politics and Communities in Bombay City, 1840–1885*. London: Oxford University Press.

Durkheim, E. 2014. *The Division of Labor in Society*. New York: Free Press.

Gardiner, M. 1996. 'Alterity and Ethics: A Dialogical Perspective', *Theory, Culture & Society*, 13 (2): 121–43.

Gellner, E. 1995. 'The Importance of Being Modular', in J. Hall (ed.), *Civil Society: Theory, History, Comparison*, pp. 32–55. Cambridge: Polity Press.

Gidwani, V. K. 2006. 'Subaltern Cosmopolitanism as Politics', *Antipode*, 38 (1): 7–21.

Hall, S. 2002. 'Political Belonging in a World of Multiple Identites', in R. Cohen (ed.), *Conceiving Cosmopolitanism: Theory, Context and Practice*, pp. 25–33. New York: Columbia University Press.

Kant, I. 2006. *Toward Perpetual Peace and Other Writings on Politics, Peace, and History*. Edited and with an introduction by P. Kleingeld; translated by D. L. Colclasure; with essays by J. Waldron, M. W. Doyle and A. W. Wood. New Haven: Yale University Press.

Long, A. A. and D. N. Sedley. 1987. *The Hellenistic Philosophers*, Vol. 1, Translations of the Principal Sources with Philosophical Commentary. Cambridge: Cambridge University Press.

McFarlane, C. 2008. 'Postcolonial Bombay: Decline of a Cosmopolitanism City?' *Environment and Planning: Society and Space*, 26 (3): 480–99.

Mendelsohn, O. and M. Vicziany. 2000. *The Untouchables: Subordination, Poverty and the State in Modern India*. Cambridge: Cambridge University Press.

Morris, R. 1998. 'Civil Society and the Nature of Urbanism: Britain, 1750–1850', *Urban History*, 25 (3): 289–301.

Mukerjee, R. 1937. 'Caste and Social Change in India', *American Journal of Sociology*, 43 (3): 377–90.

Natarajan, B. 2011. *The Culturalization of Caste in India: Identity and Inequality in a Multicultural Age*. New York: Routledge.

Pollock, S. 2000. 'Cosmopolitan and Vernacular in History', *Public Culture*, 12 (3): 591–625.

Pollock, S., H. K. Bhabha, C. A. Breckenridge and Dipesh Chakrabarty. 2000. 'Cosmopolitanisms', *Public Culture*, 12 (3): 577–89.

Rao, M. S. A. 1991. 'Traditional Urbanism and Urban Sociology', in M. S. A. Rao (ed.), *Reader in Urban Sociology*, pp. 21–41. New Delhi: Orient Longman.

Rao, N. 2013. 'Community, Urban Citizenship and Housing in Bombay, Ca. 1919–1980', *South Asia: Journal of South Asian Studies*, 36 (3): 415–33.

Rudolph, L. 1965. 'The Modernity of Tradition: The Democratic Incarnation of Caste in India', *The American Political Science Review*, 59 (4): 975–89.

Sennett, R. 2002. 'Cosmopolitanism and the Social Experience of Cities', in S. Vertovec (ed.), *Conceiving Cosmopolitanism: Theory and Practice*, pp. 42–47. Oxford: Oxford University Press.

Sheth, D. L. 1999. 'Secularisation of Caste and the Making of the New Middle Class', *Economic & Political Weekly*, 34 (34–35): 2502–10.

Simmel, G. and E. C. Hughes. 1949. 'The Sociology of Sociability', *American Journal of Sociology*, 55 (3): 254–61.

Thorat, S. and P. Attewell. 2007. 'The Legacy of Social Exclusion: A Correspondence Study of Job Discrimination in India', *Economic and Political Weekly*, 42 (41): 4141–45.

Vithayathil, T. and G. Singh, 2012. 'Spaces of Discrimination: Residential Segregation in Indian Cities', *Economic and Political Weekly*, 47 (37): 60–66.

Volland, N. 2017. *Socialist Cosmopolitanism: The Chinese Literary Universe, 1945–1965*. New York: Columbia University Press.

Waghmore, S. 2013. *Civility against Caste: Dalit Politics and Citizenship in Western India*. New Delhi: Sage Publications.

Vithayathil, T. and G. Singh, 2012. 'Spaces of Discrimination: Residential Segregation in Indian Cities', *Economic and Political Weekly*, 47 (37): 60–66.

9 Between Text and Practice

Reflections on the Sociological Study of Islam

SUDHA SITHARAMAN*

A Contested Project

'Anthropology of Islam', which forges Islam as an object located in the lifeworlds of Muslims, remains a project beleaguered by problems of definition and demarcation. In the study of Islam, anthropologists have primarily been interested in what people actually do in their lives rather than what is given in their traditions, whether textual or oral. While allegiance to the sacred texts remains the cornerstone of most Muslims world over, the anthropological focus has been on what the believer believes the teachings of the texts to be. All the same, there prevails a palpable tension in the academic discourse between 'textual' Islam and 'lived' Islam. In studying contemporary movements and trends in Islam, extant scholarship has been asking how to conceptualise Islam itself, for only then can one speak of the issues of authenticity, continuity and legitimacy of Islamism. This chapter draws attention to anthropological studies on Islam in India to argue that the concept of syncretism, which has remained the predominant lens in this scholarship, almost always disables our efforts at making sense of practices. It reveals the limits of the use of 'syncretism' and lays bare the excess that the concept cannot capture. Charting the key thematic concerns marking this scholarship on Islam, the chapter offers some thoughts on the specific question that is central to

* I acknowledge the help of R. Saravana Raja and Hashim Thadathil in copy-editing and proofreading.

the attempts to reconcile the empirical diversity of the religious beliefs and practices of Muslims in India. While dealing with this question, it is essential to situate it within the broader context of scholarship on global Islam that seeks to reconcile the multiplicity of conceptions of Islam. In addressing these concerns, I gesture towards incorporating ways of 'theologising' into the available model of 'observing', where the foundational role of texts alongside traditions of interpretation and notions of practice serve to establish particular formations of discursive practices.

Blurring Categories

The study of religion in India for a long time has remained the study of Hindu India. As Imtiaz Ahmad (1972) notes, the absence of focus on Muslims, or for that matter on any of the 'minorities', is striking. This observation mostly holds true four decades later. If one investigates the trends in religion studies, one is led to the inescapable conclusion that Islam and Muslim social life and social organisation have somehow not been of interest to anthropologists and sociologists studying Indian society. The little that does exist on these themes is also revealing in itself.

The anthropological study of Muslims in India has focused on broadly three interrelated themes: (i) Muslim social structure and practice, (ii) Islam in India and (iii) the interaction of Muslims with non-Muslims (largely Hindus).[1] It has clustered around four areas: communalism, community identity, Sufism and women. The obsessive focus on the interface between religion and politics has overdetermined the orientation of this scholarship. A major concern has been to understand the role of religion in Muslim cultural practices.

Robert Redfield, in 1956, suggested that all world religions can be divided into 'great traditions' and 'little traditions'.[2] Anthropology, with its beginnings in the study of the primitive and the exotic, was thought of as being concerned only with the little, local traditions. The first significant anthropological study focusing explicitly on Islam was Clifford Geertz's *Islam Observed* (1968).[3] Geertz sets up a maximal cultural contrast when he compares Moroccan Islam and Javanese Islam in order to grasp the specificities of Islam. Discontented with the textual focus of the orientalists who attempted to find a single universal Islam in scriptures and texts, he demonstrated that even as both Moroccan and Javanese Islam drew upon the same general set of symbols, the end result in each society was radically different because of the social climate in which each evolved (1968: 20). Geertz argues that the universality of a great tradition comes from its 'ability to engage a widening set of individual, even idiosyncratic, conceptions of life and yet somehow sustain and elaborate them all' (ibid.:14). Islam emerged not as what was left when you subtracted culture but as a set of processes through which Muslims drew on elements of their shared tradition in ways that made sense to them, in that place and at that historical moment. It is interesting to note that, for Geertz, it is the earlier, mystical forms of Islam that are more susceptible to particularisation than are the scripturalist or fundamentalist forms of Islam. Although each society has some form of veneration for Sufi saints, the exact nature of these practices varies. Further, a saint or an Islamic cultural hero in one society could be neither saintly nor heroic in another society even as scripturalism might appear as much the same regardless of the setting.

However, to draw a methodological distinction between mystical and normative Islam, as Geertz does, is a mistake as it overlooks two facts. First, a great deal of communication has always been common in the Islamic world, with philosophical texts having long been circulated. While the particular myths and parables used to communicate mystical ideas vary, the basic ideas, or at least the broad set of ideas drawn upon, are the same. Second, while fundamentalists say and do some things that may not seem out of place among fundamentalists in another country, they too have very local concerns. It is noteworthy here that Geertz sees Islam as comprising two dimensions: experience and tradition. El-Zein (1977: 232) notes that there is 'less order than in a trend within a single tradition', without explaining how much heterogeneity is allowed in a single tradition. This problem shall be taken up later, for it is critical to the approach proposed in this study.

Sometimes, Geertz, by using national or ethnic qualifiers to write about local Islamic beliefs and practices, seems to imply that there exist both a 'Moroccan Islam' and an 'Indonesian Islam', and that Islam was at once national and cultural.[4] Ahmad (1981) too spelt out a similar framework that had been implicit in much writing on Muslims in India. He said that while Muslims in India (as Muslims elsewhere) believe in and practise the cardinal pillars of the faith, the practice of Islam in India is heavily underlined 'by elements which are accretions, drawn from the local environment and contradict the fundamentalist view of the beliefs and practices to which Muslims must adhere' (1981: 7). Thus, there are at least two elements: one, 'ultimate and formal derived from the Islamic texts' and, the other, 'proximate and local, validated by custom' (ibid.: 10). These were integrated into a common religious system such that Islam in India accepted and retained the local cultural traditions but adapted them to its own requirements and needs by putting in Islamic content. Again, to draw a methodological distinction between local and normative Islam, as Ahmad does, is unsustainable for the very reasons listed earlier.

All the same, the focus was on caste among Muslims and on the mingling of 'Hindu' and 'Islamic' life cycle rituals. Theoretically, this question received rudimentary treatment as much of the work remained descriptive, as if to state the fact of interaction was sufficient. It seemed as if those writing on this subject kept in mind the theologian's notion of Islam, against which the 'syncretic' practice was being contrasted. Practices associated with rites of passage, customs, beliefs and social institutions were accordingly discussed and accounted for either as 'survivals' or as 'accretions' from Hindu customs. Rituals in particular were described as 'syncretic', thus indicating a certain identity and continuity in the social practices of Muslims and Hindus. The concept of syncretism, by and large, simply flagged the interaction between Hinduism and Islam, and it was made operational with no clear theoretical understanding of the religious pluralism and diversity that exists as a fact of social life in India. Studies on Muslims display two recurring themes: first, the relationship between 'purist' and 'syncretic' religious behaviour within Muslim communities; second, the relationship of Muslim believers to the wider non-Islamic society. But what do the terms 'purist' and 'syncretic' mean? Are they really useful categories to apply to the historical study of Muslim communities in India? These questions did not invite interrogation. Syncretism came to be a 'gate-keeping concept' to discuss Indian Islam, largely at the expense of other ways of approaching this question. It is to this that I shall now turn to.

Limits of Syncretism

Syncretism is a term most often used to describe religious communities who have assimilated rituals or concepts from other religious communities.[5] The most important illustration of Hindu–Muslim syncretism in India is always the dargah[6] and/or veneration of Sufi saints. The meeting of 'Hindu' and 'Islamic' features in the dargah has often been understood as a 'mixture' of religions—'fusion', 'amalgam', a 'patchwork model' or a form of religious 'synthesis'—and sometimes even as 'confluence' or 'convergence'. Muslims and non-Muslims frequent dargahs and Muslim shrines in India (as elsewhere), praying for the saint's intercession by participating in the rituals. The magicality of shrines is grounded in heterodox beliefs regarding the divine powers of saints, who are thought to be able to intercede for the living in their search for personal goals (fertility, worldly success, health) by granting them *baraka* or divine blessing. Such saints are described as miracle makers whose deeds are circulated orally and/or through hagiographies. The mythic narratives about saints describe supernatural events, which demonstrate the power of the pir/murshid. It is not so much saints as their shrines that became, over centuries, centres of attraction, which gradually brought in people into the fold of Islam.[7]

There has recently been a deluge of research on Sufi shrines and saints in India. These have centred on two themes: first, the ritual practices in shrines; second, the miracles of saints and the subsequent religious conversions. Most studies tend to look at symbolic meanings (and experiences) or their psychological or social functions (harmony and integration), or both.[8] For instance, Vasudha Narayanan's work is on what she calls 'mutual adaptation' found at the dargah of Shahul Hamid (ca. 1513–1579) in Nagore, Tamil Nadu. She writes that

> While terms like 'Hindu' and 'Muslim' are often used today to compartmentalize people and to articulate politically rigid categories, a nuanced understanding of the relationship between Hinduism and Islam must take into account the political, social, and intellectual contexts of the two traditions. There are, of course, some strict caste and community boundaries within the many Hindu traditions (marking, in particular, issues of diet and marriage), but there are also many permeable boundaries between the Hindu communities and Islam. A visit to the dargah of Shahul Hamid in Nagore reminds us of this permeability and helps us to understand just how frequently religious 'boundary crossings' can and do happen in India. (Narayanan 2006: 268–70)

When one visits the Nagore shrine today, she further states, 'one is struck by the number of Hindus offering worship to the saint' (ibid.: 267). According to the managing trustee of the dargah, about 60 per cent of the premises has been built by Hindus, and about 50–75 per cent of pilgrims on any given day is Hindu. Some patterns of worship at the shrine parallel Hindu worship in temples (ibid.: 267). There is a 'sharing' of a metaphoric world and the 'mutual adaptation' of religious vocabulary and rituals among Hindus and Muslims (ibid.: 266). There are other symbols of worship that suggest a Hindu cultural context like Shahul Hamid's footprint that is preserved in the dargah (ibid.: 267).

Likewise, discussing people's perceptions of dargahs in Patna, Jackson (1989) says that there is something 'Indian in ethos' about dargahs as compared to formal prayers in a mosque setting, for a large number of Hindus partake in the practices of the dargah. Thus, he argues, if the mosque separates Muslims from Hindus, the dargah often tends to bring them together (1989: 110). Because dargahs bring together 'different religious communities', serving as major nodal points for the interaction between Muslims and non-Muslims, many scholars have argued that dargah*s* bring about a 'cultural integration' (see Siddiqui 1998: 1). Similarly, Daniel Gold (2005) writes that Hindu attendance at Sufi shrines is not at all unusual. Sufi shrines have long been arenas where Hindus interact religiously with Muslims, and the activities at the shrine of Mir Badshah, for instance, illustrate how patterns of inter-communal cooperation towards the worship of a local saint still continues (p. 127). Gaborieau (1989) writes that

> the shrines continue to serve as meeting places for people belonging to every station of life and every religious tradition. Even if the management of the shrines is quasi-feudal, anybody, rich or miserable can come and partake of the *langar,* the free meals distributed every day. Women—who in South Asia are not allowed into the mosques—can come and pray here, although they are not allowed to enter the building which shelters the tomb. Frequent visitors also comprise non-Muslims, turning the shrines into places where various religious traditions of the subcontinent converge ... not only are their adepts physically present, but they find the rituals and the ideas of intercession which goes with it congenial. (ibid.: xv)

An effort is also thus made in this scholarship to distinguish the space of the dargah from that of the mosque, consequently suggesting that the former makes space for liberal democratic principles in the place of that of orthodoxy. What we also see here is that while women do not enter the mosque, they find a place in the dargah, thus levelling gender differences.

The interesting question would then be: Do descriptions and explanations of the happenings in dargahs serve us to understand the dargah as a phenomenon? Each dargah or Sufi shrine emerges as a discrete entity. There are dargahs that permit women to enter the sanctum sanctorum that shelters the mazar, the tomb, while there are others that restrict their entry. In some dargahs, the same deity is worshipped in different forms, for instance, the one in Yamanur is worshipped as Changadeva Maharaj by Hindus and as Rajabag Savar by Muslims. There are dargahs of Sufi saints, like Natharvali in Trichinapally, but there are also shrines of warriors, landed gentry, court reformers and literary men.

Thus, there are different practices, different traditions and different categories of people that dargahs cater to. Perhaps what holds these experiences of religiosity together is first and foremost their blurredness, making explicit the commitment to support dargah *practices* rather than a distinct and separate religious practice. Nevertheless, scholars working on such 'syncretic' spaces are also acutely aware that there exist Muslim communities that refuse to patronise such practices precisely because they are believed to be impure. The question that arises then is how does one explain this diversity among Muslims? And how does one understand the apparent 'synthesis', 'convergence' or 'sharing' between different religious communities in the dargah? This chapter engages with the second question first—how do we explain Hindu–Muslim interaction and/or 'convergence' between communities.

Arguments concerning 'Hindu–Muslim syncretism' flow from two distinct registers, that of religious fundamentalism and of liberal secularism. Much of the discussion on shrines and saint worship begins with a liberal secular understanding that 'syncretism' is, by definition, progressive and liberating. Scholars advocating this position believe in the unchanging essence of religion and religious identities, and they tend to treat this inter-religious convergence as a powerful resource to combat communalism and other forms of sectarian strife. I call this the secular position. According to the secular position, the recent rise of fundamentalism in India has obliterated the deep-rooted syncretism of Indian culture, and hence there is a need to recover the latter. In this position, the interaction between communities has always been perceived to be stable, positive and liberating. The secular response differs from that of Muslim revivalism/reformism, the proponents of which base their arguments on the understanding that any religion, which is conceived in terms of its pure essence, if mixed with another religion will become 'debased', 'diluted' or 'distorted'. This revivalist/reformist position is often dubbed as conservative. The practice of worshipping saints at their tombs and praying for their intercession has remained an issue for a number of theological debates among Muslims for centuries. A long-standing argument against the worship of saints is that the imputation of divine powers to the saint and his tomb goes against the fundamental concept of *tawheed*, which considers the worship of anything other than Allah as amounting to *shirk*,[9] and *bid'a*, an innovation contrary to Sunnah, the normative example of the prophet. The fundamental issue here is whether 'mediation' of the saints amounts to *shirk*.[10] However, the Sufi orders maintain that since all prayers are directed to Allah, the saint is merely a messenger, and the practice is therefore not un-Islamic. This has been reiterated by many ulemas (Sunni Islamic scholars) as well. In fact, the Barelvi Movement,[11] a scholarly movement of ulemas, came about to defend the practices at shrines and the belief in intercession. Debates between Sunni ulema and reformist religious scholars (maulvis) have been between different philosophical schools (*madhabs*). Anthropologists, however, often privilege dargah practices like the *'urs* (shrine festivals) and saint veneration against reformists who deplore tombs, saints, shrine festivals, intercessory prayers, *dikr* (remembrance chants), *moulud* (celebrating the prophet's birthday), and so on.

A review of scholarship reveals that the word 'syncretism' is used variedly: bringing together *people* of different religions, a *place* where various religious traditions of the subcontinent converge, sharing of a *metaphoric world*, mutual adaptation of *religious vocabulary* and *ritual*. Additionally, it is also understood as a 'lax' and 'spurious' form of religion, a corrupt and 'Hinduised form of Islam', an institutional form of Sufism, the worship of local saints and graves, etc. Thus, several practices with dissimilar characteristics are often brought together under the same category (not that similarity necessarily proves sameness).

Moving away from the dargahs, there are studies (e.g., Assayag 2004; Mayaram 1997; Gottschalk 2001; Eaton 1978) describing community identities and Hindu–Muslim interactions that are critical of the idea of syncretism. This scholarship demonstrates how syncretism presupposes two or more self-contained and static essences, of the Hindu and the Muslim—categories that remain internally singular and absolutely exclusive so that their resembling each other is rarely in evidence. Mayaram (1997), a proponent of the idea of liminality, argues that the problem with syncretism is that it sees cultures and particularly religion in terms of essences and ignores the ways in which human agency seeks a multiplicity of meanings and anchorage, transcending an either or status—the binary mode of thought and understanding—in its quest to comprehend, understand and explain the cosmos and to negotiate an intersubjective existence (ibid.: 37). She emphasises that we decentre our way of talking about identity so that we examine it as being constituted through processes at multiple sites rather than in terms of fixity and cultural traits as these multiple subject positions do not preclude collective identity.

In a similar vein, Assayag (2004) identifies processes at work in the context of festivals such as Ugadi and Muharram, in which both Hindus and Muslims participate, as 'acculturation' and 'counter-acculturation'. He illustrates this with the example of a shrine—the Changadeva/Rajabag Savar dargah—where an avatar of Vishnu and an intercessor of Allah are rolled into one in the persona of an ascetic who renounced the world. Assayag (ibid.) does not refer to this as 'syncretic' but as 'competitive sharing'. He demonstrates that identity may be a product of 'competitive syncretism' or 'antagonistic tolerance' where the process of interaction, identity formation and conflict pluralises the repertory of languages, behaviour, knowledge and power and does not denote distinct groups that define themselves as Muslim or Hindu. He further states that members of both communities must be understood in the context of the historical circumstances in which they have lived, including the entire range of context-specific interests with which these particular identities have interacted, as well as the larger contexts that have framed the various categories of identity (ibid.: 41).

Gottschalk (2001) goes a step further where through the example of the low-caste Chamars in western Bihar, he challenges the rigid dichotomy of Hindus and Muslims and analyses the ways in which individuals negotiate and interact with multiple identities such as class, caste, language, gender, region and nation, with the two religions being the foci of identity. He effectively demonstrates the fluid nature of all these identities and how they rise or diminish in relative importance according to particular social contexts. In this scholarship, the problem of syncretism is not a terminological one; nonetheless, religious traditions blend automatically, keeping questions of power at bay.[12] Fazalbhoy (1997) rightly points out that syncretism is not a concept that is of general sociological interest and application. It appeared much more in the discussions on Islam in India, perhaps also in the case of other minority religions (for instance, Sikhism was often referred to as 'syncretic') but it seemed as if the problematic was the impact of Hinduism on Islam, i.e., of the majority culture on the minority culture but not vice versa. In fact, in sociological discussions of religious syncretism, there is hardly any study which looks at the impact of Islam on Hinduism or considers the question of syncretism from the point of view of Hinduism. It appears that the problem of syncretism is a problem of the minority religions. Accordingly, one main issue of disagreement among scholars has centred on the degree of 'Hindu influence' and 'Hindu participation'. This is exemplified in the writings of Imtiaz Ahmad (1981). van der Veer criticises Ahmad for 'collapsing Hindu participation with the influence of Hinduism into a single phenomenon' (1992: 548). He shows that Ahmad's notions of 'syncretism' and the 'Hindu' character of saint worship do not figure in the debate on shrine worship and that neither the 'participation' of Hindus nor their 'influence' on Muslim practices, not even 'syncretism', is an issue of contention among the Muslims in Surat that he studies—the saint cult of Rifa'i (ibid.: 548).[13] van der Veer (ibid.: 546) argues that

> Sufism in general is increasingly perceived as a marginal phenomenon in modern society. Rifa'i are even more marginal than other Sufis since they are, according to common scholarly opinion, a 'heterodox order', which is to say that they are perceived to have a low, 'marginal' position in the social hierarchy.

If Islam is not to be considered as a single unified tradition, then what needs attention is the *historicity* of religious experience. Perhaps, instead of viewing dargahs or for that matter Sufi saints as constituting a single undifferentiated category, we could do well to historicise the interactions, disputes and tensions that have arisen between non-Muslims and Sufi saints, ulema and Sufi saints, kings and Sufi orders to bring out the variations in the emphasis on ideas as well as in the social roles they played. Instead of dismissing the engagement of medieval Muslim scholars with Hindu symbols as mere guises used to attract Hindus to the Islamic faith, we need to treat it as an issue requiring serious engagement with questions of how we understand the concept of religion itself. In different periods of history, the attitudes of Muslim communities to orthodoxy have varied, as have the boundaries of the communities of believers. The positing of oppositions (fundamentalism–secularism, (false) cults–(true) religion, syncretic–purist), this chapter argues, is overdetermined by the political assertion of Hindu and Muslim communities in contemporary India. When and why a particular religious custom is deemed syncretic and therefore is to be replaced by something authentic and true would reveal the work of socio-cultural contexts (Stewart and Shaw 1994). The question then is what makes something syncretic? What activities and behaviour should be coded as 'religious' and which ones as 'non-religious'? It also involves inquiring into what discursive and historical conditions gave rise to this concept. Scholars have often asked the 'when' and 'how' of 'syncretism' without answering 'What is syncretism?' This is not simply a definitional question but one which delineates our object of study—viz., Islam. An important issue is to see how Islam itself is constituted as an object of inquiry. It is to this that I turn to.

My own work on the Dada Hayath Meer Qalandar at the Bababudan dargah, Chikmagalur, Karnataka, departs from the dichotomies of elite/folk, orthodoxy/heterodoxy, tradition/modern, purist/syncretic Islam, and skirts the collapsing that van der Veer cautions against.[14] The dargah has emerged over time as a popular pilgrim centre where the rituals and practices in the shrine defy any exclusive identification of being either Islamic or Hindu. It is beyond the scope of this chapter to provide a detailed ethnography,[15] but it may suffice here to state that neither the 'participation' of Hindus nor the 'Hindu influence' on Muslim practices or for that matter notions of 'syncretism' or the 'Hindu' character of saint worship figures in the enunciation of the believers.

In the context of conversion from one religion to another and of how it oscillates between 'accretion and reform',[16] Richard Eaton identifies accretion as the process of how people add 'new deities or superhuman agencies to their existing cosmological stock, or identifying new deities or agencies with existing entities in their cosmology' (2004: 111). However, Eaton is looking at the process of conversion from a non-Muslim (Hindu in particular) perspective that finds room for Muslim powers, rather than a Muslim perspective. The question then is, are Islam (like other Semitic religions) and Hinduism of the same kind? Or would processes of accretion work differently for different religions? It appears that the scholarship works with a binary of 'accommodating Hinduism' and 'orthodox Islam' (Flueckiger 2008: 178–79). Are not the 'lax' and 'spurious' practices, which are today accretions into Islam in South Asia, deeply embedded in and shaping the local environment? It may thus be inadequate to say that anything that Muslims believe or do may be regarded as part of Islam, if only because what is practised as Islam may be contested by others for not being 'true' to Islam. Unlike the Semitic religions, Hinduism does not regard God to be central and there is neither a book nor a persona that may be considered to be the founder. There are prima facie grounds to suspect that Hindu traditions and Semitic religions are phenomena of different kinds. Besides, the construct of Hinduism is contentious and contested. From the perspective of the Hindus who come to the dargah, the practice of dargah visitation is a tradition, an accretion. For the Hindu, the tradition of following dargah practices is upheld not because it contains some exclusive truth, binding the believer to God, but because it fulfils the mundane problems of the believers. A Muslim who visits the dargah is well aware that he or she is not in a mosque and will not perform namaz. As many of my respondents said to me, 'What we do here [in the dargah] is not un-Islamic ... as we recite the *fateha*[17] here and not perform namaz. We only ask for the saints' intercession ... Muhammad is the Prophet ... and therefore we do not pray to saints ... its only supplication that we make.' Evidently, the devotee is able to distinguish correct actions from incorrect ones and thus perceives him/herself as socially distinct (as a Muslim) and consciously acts upon this perception. The meaning of 'correct actions' cannot be independent of the processes through which 'correct reading' is secured. How do Muslims then perceive the Hindu presence in the dargah? They say, 'What brings Hindus is the power of the saint.' Muslims who believe in dargah visitation do not perceive the presence of Hindus at shrines as 'Hindu influence' or as 'lax' or 'spurious', as it is for fundamentalists. To, therefore, argue that these practices are marginal to Islam is to misrecognise the centrality of processes that sustain the devotion to Muslim saints and their tombs.

Between Text and Practice

The argument here is not against the attempt to generalise about dargahs or saint veneration but against the manner in which generalisations are undertaken. Sufism and dargahs' syncretic practices are positioned against what are characterised as the essentialist and purifying logics of normative Islam with the academic's usual preference for the former.[18] Ahmad (1981: 81), for instance, identifies textual Islam and folk Islam as two mutually exclusive entities and emphasises the uniqueness of the syncretic aspects of Indian Islam.[19] Francis Robinson, on the other hand, attempts to show the gradual marginalisation of syncretic practices and how Muslim societies have moved towards a greater realisation of what he calls a 'pattern of perfection' (2000: 52), which is readily discernable in the Qur'an and the life of the Prophet. For Robinson, the course of Islamic history is clear in terms of a series of progressive stages of Islamic development. As knowledge of this perfect Islamic pattern spreads in countries like India, the process of Islamisation will sweep away the various 'dubious' practices that have crept into local Islamic cultures (quoted in

Das 1984: 294). Behind the apparent divergences between the views of these scholars, there is a remarkable similarity, wherein Ahmad and Robinson come to identify 'tradition' as an unchanging set of cultural prescriptions (elite) that stand in contrast to what is changing, contemporary or modern. The theoretical issues arising from this style of reasoning were debated by Robinson (1983, 1986), Das (1984), Minault (1984) and Lindholm (1986). The debate raised some important issues. The issue of whether the 'normative' and the 'folk' exist as separately identifiable elements or whether they could be seen as versions of one another, whether the 'folk' has a theology and the theological has a 'folk' element were raised. This opposition between Sufi-inspired (tolerant, plural, authentic) popular practices and purist Islam (intolerant, singular, inauthentic) is extremely unhelpful on a number of counts. Such a dichotomy does not bear relation to Muslims—reformists and those involved in saint veneration alike—and their close appeals to scriptural traditions to guide practice. It is of little surprise, then, if anthropologists and sociologists have paid little attention to the complex relationships and debates in Islam.[20]

Let me illustrate this point drawing from my ethnography in Kerala where religious scholars (ulema [Sunni] and maulvis [Mujahids]) have long been holding public debates (Nadapuram 2013; Kuttichara 1986, 1988; Kottapuram 1978, 2013) in which well-defined positions backed by textual evidence are presented and where audiences congregate in large numbers and are expected to be persuaded or confirmed in their judgment that one or other of the positions is rooted in the correct interpretation of the texts (Qur'an, Hadith and Sunnah). Here, groups of reformists (Tablighi Jamaat, Jamaat-e-Islami, Mujahids) are pitted against Sunnis (under the leadership of E. K. Aboobacker Musaliyar and A. P. Aboobacker Musaliyar, and popularly referred to as EK Sunnis and AP Sunnis). However, in practice, just one strand of reformism dominates Kerala—the Mujahids, consisting of two schisms from the Kerala Nadvathul Mujahideen. I have encountered the predictable ethnographic scenario of reformists (Mujahids here) battling against shrines, saints, festivals and customary practice, on the one hand, and the Sunnis, on the other, continuing to engage in a range of practices, appearing to hold on to beliefs that diverge from the reform styles of Islam. During my fieldwork, I collected audio recordings of public debates among religious scholars in Kottapuram (where Sunnis claim to have won the debate against Mujahids) and analysed the material on a plethora of issues such as shrine visitation and halal (what is allowed) and haram (what is not allowed) practices—shirk (deviation) versus tawheed (true monotheism) emerged as a recurrent preoccupation across several registers.

Ulemas and maulvis engage in highly complex arguments about *isthigasa* (help seeking), bringing in questions of help and the power of Allah, and whether divine powers are bequeathed to others or not. The maulvis argue that Sunnis who visit and seek help at a saint's shrine are effectively praying not to Allah but petitioning and praying to the saint and hence committing shirk. Additionally, they point out that isthigasa is an ordinary and natural help, which is legitimate to seek but asking for Allah's help is a different type of help seeking, which is supernatural in nature or involves soliciting divine intervention. Maulvis argue that 'nobody asks saints for ordinary help and because it is extraordinary one ends up committing shirk'. Sunni ulemas, on the other hand, defend their practices, insisting, for instance, that at a shrine they are 'praying with' and not 'praying to' the saint. They, in turn, question the Mujahids thus 'how can you possibly divide the divine power of Allah into types, when the Prophet taught that everything comes from God?' Sunni arguments display the shifting dimensions of the distinction between the human and the divine from the fixity of an insurmountable ontological difference into a fluid and indeterminate intimacy. Two things are happening here: First, Sunnis are calling upon textual authority to back up their claims that petitioning for help is permissible and that there are lesser agents or friends of God, who legitimately help humans. Second, Sunni ulemas question the Mujahid maulvis, insisting that it is the latter who must face the accusation of taking away divine power from its proper source—Allah—and of committing the dreadful mistake of not attributing His power to the saints, who may indeed be accepted as having powers of intercession, let alone any ordinary human. Here, it may be pointed out that the very existence of difference and plurality in interpretations of scripture within Muslim communities is due to the contact made by texts with different communities of readers.

Sunnis reject outright the possibility of hermeneutics based on individual understandings of the text, insisting upon the role of the ulema and following one school of practice chosen from the main four schools of *fiqh* in passing on scripture to believers. Sunnis, thereby, allow a strong role to the ulema who advocate mediated religious practices that operate through the charisma and spiritual power of Sufi saints, pirs and preachers. Mujahids present themselves as the *ijtihad* (independent interpretation) movement, which then positions Sunnis in this binarised polemic on the side of anti-text, tradition and practice. Be it as it may, there is something else that I wish to draw attention to here—the work these discursive practices do in the cultivation of pious or ethical Muslim selves. Most discussions about Islamic texts and their relationship to local Islam(s) seem to suggest a unified position of the texts vis-à-vis folk practice. As the preceding debate demonstrates, Islamic texts are themselves polyvocal. There are contradictory Hadith (sayings of the Prophet) and/or lesser texts that are much more prone to sharp disagreement on a range of theological questions. I draw attention to the work Islamic discursive practices perform in linking practitioners across past, present and future through a pedagogy of practical, scholarly and embodied forms of knowledge and virtues deemed central to the tradition. Tradition, viewed in this way, is neither a set of symbols and idioms that justifies present practices nor an unchanging set of cultural prescriptions that stand in contrast to what is changing, contemporary or modern.

Tradition may be best defined as a framework of knowledge production and consumption comprising two main elements: *method*, i.e., a particular way of doing things, making arguments, using resources, organising thought, interpreting texts as well as performing rituals or practices; and *sensibility*, i.e., a philosophical approach as well as the particular subjectivities tied to that philosophy (Iqtidar 2016: 425). Noticeably, tradition consists essentially of discourses that seek to instruct practitioners regarding the correct form and purpose of a given practice that, precisely because it is established, has a history. A tradition, then, is constituted by a set of discourses that instructs the individual in what he or she ought to do in order to be a 'correct' practitioner or a 'true' Muslim. This is where Asad's (1986) notion of Islam as a discursive tradition in which reflection upon the past through an engagement with a set of foundational texts (Qur'an and Hadith), commentaries thereon and the conduct of exemplary figures is a constitutive condition for the understanding and reformulation of the present and the future. For Asad, an engagement with the founding texts of Islam is not limited to scholarly commentaries alone but entails the practices of ordinary Muslims, such as when an unlettered Muslim invokes the authority of sacred texts to solve a practical problem or when a child argues with a parent about the correct (or incorrect) nature of an Islamic practice.[21] There is a palpable tension in the discourse in/of the world between the local situation and the universal aspects of Islam. As rightly pointed out by Bowen, looking at Islam in terms of distinct local 'Islams' runs the risk of obscuring 'both the historic connections across different Muslim societies and many Muslims' strong sense of an external, normative reference point for their ideas and practices' (Bowen 1993: 7). Of course, Muslims disagree about what is or is not acceptable, about what is or is not Islamic, but this very disagreement assumes the existence of a single true Islam. An anthropology of Islam should then begin by asking how far and in what ways a tacit understanding of coherence (texts, ideas and methods) as an everyday practice is an important dimension of the thinking of believers in different socio-historic circumstances.

Considerations in the Sociological Study of Islam

To reiterate, both positing Islam as whole and as fragmented are problematic starting points for an anthropology of Islam: such positions conflate anthropological and theological concerns (see, e.g., Robbins 2006). Anthropologists, however, are divided in their claims as to what is more 'real' (whether it is lived Islam or normative Islam) and therefore the persistent concern has been to find a framework to analyse the relationship between this single, global entity and the multiple religious beliefs and practices. It is equally clear that despite variability, Islam cannot be reduced to an infinite series of purely local peculiarities. Practices initially judged 'atypical' of Islam, and consequently deemed to be products of local culture or society, often turned out on closer inspection to have a far broader distribution within the Muslim world. Islamic discourse then is between not only texts and practice but also different practices. The question to be explored is why there are differences between various groups that identify themselves as Muslims. At core is the issue of how anthropologists define Islam.[22] Perhaps the most obvious solution to the question was to posit the existence of not one but multiple 'Islams' (El-Zein 1977: 227–54). As Launay has noted, 'for anthropologists to assert the existence of multiple Islams is, in essence, to make a theological claim, one most Muslims would not only deny but, they rightfully argue, anthropologists have no business making' (Launay 1992: 5).

Muslims—clerics and ordinary believers—are often acutely aware of alternative ideas and practices among other Muslims, either within their own communities or outside. A meaningful conceptualisation of Islam as a theoretical object and analytical category must therefore come to terms with—indeed, be coherent with—the capaciousness, complexity and, often, outright contradictions within it. These are issues addressed by two eminent anthropologists: El-Zein (1977) and Asad (1986). El-Zein's approach was to favour multiplicity or the recognition of many local Islams as integral to a social anthropological analysis of the faith that also acknowledges Islam's embeddedness within varied historical and cultural settings. Asad's critique of El-Zein rightly pointed to the foundational role played by texts such as the Qur'an and Hadith as well as the varying traditions of interpretation that have developed around these in centring the faith around a stable core of themes and practices. For Asad, this core—in its discursive, textual and practice-oriented dimensions—formed the object par excellence of investigation. Asad emphasises that 'the efforts of practitioners to achieve coherence' are to be found in the traditions of discourse developed in the Muslim world (1986:17). Asad also treats orthodoxy as a relation of power—of disciplinary regulation and subject formation—and many of his interlocutors theorise the practices Muslims embark upon to make their lives morally and ethically coherent (Scott and Hirschkind 2006). Asad's tendency to move towards tropes of 'coherence'and 'core' in his analytical framework has, however, been contested. Marsden and Retsikas point to the more centripetal orientation to Asad's analysis—one where the foundational role of texts and traditions of interpretation serves to establish relations of discursive continuity and gives rise to particular formations of orthodoxy and orthopraxy (2013: 11). The theological debates among religious scholars in Kerala, for instance, clearly demonstrate that there prevails considerable variability among ideas and practices within a single conception of Islam rather than between differing conceptions. The debates and struggles to fix authoritative interpretations of the past and visions of an ideal Muslim life and community are conducted with reference to accepted sources of authority, histories and sacred topographies. All these provide the grounding for mutual intelligibility, which allows genuine debate. This is a problem that Asad addresses.

The selectivity with which people approach their tradition does not necessarily undermine their claim to its integrity. Nor does the attempt to adapt the older concerns of a tradition's followers to their new predicament dissolve the coherence of that tradition (Asad 2003: 195). The aspiration to coherence is a necessary condition of social life. The question then is what, for instance, are the practical steps that Muslims take to materialise such coherence? How do Muslims think and behave in relationship to their own understandings of unity, often expressed in relationship to concepts of communal unity (ummah) and divine oneness (tawheed)? Sociology of Muslims/Islam in India must, perhaps, be sought in the combination of anthropology and textual scholarship that takes into consideration the ways in which both Islamic scholars and ordinary Muslims cultivate links between particular dimensions of their everyday lives and Islamic texts. Interpretative, recitational and other forms of engagements with Islamic texts, especially the Qur'an and the Hadith, illustrate the unity of thought and belief in the Islamic tradition as an ongoing normative project rather than a given. These must be placed alongside the complex genealogies of the concepts used by Muslims as they embark upon practices of unity. Such a project is markedly different from merely measuring either deviation from or proximity to the 'orthodoxy'. Encompassment (rather than conflation) of the theological and the anthropological may bring faith into sharp focus, making it of central importance to understanding particular contexts, ideas and practices.

Notes

1. With a few exceptions like Susan Bayly (1992).
2. For Redfield, great tradition is reflective, orthodox, textual and 'consciously cultivated and handed down', while little tradition is 'heterodox, peripheral, local, popular, and unreflective' (quoted in Ronald Lukens-Bull 1999: 4).The great—little tradition dichotomy arose out of the attempt to understand the social organisation of tradition, which was considered inevitable in all complex societies.
3. As Robert Launay (1992) points out, Geertz's *Islam Observed* (1968) was far from being the first anthropological study to focus on Muslim societies, and there existed a few studies that focused on various forms of religion in those societies, but that focus was always oblique. Anthropologists were expected to study specific 'cultures' or 'societies' situated in some precise and usually exotic corner of the globe. Religion in one form or another was conceived to be an essential component of such a culture or society. If some or all of the members of this culture happened to be Muslim, it was likely that the anthropologist would have something to say about Islam in that particular locality. Launay (1992: 2) adds that Geertz's was the first anthropological monograph to break away from this tradition and explicitly address the issue of Islam.
4. For a discussion on how culture and nation become synonymous after the Second World War onwards, see Irfan Ahmad (2013).

5. It would be therefore interesting to debate terms like syncretism, hybridisation and creolisation, and their relation to changes in time and space of a phenomenon. See, e.g., Stewart and Shaw (1994) and Stewart and Ernst (2003).
6. A dargah is a shrine or tomb built over the grave of a revered religious figure, often that of a Sufi saint.
7. With reference to South Asia, Thomas Arnold (1958) has described the relevance of local saints and shrines in alleviating the mundane problems of devotees. 'There is no doubt,' he wrote, 'among the lower classes prayers are directly addressed to the saint and the desired result is believed to lie within his power' (p. 70). Eaton (2004) contests Arnold's 'fervent portrayal of Sufis' as Islamic missionaries among non-Muslims. He argues, 'a close reading of primary sources, however, would not support this graphical accounts of them. Sufis do not appear to have been concerned with conversion' (p. 117). Further, he notes, 'if a living Sufi had only minimal influence in the religious life of non-Muslim Indians, a deceased Sufi, especially one blessed with sainthood by the local population, could literally work miracles. This was because the charisma or the *baraka* of a spiritually saturated Sufi saint became, with time, transferred to this tomb. And since brick and mortar shrines have much greater longevity than flesh and bone Sufis, self-sustaining centres of religious power were able in this way to grow and span many centuries' (ibid.).
8. See, e.g., Currie (2006); Dale and Menon (1978); Khan and Moir (1999); Eaton (1978); Gaborieau (1989); Gold (2005); Hasan and Roy (2005); McGilvray (2004); Moini (1989); Narayanan (2003); Pfleiderer (1981); Desiderio Pinto (1987); Roy (1982); Saheb (1998); Saiyad (1989); Sikand (2003, 2004); Troll (1989); van der Veer (1992); Werbner (2003); Werbner and Basu (1998).
9. 'Shirk' refers to the sin of practising idolatry or polytheism or the tendency to deviate from true monotheism.
10. Sufi Islam is often perceived and understood in juxtaposition with what is commonly constructed as 'normative Islam'. This understanding emanates from the notion that the Sufi way of life went beyond the tenets of Shari'at or Islamic law. However, recent studies connect Sufi literature to the greater vehicle of Muslim piety, reminding us of the danger that often lies in talking about Sufism in a different breath from Islamic law or the study of the Hadith. Green (2004), in recounting Sufi writings in Persian, cites a work by al-Hujwiri titled *Kashf al-mahjub,* composed in the mid-eleventh century, and its emphasis on morality and etiquette (*akhlaq* and *adab*), to argue that Sufism was a path to perfecting one's adherence to normative Islam rather than an alternative to it (p. 125).

11. The Barelvi Movement, one of the most influential modern religious movements among the Muslims in the subcontinent, was initiated by Maulana Ahmad Raza Khan Barelvi (1856–1921), who tried to inculcate in individual Muslims a stricter adherence to the Shari'at or Islamic law to bring about reform or to engage in *tajdid* (renewal of faith). The importance of Ahmad Riza Khan and the Barelvi Movement lay in their efforts to define, within the reforming discourse of the late-nineteenth and twentieth-century, a position stressing Sunnah, the following of the Prophet's path, with the help of saintly intermediaries (for details, see Sanyal 1996).
12. Against this background, for instance, Stewart and Shaw (1994) explore a range of ways in which people promote or resist syncretism. They understand syncretism and anti-syncretism as continually created and recreated in conditions of contestation and struggle.
13. Rifa'i is a Muslim Sufi brotherhood (*tariqat*). It is a saint cult in Islam and the structure of the cult comprises the 'holy man (pir) and his family, his lay followers, the Rifa'i faqirs' (van der Veer 1992: 545).
14. Madan (2007) has recently argued that Islam as lived is in significant respects not only different from scriptural Islam but also opposed to it. He writes, 'It could yet be argued that Islam as lived is included in, or (to use Dumontian phraseology) encompassed by, scriptural Islam, not as an alien *entity* by itself, but *in a dialectical relation to it* as a contrary' (ibid.: 20, emphasis original). Viewed from such a perspective, 'lived' Islam emerges as varieties of integral religious experience rather than so many cases of incomplete Islamisation or degeneration and, therefore, of imperfection (ibid.: 1–25). Also see Roy (2005: 29–61) for a discussion on 'incomplete conversion and degeneration' concerning Islamisation.
15. For details, see Sitharaman (2013).
16. Eaton has identified three theories regarding the accretion aspect of conversion—'religion of the sword' theory, theory of 'political patronage' and 'religion of social liberation theory' (2004: 105–27).
17. Fateha is combination of reciting few *suras* of the Qur'an, supplications (*dua*) for the diseased and the Muslim ummah, feeding family, relatives, neighbours, near and dear, and the poor, and passing on the reward for these virtuous acts to the diseased.
18. Ever since Goldziher, Sufism has been understood as a separate part in the history of mystical Islam, as the mutually exclusive part of binaries such as 'orthodox Islam' versus 'Sufi Islam' and 'rule following' versus 'mystical experience'. To understand why this has been so, see among others, Carl Ernst (1997).
19. Ahmad's observations, writes Roy (2005: 41), were very largely grounded in the empirical studies of a number of other sociologists and social

anthropologists, covering Islamic beliefs and practices in various parts of South Asia, for instance, Mattison Mines (1981) on Tamil Muslims, Ismail Lambat (1976) on the Sunni Surati Vohras (Bohras), Pratap Aggarwal (1976) on the Meos of Rajasthan and Harayana, and Lina Fruzzetti (1981) on the rites of passage and rituals of the Muslims of Bishnupur in West Bengal. The realities of living and practising Islam emerging from these studies constitute a significant challenge indeed to some long-standing assumptions concerning Islamisation at the ground level.

20. A few notable exceptions were Metcalf (1982), van der Veer (1992) and Sanyal (1996). A historical study that makes clear how ideological positions are negotiated by and between the ulema (religious scholars) and ordinary Muslims and are constantly subject to modifications, see Metcalf (1993: 584–608).
21. Quite often, elements of the 'folk' rather than being rejected or eliminated are actually accepted through Islamisation and 'incorporated into the corpus of the orthodox religious complex'. Eaton speaks of how this literature employed indigenous themes and imagery for the propagation of complex mystical doctrines in Sufism (1974: 117–27). We also find orientations that blur categories, such as 'Sufi reformism' (Green 2005) and 'reformist traditionalism' (Metcalf 1982), as in Deoband's early support of some Sufi practices. Indian Deobandi reformists in the nineteenth century, for example, self identified as Sufis but argued that Sufi practices should be internalised; they objected, in particular, to what looked like worship of the saint (ibid.: 158).
22. To ask 'what is Islam?' is to ask both a theoretical and a theological question, and these are not the same. The theoretical question is what must be included and what can be excluded in our analyses of things, a question that must be addressed by all anthropologists of the Muslim world. The theoretical problem is that of level of analysis. The theological question addresses the ontological status of things and seeks the foundations of faith within the tradition. These two questions, while dealing with similar cultural forms, are fundamentally different. However, because the forms and the discourses about them overlap, there is a danger that these questions become conflated.

References

Aggarwal, P. C. 1976. 'Kinship and Marriage among Meos of Rajasthan', in Imtiaz Ahmad (ed.), *Family, Kinship, and Marriage among Muslims in India*, pp. 265–96. Delhi: Manohar.

Ahmad, Imtiaz. 1972. 'For a Sociology of India', *Contributions to Indian Sociology* (n.s.), 6 (1): 172–78.

———. (ed.). 1981. *Ritual and Religion among Muslims in India*. New Delhi: Manohar.

Ahmad, Irfan. 2013. 'Margins of Knowledge: Nation-State, "the Other" and the Discipl(e)ining of Sociology/Anthropology', key lecture for the conference 'Questioning Marginality', Brown University, Providence.

Arnold, T. 1958. 'Saints and Martyrs: Mohemmedan in India', in J. Hastings (ed.), *Encyclopaedia of Religion and Ethics*, pp. 70–71. Edinburgh: T. & T. Clark.

Asad, T. 1986. 'The Idea of an Anthropology of Islam', Occasional Papers Series, George Town University, Washington.

———. 2003. *Formations of the Secular: Christianity, Islam and Modernity*. California: Stanford University Press.

Assayag, J. 2004. 'Can Hindus and Muslims Coexist?' in Imtiaz Ahmad and H. Reifeld (eds), *Lived Islam in South Asia: Adaptation, Accommodation, and Conflict*, pp. 40–60. Delhi: Social Science Press.

Bayly, S. 1992. *Saints, Goddesses and Kings: Muslims and Christians in South Indian Society 1700–1900*. Cambridge: Cambridge University Press.

Bowen, J. 1993. *Muslims through Discourse: Religion and Ritual in Gayo Society*. Princeton: Princeton University Press.

Currie, P. M. 2006. *The Shrine and Cult of Mu'in al-din Chisti of Ajmer*. New Delhi: Oxford University Press.

Dale, S. and G. Menon. 1978. 'Nerccas: Saint Martyr Worship among the Muslims of Kerala', *Bulletin of the SOAS*, 41 (3): 523–38.

Das, V. 1984. 'For a Folk-Theology and Anthropology of Islam', *Contributions to Indian Sociology* (n.s.), 18 (2): 293–300.

Desiderio Pinto, S. J. 1987. 'The Mystery of the Nizamuddin Dargah: The Accounts of Pilgrims', in C. W. Troll (ed.), *Muslim Shrines in India*, pp. 112–24. Delhi: Oxford University Press.

Eaton, R. M. 1974. 'Sufi Folk Literature and the Expansion of Indian Islam', *History of Religions*, 14 (2): 117–27.

———. 1978. 'The Profile of Popular Islam in the Pakistani Punjab', *Journal of South Asian and Middle Eastern Studies*, 2 (1): 74–92.

———. 2004. 'Approaches to the Study of Conversion to Islam in India', in D. N. Lorenzen (ed.), *Religious Movements in South Asia 600–1800*, pp. 105–27. New Delhi: Oxford University Press.

El-Zein, A. H. 1977. 'Beyond Ideology and Theology: The Search for an Anthropology of Islam', *Annual Review of Anthropology*, 6: 227–54.

Ernst, C. W. 1997. *The Shambhala's Guide to Sufism*. Boston: Shambhala.

Fazalbhoy, N. 1997. 'Sociology of Muslims in India: A Review', *Economic and Political Weekly*, 32 (26): 1547–51.

Flueckiger. J. B. 2008. *In Amma's Healing Room: Gender and Vernacular Islam in South India*. Hyderabad: Orient Longman.

Fruzzetti, L. M. 1981. 'Muslim Rituals: The Household Rites vs. the Public Festivals in Rural India', in Imtiaz Ahmad (ed.), *Rituals and Religion among Muslims in India*, pp. 91–112. New Delhi: Manohar.

Gaborieau, M. 1983. 'The Cult of Saints among Muslims in Nepal and North India', in Stephen Wilson (ed.), *Saints and Their Cults: Studies in Religious Sociology, Folklore and History*, pp. 291–308. Cambridge: Cambridge University Press.

———. 1989. 'Introduction', in C. W. Troll (ed.), *Muslim Shrines in India*, pp. v–xxi. New Delhi: Oxford University Press.

Geertz, C. 1968. *Islam Observed: Religious Development in Morocco and Indonesia*. London: University of Chicago Press.

Gold, D. 2005. 'The Sufi Shrines of Gwalior City: Communal Sensibilities and the Accessible Exotic under Hindu Rule', *Journal of Asian Studies*, 64 (1): 127–50.

Gottschalk, P. 2001. *Beyond Hindu and Muslim: Multiple Identities in Narratives of Village India*. New Delhi: Oxford University Press.

Green, N. 2004. 'Emerging Approaches to the Sufi Traditions of South Asia: Between Texts, Territories, and the Transcendent', *South Asia Research*, 24 (2): 123–48.

———. 2005. 'Mystical Missionaries in the Hyderabad State: Mu'in Allah Shah and His Sufi Reform Movement', *The Indian Economic and Social History Review*, 42 (2): 187–212.

Hasan, M. and A. Roy. (eds). 2005. *Living Together Separately: Cultural India in History and Politics*. New Delhi: Oxford University Press.

Iqtidar, H. 2016. 'Redefining "Tradition" in Political Thought', *European Journal of Political Theory*, 15 (4): 424–44.

Jackson, P. 1989. 'Perceptions of the Dargahs of Patna', in C. W. Troll (ed.), *Muslim Shrines in India*, pp. 98–111. New Delhi: Oxford University Press.

Khan, D-S and Z. Moir. 1999. 'Co-existence and Communalism: The Shrine of Pirana in Gujarat', *South Asia: Journal of South Asian Studies*, XXII (Special Issue): 133–54.

Lambat, I. A. 1976. 'Marriage among the Sunni Surati Vohras in South Gujarat', in Imtiaz Ahmad (ed.), *Family, Kinship, and Marriage among Muslims in India*, pp. 49–82. Delhi: Manohar Publications.

Launay, R. 1992. *Beyond the Stream: Islam and Society in a West African Town*. Berkeley: University of California Press.

Lindholm, C. 1986. 'Caste in Islam and the Problem of Deviant Systems: A Critique of Recent Theory', *Contributions to Indian Sociology* (n.s.), 20 (1): 61–73.

Lukens-Bull, R. 1999. 'Between Text and Practice: Considerations in the Anthropological Study of Islam', *Marburg Journal of Religion,* 4 (2): 1–21.

Madan, T. N. 2007. 'One from Many: Explorations in the Anthropology of Islam', *Eastern Anthropologist,* 60 (1): 1–25.

Marsden, M. and K. Retsikas. 2013. *Articulating Islam: Anthropological Approaches to Muslim Worlds*. Springer: London.

Mayaram, S. 1997. 'Rethinking Meo Identity: Cultural Faultline, Syncreticism, Hybridity or Liminality', *Comparative Studies of South Asia, Africa and the Middle East,* 17 (2): 35–44.

McGilvray, D. B. 2004. 'Jailani: A Sufi Shrine in Sri Lanka', in Imtiaz Ahmad and H. Reifeld (eds), *Lived Islam in South Asia: Adaptation, Accommodation, and Conflict,* pp. 273–90. Delhi: Social Science Press.

Metcalf, B. D. 1982. *Islamic Revival in British India: Deoband, 1860–1900.* Princeton: Princeton University Press.

———. 1993. 'Living Hadith in the Tablighi Jamaat', *The Journal of Asian Studies,* 52 (3): 565–84.

Minault, G. 1984. 'Some Reflections on Islamic Revivalism vs. Assimilation among Muslims in India', *Contributions to Indian Sociology* (n.s.), 18 (2): 301–05.

Mines, M. 1981. 'Islamization and Muslim Ethnicity in South India', in Imtiaz Ahmad (ed.), *Rituals and Religion among Muslims in India,* pp. 65–90. New Delhi: Manohar.

Moini, S. L. H. 1989. 'Rituals and Customary Practices at the Dargah of Ajmer', in C. W Troll (ed.), *Muslim Shrines in India,* pp. 60–75. New Delhi: Oxford University Press.

Narayanan, V. 2003. 'Religious Vocabulary and Regional Identity: A Study of Tamil Cirappuranam', in R. M. Eaton (ed.), *India's Islamic Traditions, 711–1750,* pp. 393–410. New Delhi: Oxford University Press.

———. 2006. 'Tolerant Hinduism: Shared Ritual Spaces—Hindus and Muslim at the Shrine of Shahul Hamid', in J. Hawley and V. Narayanan (eds), *The Life of Hinduism,* pp. 266–70. Berkeley: University of California Press.

Pfleiderer, B. 1981. 'Mira Datar Dargah: The Psychiatry of a Muslim Shrine', in Imtiaz Ahmad (ed.), *Rituals and Religion among Muslims in India,* pp. 195–234. New Delhi: Manohar Publications.

Robbins, J. 2006. 'Anthropology and Theology: An Awkward Relationship?' *Anthropological Quarterly,* 79 (2): 285–94.

Robinson, F. 1983. 'Islam and Muslim Society in South Asia', *Contributions to Indian Sociology* (n.s.), 18 (2): 301–05.

———. 1986. 'Islam and Muslim Society in South Asia: A Reply to Das and Minault', *Contributions to Indian Sociology* (n.s.), 20 (1): 97–104.

———. 2000. *Islam and Muslim History in South Asia.* New Delhi: Oxford University Press.

Roy, A. 1982. 'The Pir Tradition: A Case Study in Islamic Syncretism in Traditional Bengal', in F. Clothey (ed.), *Images of Man: Religious and Historical Processes in South Asia*, pp. 112–41. Madras: New Era.

———. 2005. 'Thinking over Popular Islam in South Asia: Search for a Paradigm', in M. Hasan and A. Roy (eds), *Living Together Separately: Cultural India in History and Politics*, pp. 29–61. New Delhi: Oxford University Press.

Saheb, S. A. A. 1998. 'A Festival of Flags: Hindu–Muslim Devotion and the Sacralising of Localism at the Shrine of Nagore-e-Sharif in Tamil Nadu', in P. Werbner and H. Basu (eds), *Embodying Charisma: Modernity, Locality, and the Performance of Emotion in Sufi Cults*, pp. 55–76. London: Routledge.

Saiyad, A. R. 1989. 'Saints and Dargahs in the Indian Sub-continent: A Review', in C. W. Troll (ed.), *Muslim Shrines in India*, pp. 240–56. Delhi: Oxford University Press.

Sanyal, U. 1996. *Devotional Islam and Politics in British India: Ahmad Riza Khan Barelwi and His Movement 1870–1920.* New Delhi: Yoda.

Scott, D. and C. Hirschkind (eds). 2006. *Powers of the Secular Modern: Talal Asad and His Interlocutors.* California: Stanford University Press.

Siddiqui, I. H. 1998. 'The Early Chisti Dargahs', in C. W. Troll (ed.), *Muslim Shrines in India*, pp. 1–23. New Delhi: Oxford University Press.

Sikand, Y. 2003. *Sacred Spaces: Exploring Traditions of Shared Faith in India.* New Delhi: Penguin.

———. 2004. 'Shared Hindu–Muslim Shrines in Karnataka: Challenges to Liminality', in Imtiaz Ahmad and H. Reifeld (eds), *Lived Islam in South Asia: Adaptation, Accommodation and Conflict*, pp. 166–86. Delhi: Social Science Press.

Sitharaman, S. 2013. 'Limits of Syncretism: Bababudhan Dargah in South India as a Paradigm for Overlapping Religious Affiliations and Co-existence', in A. Pries, L. Matzolff, R. Langer and C. Ambos (eds), *'Synkretismus' Negation und New Definition*, Studies in Oriental Religions, 67, pp. 79–111. Wiesbaden: Harrassowitz.

Stewart, C. and R. Shaw. 1994. *Syncretism/Anti-Syncretism: The Politics of Religious Synthesis.* London: Routledge.

Stewart, T. K. and C. W. Ernst. 2003. 'Syncretism', in P. J. Claus and M. A. Mills (eds), *South Asian Folklore: An Encyclopaedia*, 586–88. New York: Routledge.

Troll, C. W. 1989. *Muslim Shrines in India*. New Delhi: Oxford University Press.

van der Veer, P. 1992. 'Playing or Praying: A Sufi Saint's Day in Surat', *Journal of Asian Studies*, 51 (3): 545–64.

Werbner, P. 2003. *Pilgrims of Love: The Anthropology of Global Sufi Cult*. New Delhi: Oxford University Press.

Werbner, P. and H. Basu. 1998. *Embodying Charisma: Modernity, Locality and the Performance of Emotions in Sufi Cults*. London: Routledge.

10 Catholic Citizens

Faith as Activism in Mumbai

ROWENA ROBINSON and NANDINI PALIYATH*

The anthropology of Christianity has emerged as an exciting field in the last decade or so. Several interesting works on global Christianity, particularly Protestant denominations, have emerged, though there has been some work on Catholicism as well. Of course, the interest in the anthropological understanding of Christian communities, especially in postcolonial societies, preceded as well as continues alongside the establishment or acceptance of the field now known as the 'anthropology of Christianity' (see, for instance, Comaroff 1985; Ram 1991; Robinson 1998; Anderson 2013). Themes of interest for us in India in particular and South Asia in general include the issues of caste, conversion and belief, the ideas of sin and morality, commitment, community and individualism. Christianity in different parts of the world, particularly in Asia, South America and Africa, has been explored, for instance, Papua New Guinea (Robbins 2004), the Philippines, Madagascar, Indonesia, Bolivia and Melanesia (Cannell 2006), India (Mosse 2012), Fiji (Tomlinson 2009), Guatemala (O'Neill 2010) and Botswana (Werbner 2011).

O'Neill (2009) points out that the anthropology of Christianity has yet to occupy itself seriously with the question of citizenship

* We would like to thank the Indian Council of Social Science Research (ICSSR), which funded the project on which this chapter is based. Nandini Paliyath is one of the two research associates on the project responsible for field data collection in Mumbai city.

despite the fact that Christian theology itself continually references the notion. He suggests the possibilities of looking at everyday understandings of the idea of citizenship and engagements with it by Christians, particularly in the context of democracies (or emerging ones) in the Global South wherein transnational religious movements such as those of Pentecostal and Charismatic Christianity are increasingly spreading their influence. The location of his study is Guatemala and his dense ethnography explores the activities of mega-churches, which operate on the ground through hundreds of small cells. He shows how fasting, prayer, anointing with oil, weeping and the examination of one's conscience are not merely Christian practices but real acts of citizenship. Christianity is thereby not incidental to or merely supplementary to citizenship. Christianity is central to citizenship—what is being practised in Guatemala is *Christian citizenship*.

Drawing on in part from Robbins' (2003) call for a self-conscious anthropology of Christianity in which researchers recognise the relevance of and read each other's work across geographical locales, thereby beginning to address questions in a comparative perspective, this chapter keeps O'Neill's insights in view while examining data on lay Christian organisations in Mumbai. At the same time, it takes the study of Christianity and citizenship into previously unexamined directions. Focusing not merely on the personal adjustments of individual Christians or on interactions within the private sphere, the study looks at the engagements of lay Christians across a cluster of associations such as the Association of Concerned Catholics, Satya Shodhak, Catholic Secular Forum and various women's bodies within the Catholic archdiocese. In such associations, which have so far not been the subject of study of scholars, Christians (particularly Catholics) come together as Christians but their concerns cut across social and political issues and specifically church affairs.

In other words, as O'Neill (2010) suggests, Christianity and citizenship are entangled but as this study will show, Christians in these organisations often take on their churches, questioning them and maintaining a position of critical and interrogative distance from them. In the process, they employ not only alternative understandings of what it means to be Christian, which split personal faith from institutionalised religion, but also terminologies and ideas of citizenship including of equality, participation, democracy and transparency. Interrogation of both church and state implicates the dissolution of lay understandings of citizenship, for instance, along the lines of caste, class or gender.

Citizenship, Civil Society and Christianity

It has been some time now since scholars writing in the context of multiculturalism, more prominently Will Kymlicka and Wayne Norman (2000) and Iris Marion Young (1989, 1990), suggested that a common set of civil and political rights for all citizens in societies with a diversity of races, creeds, ethnicities and language groups is insufficient, because the needs of minority groups are not addressed by it. Young, in particular, raised the idea and possibility of 'differentiated citizenship', thereby acknowledging that a notion of citizenship based singularly on individual rights, without reference to group identities marginalises groups with histories of oppression. Simultaneously, it may be pointed out that such discussions also have the potential of becoming primarily concerned with the unity and viability of democratic nationhood and the perceived threats posed to citizenship by minority rights and multiculturalism (see Kymlicka and Norman 2000).

These studies have had more influence in Anglo-American scholarship, though European societies have also been considered from the perspective of such ideas. For India, it has been pointed out that the practice of multiculturalism and attention to minority rights has been in place for long, and the Indian experience constitutes a critique of certain central concerns in Western discourses (see Mahajan 1999). In Western democracies, minority rights deal largely with the cultural rights of communities. In India, on the other hand, social and political representation has always been included as an element in minority demands and not merely cultural recognition. Further, in Western societies, minorities claimed rights against the state's hegemonic tendencies, while in India these rights were put in place precisely to forestall the overwhelming of minority cultures by the majority and their institutionalisation was coeval with the constitution of the nation state (Mahajan 1999; Mahajan and Sheth 1999).

The idea of citizenship has not found much purchase in the context of India. Moreover, whether in scholarship here or elsewhere, all of these questions concerning religion and the state, citizenship and minorities are addressed at the level of philosophy and larger political systems. Thus, the question of what citizenship looks like in the everyday practices and activities of individuals or associations on the ground has usually not been taken up for analysis even where efforts in citizenship studies have been made. In this regard, Kevin O'Neill's *City of God* (2010) perhaps marked the initiation of a distinctive field for anthropological analysis: the study of active Christian citizenship. As he remarks elsewhere, 'For a field whose continual points of departure have been such Christian themes as belonging, responsibility, and stewardship, and whose current conceptual framing prioritizes transnational processes and globalization's cultural complexities, astoundingly little has been written in citizenship studies . . . about the formation of Christian citizenship . . . in Asia, Africa, and Latin America'(O'Neill 2009: 333). Among other references, he quotes Philippians 3:20 ('But our citizenship is in heaven. And it is from there that we are expecting a Savior, the Lord Jesus Christ') to argue that ideas of citizenship have always had a life in Christian discourses and in Christian self-understanding (ibid.).

The relationship between Christianity and citizenship as framed by the secularisation thesis is constructed in terms of the 'pedagogical paradigm'. This paradigm partakes, to some extent, of the biblical understanding of separating what is God's (spiritual authority) from what is Caesar's (political authority). It suggests that in the private sphere of the churches, the clergy inculcate good character and teach their congregants to be good citizens. As learners and students, congregants go outside into the public sphere to practise the lessons of care, responsibility and respect for authority, which make them upstanding, law-abiding members of civil society and respectable citizens (O'Neill 2009). Thus, the church is the realm of thought and convictions. In the outside world, the space of action, these are put into practice. However, the author argues that this paradigm makes several assumptions, which do not hold in many countries, especially in those of the Global South. In particular, the notion of the separation of state and church, of private and public spheres and of thought and action are largely inapplicable in these societies.

While acknowledging the potential for anthropology in this turn in citizenship studies, I would argue that there are several limitations in this particular analysis. First, O'Neill (2009, 2010) focused solely on the idea of self-regulation within the Foucauldian paradigm of governmentality. Thus, in his study of Guatemala, he is interested in looking at how the Pentecostal cells call upon Christians to 'craft painstakingly their characters, conduct, actions, and thoughts through elaborate efforts at self-governance' (2010: 71). Further, though there is awareness that public and private spheres are not held apart or isolated from each other in such societies, the analysis of their engagement through the practices of prayer, fasting or examination of the conscience of individual Christians is surely inadequate. What this analysis does is to examine the engagement with citizenship at the level of individual persons and in small prayer cells, but apart from formal political participation, it does not mention the possibility of other kinds of informal associations within which Christian participative citizenship could be exercised. It also suggests that it is within Pentecostal and Charismatic Christianity that these ideas are more worthy of study, partly perhaps because such cultic movements are transnational and challenge the finitude of national political boundaries taken for granted in the 'pedagogic paradigm'.

As mentioned earlier, the engagement with citizenship studies in India is largely non-existent. In fact, even where such research is conducted, only recently has the focus been on activities and practices of citizenship among individuals or groups in everyday life. This chapter looks at individuals belonging to a clutch of

Catholic lay associations (which might also bring together persons from other denominations) in which they are members because of their religious affiliation. However, their concerns have to do with not only matters of ritual, worship or religious practice but also other social and political questions. Their activities as part of these associations are voluntary and 'achieved' rather than 'ascribed'. These activities may be performed both for the church as well as for others outside of it. These associations straddle the presumed divide between the private and the public sphere in that while their membership is restricted by religious affiliation, they are defined by their consideration of and activism in issues that have wider implications.

What is even more interesting is that though brought together by faith, the individuals discussed in this chapter stand at a certain critical distance from the traditional clerical and religious authorities and question them on all sorts of issues including those related to parish property, participation and transparency in decision making, inequality in the church, liturgical matters and gender. This is apart from the other social and political themes that they are concerned about such as the representation of Catholics in the media, communal attacks on churches and the legal status of Christian women in the context of divorce.

Engagement with such themes, which so deeply implicate society and politics and raise questions about minority rights, law, secularism and national belonging in a complex, multicultural and multireligious environment, indubitably predicate certain notions of citizenship. In particular, it must involve an understanding of what it means to be a citizen. Indeed, the questioning of clerical authorities by lay Catholics on grounds that they are not 'participative' enough or not 'transparent' enough bring to interior church discussions notions from the discourse of representative democracy. Contrary to received understandings, this suggests that Christians carry their citizenship *into* the church rather merely taking lessons in citizenship out from it to the outside world.

Apart from the idea of citizenship, the other concept that calls for some consideration here is civil society, since the chapter focuses on the engagements of Christians, particularly Catholics, in movements and groups in the domain of civil society. Civil society definitions abound and what will be set out here will only be a brief explication of the way in which the term is employed here. In general, civil society is understood as constituting the realm of modern society outside of both the state and the market. It is usually theorised as being composed of the private and the public spheres. In Habermas (1989), for instance, this distinction is clear, and he characterises the public sphere as the domain wherein private individuals participate in the discussion of matters of public concern. It is in theory open to all and is thereby distinct from the family or private associations in which individuals participate as members of particular groups with particular shared characteristics such as business clubs or caste groupings. Such groups are marked by the exclusion of those who do not share in or have access to the specific characteristics that unite the group and are thereby understood to belong to the private sphere.

This distinction is, however, a matter of debate among scholars, and there are some who do not adhere to it. For instance, Robert Putnam (2000) does not separate the private and public spheres of civil society. In his focus on the problem of civic engagement in contemporary American society, he includes within the definition of civil society groups and organisations, groupings ranging from card parties, bowling leagues and ball games to religious bodies, social clubs and unions. He also locates voluntary associations, social movements and even the Internet within the scope of civil society. On the other hand, like Habermas, other scholars too would like to limit the public sphere to those organisations or movements that are associated with a concern for increasing people's democratic involvement. Thus, Powell (2007: 15) argues that even if certain civic associations may be circumscribed by space or identity (for instance, neighbourhood associations or associations on the basis of race, sexuality or gender), they are basically oriented towards democratic participation and its enhancement and deepening (see also Young 2000).

Given this trajectory in the literature, it would appear somewhat indiscriminate to include groups such as the ones discussed in this chapter—framed first and foremost by belongingness to faith—in the domain of civil society. However, I would argue that there is something other than mere theoretical and conceptual confusion here. On the one hand, Putnam's influential example of the merging of different kinds of associations in the space of civil society does force us to consider certain significant issues. In particular, it may be argued that the public–private divide is not always so easy to maintain when considering the variety of forms of engagement available in civil society. It is true that the subjects of this chapter are members of groups that are defined by religious affiliation and can therefore be dismissed as belonging appropriately to the domain of the private sphere. However, they are in these groups by their own active choice and the groups are particularly concerned with issues of democracy and participation, with the deepening of involvement of Christians as active citizens and even with questions of legal representation.

Faith as Activism

This chapter records the initial reflections on extensive, structured and unstructured interviews conducted with eight individuals, women and men, who are leading members of lay Catholic associations in Mumbai. It looks at pan-Mumbai, indeed even pan-Indian, associations in which members engage in a wide variety of activities that may be performed under the umbrella of the church but extends beyond it (and often against it). The interviews were conducted over a period of several months, and individuals were often interviewed or conversed with more than once. For reasons of privacy and in some cases because of explicit requests, informants' names have not been revealed in the text of this chapter. The literature produced by these groups as well as the websites they maintain have also been examined. The chapter is part of a wider study, which also includes the study of Dalit Catholic organisations in Chennai. However, the analysis here is confined to the research done in Mumbai.

Mumbai is a complex, crowded megacity with aspirations to be world class, even as its flailing infrastructural development and gross inequalities of wealth push in another direction. From the time of its growth as a commercial and industrial centre, the coastal city has been home to multiple ethnic, linguistic and religious groups. Catholicism is relatively old in Mumbai, going back to the time of the Portuguese. Apart from communities of converted fisherfolk, from the nineteenth century if not earlier, Goans moved into the city in more and more numbers, taking up all kinds of work including on ships, in restaurants and workshops and, for the more educated, in the offices of colonial enterprises. Since then, Christians of other ethnicities have come to Mumbai, mostly from the south but also other parts of the country, and they are to be found in jobs across the urban occupational structure. The individuals interviewed for this chapter, leaders of associations, tend to be from middle-class or professional backgrounds or at least old, well-established Catholic families.

Faith above Religion

One of the first things that stands out in the testimonies of these individuals is the sharp distinction made between personal faith, one's own spiritual beliefs and the bounded domain of religion defined by clericalism and a rigid institutional structure. For all the informants, it was the first to which they attached themselves, not the second. They took from Christianity 'the religion' but most often just from the Bible itself or theological lessons, values and beliefs that they commit their lives to and abide by. As P said, 'I wouldn't claim to be a religious person, I believe more in spirituality.' D, working for women's rights within the church, also would not describe herself as religious. She distinguished the presence of Jesus in her life from the straitjacket of formulaic Catholic prayer.

> Prayer is not that much, but Jesus is always there. Without him, I would not have existed. I would not have had the stamina, energy or the perspective. Because I don't actually say 'Hail Marys

> and Holy Marys' and rosaries or some Novena books and all. But it is like, every time I do something, it is Jesus, I cannot do anything without. So, it is like he is my talking friend, I keep talking to him.

L, another well-known activist working with a feminist collective to dismantle patriarchal structures in the church, said,

> I had the strangest experience. Some of my very best friends decided let us go to Rishikesh ... and I was the only Catholic in the group ... we didn't do the Char Dham ... we just did two I guess ... we all went in this wonderful van that we had hired ... we were three families and two others ... a friend of my son and one another person ... they are all Hindus, it was a very holy pilgrimage for them ... I went everywhere with them and they never felt they have a Catholic in their midst ... so at one point ... we were at the Gaumukh, the mouth of the Ganges ... and I tell you it was such a wonderful experience ... I call it an experience of god, maybe someone who does not believe in god may have felt it was a wonderful experience ... so I was so moved by the experience, I wrote a poem, I am not a great poet and I called it 'I saw god'. So it is a wordless kind of experience, so unless you have it, you can't experience it and other people will call you a nut. Fair enough. So I have experienced god in different ways in terms of interventions in life. People would say coincidence; I would say god. So when you ask what will be the future of religion, may be there will be a world without a religion, may be it will be a better place, my children say so, I don't know.

For these persons, the experience of God is not restricted to ideas framed by Catholic teaching. In a plural society, they meet and engage with a variety of individuals from other faiths and they may encounter God in disparate places. The most holy sites of other religions can trigger a sense of communion with God.

Christian Values, Citizenship and Activism

> *Question*: What, according to you, is the essence of Christianity?
>
> *Answer*: You have to be a good citizen.

In the course of thinking about the concerns of this chapter, certain insights from the recent scholarship on the anthropology of Islam kept suggesting themselves as relevant. It is certain that for each of these individuals, community and social activism is a way through which each fashions for herself an ethical self. Mahmood (2005: 29), in discussing Muslim women in the piety movements in Egypt, follows Foucault in arguing that in each case the ethical self is a product of a particular set of relationships between the 'capacities of the self (will, reason, desire, action, and so on) and a particular norm … [Only] through an analysis of the specific shape and character of ethical practices can one apprehend the kind of ethical subject that is formed.'

Foucault asserts that ethics is the 'conscious practice of freedom' (2000: 284), an idea which is used by Laidlow (2002) to imagine an anthropology of freedom that seeks to understand an individual's project to make of herself a certain kind of person. In this conceptualisation, freedom is understood as being of a 'definite, historically produced kind' (2002: 323), and the practices through which a subject shapes a self may be 'proposed, suggested, imposed upon' her by society, culture, authoritative groups or voices (Foucault 2000: 291). Even so, the act of cultivating a self remains one of freedom.

What is of further interest to the concerns of this chapter is that the idea of ethical self-constitution enables us to think not merely of the domain of religious belief but also perhaps of other values such as liberalism, civic responsibility and citizenship or secularism 'as moral fields enacted through everyday practices' (Fadil and Fernando 2015: 64). Thus, each may be perceived as including 'a range of ethical, social, physical and sexual dispositions' (ibid.) that need to be appreciated apart from the political. For JD, it is important to speak both of 'Indian Christians as citizens of the country as well as upholders of the faith. On the one hand, we have the Constitution of India; on the other hand, we have the Bible. So whatever we do, we draw our inspiration from both these sources.'

The individuals in this chapter are perceived as subjects cultivating selves in relation to a range of available values and norms and in accordance with each one's particular capacities and disposition. While seeking to comprehend how Christianity shapes ideas of citizenship, neither Christianity nor citizenship is treated as a closed concept. What is central is the work of the faithful self in forging connections between a range of available norms or values that she commits to living by. One may quote at length L's words with regard to what shapes her activism as a citizen:

> You know, more and more as I move outside the church, I realise what we call Christian values, the Hindus call Hindu values ... a Buddhist might call it Buddhist values ... so I don't know ... we all claim it as our values ... which is fair enough ... because we all work within our framework and it is important to realise that ... the language you use is the language of your framework which is acceptable as long as you acknowledge this. If you make it an absolute, then you have a problem. So I would say Christian values because that was how it was introduced to me. But I can well understand that they are not 'only' Christian. They could even be just human values. It is difficult to ... let me see ... I will give you some phrases which have meant a lot to me. For instance, 'judge not and you will not be judged' ... this has been a very important thing to me with regard to when you deal with other people. Then the basic Christian value which I am sure everyone will tell you, which is 'Love yourself and love your neighbour' ... this is also tied up with the judge part because that is also love ... the third one which has meant a lot to me is you see Christ in the other ... so may be in this sense this is very Christian. Now this is when Jesus talks about the end times ... sorry I cannot quote the chapters ... you know, he asks, 'When I was thirsty, did you give me to drink ... did you feed me when I was hungry, when I was sick, when I was in prison, did you come to see me?' And people say, 'But Lord, did we see you like that?' And he says, 'When you did it to the least of my brethren, that you did to me.' So basically, to me it is that you see Christ in everyone. It also means that you have a responsibility to reach out to everyone. This is definitely something I have strongly got from my Christian upbringing, in terms of reaching out, in terms of giving back ... now at this stage in my life, I think that I have received so much ... and that is what I have given back ... so

> a lot of all this work I do is my way of giving back ... So I feel this is what god wants and the spirit is calling me and I know the spirit will help me and it has never failed me all these years ... I realise it isn't just me. I am just an instrument. So maybe that is my Christian upbringing in that sense.

Contesting the Church

Catholic upbringing, parental influence, theological learning and a close reading of the Bible shape the way in which individuals think about themselves as citizens, as opposed to mere conformity to church injunction. At the same time, the performance of citizenship in everyday life involves questioning the church itself. Some of the persons spoken of in this chapter are part of associations such as the Association of Concerned Catholics and even organisations that work under the overall umbrella of the church such as the Commission for Women. However, they function as largely independent of the church itself and even as oppositional entities to it. What one begins to perceive with these individuals and associations is that ideas of citizenship including notions of rights are turned back and applied to the church institutions and structures themselves. On the one hand, we see Christian inflections on the performance of citizenship but also the use of the latter to interrogate the church itself: citizenship *against* Christianity, democracy *against* discrimination.

Two particular areas may be briefly mentioned here: gender equality and social justice. Regarding the first, L's critical analysis of the stance of the church was that while it has been very supportive of the cause of women in society with respect to education or capacity building, it declines to look inside where patriarchy remains firmly entrenched and, in particular, the ordination of women continues to be opposed. Almost all the activists interviewed felt that the church does not do enough for social justice, for Dalits, for the poor. There was also the more specific concern raised by at least one of the activists about the church as administrator, holder and manager of certain properties and the lack of transparency and democracy in decision making exercised in this regard. He argued,

> The Bible says that it is your duty to bring it to the notice of the person that is doing it that what he is doing is wrong and if you don't do it, the fault is on you. You also are partaking in that offense ... I have told them [clergy] ... I won't touch your religious duties. I am attacking you when you are an administrator. There you are no longer Christ's disciple.

Final Reflections

Despite some of the more problematic assumptions of Joel Robbins' (2014) declaration on past research on Christianity, his assertion regarding the new and growing field of the anthropology of Christianity is certainly valuable: that such studies illuminate each other through a comparative perspective. This chapter thinks through the engagement of Christianity and citizenship as richly examined in O'Neill's (2010) ethnography of Guatemala. However, several dissonant threads emerge from our analysis. The cultivation of an ethical self is understood here as an act of freedom and not perceived through the lens of congregational indoctrination or governmentality per se, which O'Neill (2010: XVIII, 15-16) pursues. Moreover, the field here is one of activism framed by faith and not solely of religious observances.

Again, the notions of self-cultivation and self-reformation are seemingly easier to apply when discussing Pentecostal and Protestant belief systems, and have now—thanks largely to feminists—sown deep roots in the anthropology of Islam. Such ideas are usually considered problematic when posed in the context of Catholicism, perceived from a Weberian perspective to be more attuned to magic and irrational adherence. This chapter sees the production of the ethical self as a relationship of a definite, historical kind between the capacities of the self and available values or norms. It is thus, in sharp contrast, able to *return* the idea of the constitution of piety to individual selves with Catholic leanings. It highlights faith as activism and Catholic-inflected, 'differentiated' citizenship on the ground. In doing so, it argues that for these Catholics, faith or spirituality is what they identify themselves by, while institutionalised or clerically defined religion is set aside or sharply questioned. Thus, not only do we see the idea of citizenship as constituted by Catholic faith but also the church castigated for failing both in terms of Christ's teachings (with regard to social justice for instance) and constitutional principles (of transparency, democracy, equality and the like).

The chapter interrogates the somewhat evasive assertion of the 'uniqueness' of Christianity that Robbins appears to make when he says: 'One would not want to set the search for Christian uniqueness as the only or even the primary goal of *every* contribution to the anthropology of Christianity' (2014: S164, emphasis added). The statement, which in effect makes the search for uniqueness one of the goals to be pursued, is challenged here by showing the differences in the ways in which Christianity operates in civil society in areas of the world where it is not a majority religion and must engage with multiple faiths as well as challenges of gender, caste or class. The chapter raises the potential of new understandings of the intersections of religious and civil activism and the making of citizens in a region marked by certain specificities that include, first, long-standing pluralism and multiculturalism, second, deep social divisions despite constitutional and legal provisions of equality, and finally, the difficulty of neatly separating the private and public spheres of civil society.

References

Anderson, J. 2013. *Community and Worldview among Paraiyars of South India: 'Lived' Religion*. London: Bloomsbury.

Cannell, F. (ed.). 2006. *The Anthropology of Christianity*. Durham and London: Duke University Press.

Comaroff, J. 1985. *Body of Power, Spirit of Resistance: The Culture and History of a South African People*. Chicago: University of Chicago Press.

Fadil, N. and M. Fernando. 2015. 'Rediscovering the "Everyday" Muslim: Notes on an Anthropological Divide', *HAU: Journal of Ethnographic Theory*, 5 (2): 59–88.

Foucault, M. 2000. *Essential Works of Michel Foucault*, Vol. 1: Ethics, Subjectivity and Truth, edited by P. Rabinow. London: Allen Lane.

Habermas, J. 1989. *The Structural Transformation of the Public Sphere: An Inquiry into a Category of Bourgeois Society*. Cambridge: MIT.

The Holy Bible. New Revised Standard Version. Catholic Edition.

Kymlicka, W. and W. Norman (eds). 2000. *Citizenship in Diverse Societies*. New York: Oxford University Press.

Laidlow, J. 2002. 'For an Anthropology of Ethics and Freedom', *Journal of the Royal Anthropological Institute* (n.s.), 8: 311–32

Mahajan, G. 1999, 'Contextualizing Minority Rights', in D. L. Sheth and G. Mahajan (eds), *Minority Identities and the Nation-State*. New Delhi: Oxford University Press.

Mahajan, G. and D. L. Sheth. 1999. 'Introduction', in D. L. Sheth and G. Mahajan (eds), *Minority Identities and the Nation-State*, pp. 1–17. New Delhi: Oxford University Press.

Mahmood, S. 2005. *Politics of Piety: The Islamist Revival and the Feminist Subject*. Princeton: Princeton University Press.

Mosse, D. 2012. *The Saint in the Banyan Tree: Christianity and Caste Society in India*. Berkeley and Los Angeles: University of California Press.

O'Neill, K. 2009. 'But Our Citizenship is in Heaven: A Proposal for the Future Study of Christian Citizenship in the Global South', *Citizenship Studies*, 13 (4): 333–48.

———. 2010. *City of God: Christian Citizenship in Postwar Guatemala*. Berkeley: University of California Press.

Powell, F. 2007. *The Politics of Civil Society: Neoliberalism or Social Left?* Bristol: Policy Press.

Putnam, R. 2000. *Bowling Alone: The Collapse and Revival of American Community*. New York: Simon & Schuster.

Ram, K. 1991. *Mukkuvar Women: Gender, Hegemony and Capitalist Transformation in a South Indian Fishing Community*. London and New Jersey: Zed Books.

Robbins, J. 2003. 'What Is a Christian? Notes toward an Anthropology of Christianity', *Religion*, 33 (3): 191–99.

———. 2004. *Becoming Sinners: Christianity and Moral Torment in a Papua New Guinea Society*. Berkeley: University of California Press.

———. 2014. 'The Anthropology of Christianity: Unity, Diversity, New Directions', *Current Anthropology*, 55 (Supplement 10): S157–71.

Robinson, R. 1998. *Conversion, Continuity and Change: Lived Christianity in Southern Goa*. New Delhi: Sage Publications.

Tomlinson, M. 2009. *In God's Image: The Metaculture of Fijian Christianity*. Berkeley: University of California Press.

Werbner, R. 2011. *Holy Hustlers, Schism and Prophecy: Apostolic Reformation in Botswana*. Berkeley: University of California Press.

Young, I. M. 1989. 'Polity and Group Difference: A Critique of the Ideal of Universal Citizenship', *Ethics*, 99 (2): 250–74.

———. 1990. *Justice and the Politics of Difference*. Princeton, New Jersey: Princeton University Press.

———. 2000. *Inclusion and Democracy*. Oxford: Oxford University Press.

SECTION THREE

On Education and Learning in India

11 Ritualising Higher Education Reforms in India*

N. JAYARAM

On Rituals and Ritualisation

India is land of rituals. The daily life of her people is organised around rituals; their calendar and life-cycle events are organised around rituals. In a predominantly oral society, it is hardly surprising that there is a strong and persistent tendency towards ritualising any norm or practice that is introduced in social life.

Adapting from its usage in zoology, the term 'ritualisation' may be defined as the process by which a behaviour pattern is retained as 'a form of display or interaction, without its original function', that is, it involves making something into 'a ritual by following a pattern of actions' (Soanes and Stevenson 2004: 1242). In ritualisation, thus, the original intent of the norm or practice is lost, but its form is maintained and repeated mechanically.

Catherine Bell, in her book *Ritual Theory, Ritual Practice* (2009 [1992]), has argued that ritualisation in the sphere of religion is best understood as a strategy: a culturally strategic way of acting

---

* This chapter was first presented at the International Seminar on 'Pathways for Change: Comparative Reflections for Reforms in Public Universities and Higher Education in India', organised by the National University of Education Planning and Administration, New Delhi, 4–5 March 2016. It was subsequently presented in the panel discussion on 'Higher Education: Current Crisis', organised as part of the 42nd All India Sociological Conference held at Tezpur University, 28–30 December 2016. I am grateful to the participants at these two fora for their comments and suggestions.

in the world. Ritualising a behaviour pattern, norm or practice is important when its original rationale is either not understood by people or they cannot understand it because of its complexity or indeterminacy in the short run. When ritualised action takes places despite the underlying rationale being clear and understandable, the norm or practice is subverted. In the realm of public policy, ritualisation is tantamount to subversion and that too at a high cost to the public exchequer. This chapter argues that well intentioned as they may be, policy reforms in the realm of higher education in India since Independence have by and large been ritualised.

The chapter is divided into five sections, including this introductory section. The second section discusses the colonial legacy of higher education in the country and the nature of the crisis it has been confronting. The third section documents the salient policy proclamations in higher education. The fourth section discusses a few cases of ritualisation of policy reforms in higher education. Taking an overview of the history of higher education in the country, the concluding section reflects on the explanation for ritualisation and the resulting drift in higher education in the country.

Higher Education in India: A Crisis-Ridden Colonial Legacy[1]

The foundation for India's present system of higher education was laid down by the British colonial regime in the mid-nineteenth century (Ashby and Anderson 1966: 54–146). The initial efforts of Christian missionaries and the East India Company generated a protracted controversy between the 'Anglicists' recommending a Western approach and the 'orientalists' favouring an indigenous direction. William Bentinck finally resolved this controversy in favour of the Anglicist orientation, barely a month after Thomas Babington Macaulay had penned his (in)famous 'Minute' on 2 February 1835. Charles Wood's Despatch of 19 July 1854 reaffirmed Bentinck's policy. Upon recommendation of the committee set up on 26 January 1855 on the direction of the Hon'ble Court of Directors to prepare a scheme for the establishment of universities in Presidency towns in India, the first three universities were established at Bombay (now Mumbai), Calcutta (now Kolkata) and Madras (now Chennai) in 1857 (Pranjpe 2005: 95).

Modelled after the University of London (established in 1836), these pioneering universities were largely affiliating and examining bodies, with very little intellectual life of their own. All the universities that were subsequently established developed in an isomorphic fashion set on the pattern of the original universities. The British educational implantation in India was conceived to serve the economic, political and administrative interests of the British and, in particular, to consolidate and maintain their dominance in the country.[2] It emphasised English, which was not only taught as a language but also made the exclusive medium of instruction in higher education. The content was biased in favour of languages and the humanities, and against science and technology.

It is not as if the British rulers did not realise the problems associated with such an educational implantation or its adverse consequences for the colonised society. Yet, it was only during the early years of the twentieth century—thanks to the initiative of Lord Curzon, the then viceroy of India (1898–1905)—that efforts were made to 'rescue the original concept of the university from its corrosive narrowness' (Tickoo 1980: 34). Several inquiries were instituted during the last three decades of the colonial rule, but 'hardly any of their major recommendations were translated into university policy or practice' (ibid.).

Thus, the legacy of higher education inherited by India at the time of Independence in 1947 was already crisis-ridden. As an integral element of colonial underdevelopment, higher education was anaemic, distorted and dysfunctional. Low levels of enrolment, the 'liberal' nature of education, 'enclavisation' of the institutes of higher learning and spurious modernisation were its festering features (Raza et al. 1985: 100–09). While the general obsolescence of the inherited system of higher education persisted, the system itself underwent a phenomenal expansion.

Prior to the adoption of structural reforms by the Government of India in the 1990s, that is, in the 40 years between 1950–51 and 1990–91, the education system expanded steadily under state patronage, with the number of universities increasing from 30 to 190 and the number of colleges from 695 to 7,346. Since then, however, the system has expanded rapidly both under the aegis of the state and under private entrepreneurship, which found in higher education a lucrative investment proposition. By 2015–16, the number of universities had risen to 753, that of colleges to 41,435 and that of stand-alone (non-university-level) institutions to 11,445.[3] With 14,37,753 teachers (UGC 2016: 128–29), excluding those in stand-alone institutions, and 2,84,85,000 students (ibid.: 123), India today has one of the three largest higher education systems (the other two being those of the US and China).

It is important to note that the bulk of the student enrolment in higher education has taken place in affiliated colleges in state universities in first-degree courses and in general education (arts, science and commerce) (UGC 2016: 125). Most of the teachers are also working in these institutions (ibid.: 129), and their work almost exclusively entails teaching and examining candidates at the undergraduate level. Obviously, much of the crisis in higher education in the country relates to this sector and its residual effect on the other sectors.

Among degree-awarding higher education institutions, only in the institutions of national importance, central universities and select departments in state universities is research a priority. The university system has largely concentrated on dissemination of knowledge rather than creating and refining knowledge—a function assigned to specialist institutes treated as institutions of national importance and laboratories outside the university system. This peculiar disjunction between universities and research institutes, a legacy of the colonial era, explains the paradox that the large and experienced system of higher education in India is hardly known for its excellence in research (see Jayaram 2007). No wonder, the National Knowledge Commission (NKC) noted with concern that 'There is ... a quiet crisis in higher education in India that runs deep. It is not yet discernible simply because there are pockets of excellence, an enormous reservoir of talented young people and an intense competition in the admissions process' (NKC 2007: 48).

Post-Independence Policy Initiatives

Not that the question of the fit of the university system with our socio-economic and cultural realities has never been questioned or debated. Immediately after Independence, the Government of India appointed the University Education Commission (1948–40)[4] to examine the development of higher education and make proposals for its future expansion and improvement (MoE 1962 [1950]). Covering practically all aspects and issues of higher education in the country in the immediate aftermath of Independence,[5] the commission's 700-page report remains a masterly study on the subject. The commission was candid in its admission that

> The marked deterioration of standards in teaching and examinations and increasing dissatisfaction with the conduct of University administration and elections to university authorities are matters of great concern.... A policy of drift in the vague hope that, if the universities are granted autonomy and are permitted to pursue their own ends with intelligence and imagination, higher education will take care of itself, will be dangerous. (ibid.: 6)

The commission thought it wise 'to concentrate our attention on the major defects of our university system ... and on measures which would tend to remove them' (ibid.: 512). Regrettably, a golden opportunity was lost for making a new beginning in higher education. The commission's report was soon consigned to library shelves and has been referred to ritualistically down the last 67 years.

The Education Commission (1964–66)[6] was the first commission in India's educational history to look comprehensively at almost all aspects of education and to develop a blueprint for a national system of education. Having influenced the two statements on the National Policy on Education (1968 and 1979) and through them the policies and programmes adopted in the Fourth, Fifth and Sixth Five Year Plans (1968–83), the report of the Education Commission (MoE 1971 [1966]) was on the anvil for nearly two decades. However, the Ministry of Education, which processed the report, obliterated it by treating in a piecemeal fashion aspects of what was conceived to be a package deal (Naik 1982: 31–32).

In 1985, the Congress government, led by Rajiv Gandhi, proposed to embark on the complex task of restructuring the system of education. Toward this end, in August of that year, the Ministry of Education (since then reorganised as the Ministry of Human Resource Development [MHRD]) presented to the Parliament a 119-page document titled *Challenge of Education: A Policy Perspective* (MoE 1985). This document placed the utmost emphasis on higher education, since it 'can provide ideas and men to give shape to the future and also sustain all other levels of education' (ibid.: 6). This was a 'somewhat unorthodox exercise in policy formulation' (Jayaram 2015 [1990]: 333). Unlike in the past when a committee or commission was appointed to survey the situation and counsel the government, this time the government itself came out with a document that was intended to act as a catalyst and elicit the views and opinions of all those dealing with or interested in the complex task of restructuring the system of education confronted by a crisis.

This document is perhaps the most remarkably candid and forthright one to have come from the government, admitting failures on several fronts and acknowledging innumerable mistakes. The key policy measures it contemplated included the delinking of degrees from jobs; the diversification of courses; placing a moratorium on the expansion of the conventional pattern of colleges and universities; selective admission to higher education based on 'scholastic interest and aptitude'; establishment of new centres of excellence; decentralisation of educational planning, administration and monitoring; and depoliticisation of academia (Jayaram 2006: 749).[7]

Based on this document and the public discussion that ensued, a programme of action was contemplated for the national policy on education (MHRD 1986). This programme of action was reviewed by the Acharya Ramamurti Committee (MHRD 1991). The recommendations of the Central Advisory Board on Education that considered the review report were adopted by the Parliament in May 1992. Still, considering the nature of the constraints that had to be encountered, one could hardly have been too optimistic about their outcome. As with earlier policy reform initiatives, this policy too resulted in ad hoc piecemeal tinkering with the system, rather than its overhaul with grit and determination.

Besides these major policy initiatives, there were other commissions and committees set up by the government to look at issues concerning higher education, for instance, the Committee to Advise on the Renovation and Rejuvenation of Higher Education (see MHRD 2009)[8] and the Committee on Corporate Participation in Higher Education (see Planning Commission 2012).[9] The aforementioned committees had as their members some of the best statespersons, academicians and administrators in the country. Notwithstanding their ideological predilections, their concern for higher education was never in question and their reports were based on painstakingly collected data and wide-ranging consultations. But they all invariably met with the same fate, namely, inaction or truncated action on the part of the government. Considering this, one can hardly hope anything significant to come out of the report of the Committee for Evolution of the New Education Policy (see MHRD 2016).[10]

Thus, policy formulation in the sphere of higher education has been ritualised, and it hardly evokes the kind of expectations that it did in the first two decades of Independence. It is true that to address some pressing issues with regard to higher education, some programmes of action were implemented, even if the policy recommendations contemplated to be implemented in totality were truncated. A closer examination of some of the programmes of action reveals that they were well thought-out and were justifiably expected to improve the quality of higher education. However, all of these programmes were ritualised within a few years of their implementation. In the following section, the ritualisation of three such programmes of action concerning teacher quality, career advancement and curriculum development respectively are discussed.

Case Studies of Ritualisation of Reforms in Higher Education

Teacher Quality

One consequence of the rapid expansion of higher education was the unprecedented demand for teachers. Many postgraduates churned out by the state university system found in teaching an easy employment avenue. The cumulative, adverse consequences of the reckless manner in which teachers were recruited and allowed to function soon became evident. In its nationwide sample survey of teachers and students in higher education and members of the wider community, the National Commission on Teachers (NCT) recorded the 'widespread feeling that no profession has suffered such downgrading as the teaching profession' (NCT 1985: 21).

Studies on college teachers have invariably stressed the sad deficiency of academic preparation for and declining commitment to the profession. The NCT (1985) also bemoaned the fact that most teachers are simply making a living rather than following a vocation. This has, no doubt, a lot to do with the deplorable standards obtained at the master's level education. More important, however, is the fact that for decades, most master's degree holders easily found employment in colleges, and even universities, with absolutely no training in (or orientation to) teaching and with a doubtful aptitude for the vocation.

National Eligibility Test

To ensure proficiency in the subject and aptitude for teaching and research on the part of candidates aspiring to become teachers, the University Grants Commission (UGC) introduced an 'eligibility test' in 1986.[11] Called the National Eligibility Test (NET), this test is held twice a year (in June and December) in 79 subjects and at 89 centres spread across the country (UGC 2016: 203).[12] The eligibility test for five core science subjects—chemical sciences, life sciences, physical sciences, mathematical sciences and Earth/atmospheric/ocean/planetary sciences—is also conducted twice a year by the Council of Scientific and Industrial Research (CSIR) under the Joint CSIR–UGC NET. There is no time bar on the eligibility certificates issued by the UGC.

The percentage of candidates successfully qualifying the NET to enter the academic profession is miniscule.[13] This partly reflects the poor quality of education and the liberal standards of evaluation at the master's level. To increase the number of candidates qualifying the NET, from June 2010 onwards, the UGC abolished negative marking (i.e., deducting marks for wrong answers) in the multiple-choice questions of the test.

To address regional specificities, many state governments had been permitted by the UGC to conduct a State Eligibility Test (SET), which was treated as equivalent to the NET. In some states, the standard of the SET had been so appallingly diluted and the norms so brazenly flouted that the UGC had to withdraw the permission granted to them to conduct the SET (Jayaram 2003). The UGC has since introduced a system of accrediting the SET conducted by state governments to ensure that the pattern and standard of SET is the same as that of the NET. The accreditation is renewed periodically based on a review by an expert committee. Moreover, since June 2002, candidates qualifying the SET are eligible for assistant professorship only in universities and colleges in the respective states and not throughout the country as earlier.

Since the NET is now an established bi-annual test, prospective candidates start preparing to 'crack' it in the second year of their master's programme, even if it is an infructuous attempt for the overwhelming majority of them. It is a ritual that they compulsively perform. As part of the ritual, coaching classes, guidebooks and lessons on compact discs to prepare the candidates are already in place and thriving too. Instead of the test being a means to an end, it has become an end in itself. So much so that the MHRD and the UGC even contemplated abolishing the NET. Many academicians and academic administrators surveyed as part of a study of the structure and functioning of NET felt that 'the NET in its present version does not always help to identify the best for teaching', but 'in the absence of other reliable mechanisms to identify the best candidates for teaching, the NET should be continued' (Varghese et al. 2015: 75).

Academic Staff College

Starting in 1987, the UGC established at least one Academic Staff College (ASC) in each state with the mandate to improve standards of teaching through 'orientation courses' (focusing on pedagogy and on the social relevance of education) for new entrants to the profession and 'refresher courses' (providing up-to-date information on the content of various disciplines) for those already in the profession. In 2014–15, there were 66 ASCs spread across the country. The duration of the 'orientation course' is 24 working days and involves 144 contact hours, while that of the 'refresher course' is 18 working days and involves 108 contact hours.

As early as 1993, Jayalakshmi Indiresan, who reviewed the working of ASCs, observed,

> Often the[ir] implementation is unplanned, and the approach is ad hoc particularly in the appointment of directors, in selecting resource persons and in conducting programmes. There has been very little monitoring. The overview of the functioning of ASCs indicates that while some of them are functioning well, mainly due to the competence and enthusiasm of the director, about a third have been observed to be decidedly poor. (Indiresan 1993: 317)

To instil a sense of seriousness among participants, which appeared lacking, an element of compulsion came to be introduced: those entering the profession are required to attend an 'orientation course' before they complete their probation and those in service are required to attend two 'refresher courses' to become eligible for promotion to the next stage in the academic career. Since the participants at these courses were found to be indifferent, an examination was introduced, whose successful completion is mandatory for obtaining a certificate of participation in the course. Of course, this examination is now treated more as a formality than as a test of acquisition of knowledge and skills at the programme.

Thus, as with all such well-intentioned innovations by the UGC, the orientation and refresher courses are now trivialised at the ASCs (Jayaram 2003: 209–11). Recognising this, the National Assessment and Accreditation Council (NAAC) has advised that the ASCs should be renamed Human Resource Development Centres, which should make induction training mandatory for all entrants into the academic profession, including those appointed in private institutions and on a temporary basis (*Times of India* 2012). It is doubtful if the NAAC's advice will be heeded and, if heeded, it is doubtful if it too will not be ritualised.

Career Advancement

In India, the professoriate is pyramidal in structure: there are fewer positions of professor than that of associate professor and fewer positions of associate professor than that of assistant professor. This is more so in the affiliated colleges. To improve the opportunities of teachers for moving up in the career ladder and as an incentive to performance, a six-stage Career Advancement Scheme (CAS) has been introduced. An important component of the guidelines formulated by the UGC (2010) is about performance appraisal of teachers. There are three categories of a teacher's performance for appraisal, namely, (i) activities related to teaching, learning and evaluation, (ii) activities related to co-curricular, extension and professional development and (iii) research and academic contributions. For each category, indicators and weights are specified (ibid.: 103–07).

It is well known that for several decades, the job performance of teachers in higher education institutions remained unevaluated, and any attempt at evaluation was either resisted or done perfunctorily. Only in state government–run colleges were confidential reports of teachers written by their principals and filed in their personal files called 'service registers'. In universities and institutes, teachers on probation were confirmed generally on the basis of confidential reports by the head/chairperson of the department or the dean if the teacher was the head/chairperson of the department.

However, as part of the package of pay revision and raises, performance evaluation of teachers in all public-funded universities and colleges has been introduced since 2010. This time around, the institutions of higher education and the teachers working there did not (because they could not) resist it, but they soon subverted it by ritualising it. Since teaching and evaluation are prescribed elements of academic performance, these tend to be measured quantitatively in terms of the number of hours spent on these activities. But in the matter of professional development–related activities and in research and academic contributions, the ritualisation is most manifest. Teachers attend seminars and conferences for the certificate that they will get and because they can accrue the necessary number of points by such attendance. In fact, attendance at seminars and conferences has increased by leaps and bounds, and there is a scramble for certificates issued by their organisers.

A more serious concern is in the area of publications (i.e., academic contributions) as it carries greater weight. 'Predatory journals' and 'predatory publishers'[14] have mushroomed in India.[15] With bogus academic achievements already in place, CAS has already been reduced to a formality of putting in the requisite years of service. It has virtually been reduced to its earlier avatar of the Merit Promotion Scheme, which in its heyday had been dubbed the 'Mass Promotion Scheme'. Thus, a mechanism conceived for rewarding academically active teachers has already been ritualised and subverted.

Curriculum Development

Curriculum is an integral component of education. It defines what is to be taught and learnt in an educational programme; it not only lists out courses—major and minor, core/compulsory and optional/elective, requisite and audit—but also details the contents of each course, the reading lists (prescribed or recommended texts), the pedagogy and the mode of evaluation. Ideally, each course in every programme carries with it the rationale, objectives and expected learning outcomes. Curriculum development, therefore, is a serious academic exercise at all levels of education, particularly in higher education, as it is supposed to guide the formulation and transaction of curriculum at the lower levels of education.

Curiously, very few institutions of higher education invest their time, energy and money in curriculum development.[16] In most state universities, curriculum development is unheard of. The board of studies in a given discipline is entrusted with the responsibility of formulating the curriculum. Anyone associated with any board of studies in state universities, and in some central universities, would be familiar with the way the board goes about its business and 'passes' the 'syllabus' for consideration and approval by the higher bodies before it is prescribed in the teaching programme. There is very little or no meaningful discussion on curriculum in these bodies, as most of the time they are busy with other matters.

Of course, as a ritual, the boards of studies in each university carry out periodical revision of the curriculum, as this is a criterion on which NAAC grades universities. However, substantively, there is very little or no change in the curriculum. The standard practice is to copy the curriculum of another university, with little or no thought on its relevance. One should not, therefore, be surprised to find archaic content and outdated reading lists in the prescribed curriculum. This state of affairs is partly explained by the system of external examination that state universities follow. Thus, whatever may be the contents of the curriculum and the reading list prescribed, what determine transactions in classrooms are the question papers of the previous years. Any new curriculum, whatever effort may have gone into its development, if at all, will soon be replaced by the question papers of the previous years.

Appreciating the importance of curriculum development and being aware of its absence in state universities, the UGC constituted Curriculum Development Committees in 30 subjects in March 2000 (UGC n.d.-a) 'to address issues such as the development of multi-disciplinary skills among students, modular systems, flexibility in respect of the credit based systems, and introduction of bridge courses allowing for vertical as well as horizontal academic mobility' (UGC n.d.-b: 1). It was also suggested that 'the proposed exercise should reflect the Indian contributions to the subject' (ibid.). These committees met several times and held consultations with senior teachers, academic administrators and others. Most of these committees submitted their reports and the model curriculum in their respective subjects in 2001.

The UGC circulated the model curriculum in different subjects to the universities, emphasising that the curriculum was in the nature of a guideline, which the universities could adapt to suit their requirements and context. The UGC circular received a mixed response from universities: most of them just ignored it, as they would do with circulars that do not require mandatory compliance or that do not have financial benefits; some adopted it as it is, without applying their mind to it; and a small number of universities took it seriously and adopted it after due deliberation. With a ritual over, soon the model curriculum was forgotten.

While on curriculum, one interesting point needs worth making. In 2007, the UGC decided to do away with the annual examination system and asked universities to shift to the semester system, because the latter was thought to be functionally more efficient (*Times of India* 2007). Almost all universities switched to the semester system in due course, if not immediately. But in implementing the semester system, they ritualised it by ignoring the rationale behind it. For instance, instead of one examination at the end of the year, they introduced two examinations, one at the end of each semester; instead of 100 per cent weightage to the final examination, they introduced a component of about 20 per cent weightage to 'internal assessment'. But the greater ritualisation was with regard to the curriculum: instead of formulating syllabus for each semester de novo, they just split the existing syllabus into two parts to be taught in two semesters. Going by the past experience, one should not be surprised if the choice-based credit system (CBCS) introduced by the UGC in April 2015 (UGC 2015) is also ritualised.

Whither Reforms?

The history of higher education in India, especially since Independence, is replete with attempts at reforms, often based on an extensive review of its status and problems. Going by the sincerity of purpose and the seriousness of thought that have gone into the making of these reforms, one would have expected a different scenario of higher education. However, the fact of the matter is that no serious scholar talks of higher education in India without bemoaning the crisis it has been confronting over several decades now. So much so that one even wonders if reflecting on higher education, which S. C. Dube (1988) long ago dubbed as 'an immobile colossus', is worth one's while.

Why do reforms in higher education get ritualised? In the absence of any definitive study seeking to answer this question, we can only reflect on our engagement with higher education. To start with, though the UGC is expected to play a lead role in higher education, it is endowed with very little power. Considering the inordinate number of universities and colleges it is required to oversee, and the limited human power and resources it has at its disposal, the UGC has been virtually reduced to a fund-disbursing agency, incapable of enforcing its own recommendations. Also, given the diarchy in higher education—with the UGC expected to oversee it and the state governments regulating it in practice—higher education has virtually remained an unbridled horse (see Pinto 1984: 63–107).

In its *Report to the Nation 2006*, the NKC observed that

> The present regulatory system in higher education is flawed in some important respects.... The system, as a whole, is over-regulated

> but under-governed. NKC perceives a clear need to establish an Independent Regulatory Authority for Higher Education (IRAHE). The IRAHE must be at an arm's length from the Government and independent of all stakeholders including the concerned Ministries of the Government. (NKC 2007: 43)

Further, the NKC contemplated redefining the UGC's role 'to focus on the disbursement of grants to, and maintenance of, public institutions in higher education' (ibid.: 44).

As of now, the UGC's functioning itself is ritualised. The standard operational procedure at the UGC for addressing any academic or academic–administrative issue is to constitute a committee and circulate the committee's reports or its own recommendations to universities and colleges. No one seems to bother if these recommendations are implemented or if the stipulations are complied with. And the universities and colleges and their teachers resist any change unless it benefits them.

Since Independence, like a rudderless ship, the system of higher education in the country has been drifting. There are three possible responses to policy reforms in this scenario. First, those who are incorrigibly optimistic will live with the hope that something will come out and that something is better than nothing. Second, those who are irredeemably pessimistic will deny anything significant will ever come out. Third, those who are avowed realists will focus on some small-scale, isolated practices by committed teachers, educators and even institutions and try to replicate meaningful reform in a world of ritualism.

Notes

1. In writing this section, I have drawn from my earlier work on higher education (see Jayaram 2006, 2009).
2. The British rule gradually supplanted the pre-colonial indigenous system of education consisting of Buddhist *viharas*, Hindu *pathashalas* and *tols*, and Muslim madrasas by stopping financial aid to these. The Indian urban elite, too, welcomed English education as it was viewed not only as an avenue to jobs but also an instrument for social and political regeneration of India (Basu 2002: 168).

3. Thus, between 1950–51 and 2015–16, there was an increase in the number of degree-awarding universities/institutions by 25.1 times and an increase in the number of colleges by 59.6 times. Additionally, there was an increase in the number of teachers by 52 times and an increase in student enrolment by 71.8 times.
4. This commission is better known as the Radhakrishnan Commission, after its chairman Sarvepalli Radhakrishnan, philosopher and statesman, who was also the first vice president of India (1952–62) and the second president of India (1962–67).
5. Of particular interest to sociologists, the commission observed:

   Research in rural sociology ... should prevent any impulsive rejection of India's past as being out of date, and may help bring an end to blind acceptance of harmful or useless elements, now retained because they are old and deeply entrenched. Such evaluation will objectively and critically examine, explore, test and appraise in order to disseminate what is good, and to purify the cultural inheritance from that which has prevented fulfilment of possibilities. (MoE 1962 [1950]: 690–91)

   It recommended the application of 'disciplined critical objective inquiry to a study of rural India' (ibid.).
6. Popularly known as the Kothari Commission after its chairman Daulat Singh Kothari, the then chairman of the University Grants Commission (UGC).
7. For a detailed review of this document, see Jayaram (2015/1990: 333–44).
8. Popularly known as the Yash Pal Committee after its chairman Yash Pal, a former chairman of the UGC.
9. Popularly known as the Narayana Murthy Committee after its chairman N. R. Narayana Murthy, founder of Infosys, Bengaluru.
10. Popularly known as the Subramanian Committee after its chairman T. S. R. Subramanian, a former cabinet secretary of the Government of India. Interestingly, the Government of India seems to treat the report of this committee (MHRD 2016) as an interim report; it has set up a nine-member committee headed by eminent scientist K. Kasturirangan 'to prepare a final draft of the ... national education policy' (*Deccan Herald* 2017: 1 and 8).
11. Candidates who have completed their PhD or registered for one before 2009 are exempt from the requirement to clear the NET.
12. With effect from June 2015, on behalf of the UGC, the Central Board of Secondary Education conducts the NET.
13. In the NET conducted in June and December 2015, of the 1,476,509 candidates who registered, 1,084959 (or 73.48 per cent) appeared

for the test. Of the 1,084959 who appeared for the test, 48,513 (4.47 per cent) qualified to enter the academic profession (UGC 2016: 204).

14. The terms 'predatory journal' and 'predatory publisher' were coined in 2010 by American librarian Jeffrey Beall to describe unscrupulous open-access publishers who were publishing articles with little or no real peer review. So one could get one's article/manuscript published, irrespective of its quality, by paying the journal/publisher concerned (see https://www.quora.com/What-is-a-predatory-journal, accessed on 5 July 2017). The list of such journals that Beall initially compiled has become the basis for 'Beall's List' of predatory journals and predatory publishers (see https://jefferson.libguides.com/c.php?g=250298&p=1666257, accessed on 5 July 2017). From 18 such publishers in 2011, the list had grown to 923 by early 2016 (Mascarenhas 2017).
15. Predatory publishing has become a matter of serious concern in India. As many as 3,300 articles by Indian first authors published during September 2015–February 2016, randomly downloaded for analysis by G. S. Seethapathy and other researchers, were published in 350 journals marked as 'predatory' by Jeffrey Beall (Mascarenhas 2017). Forty-five per cent of these articles were by teachers and 32 per cent by PhD scholars. Of the 480 authors who responded to an online questionnaire, '20 per cent said they were unaware that their paper was published in a predatory journal, 10 per cent said they knew, while the remaining 70 per cent were not willing to reply' (Mascarenhas 2017; see also Pulla 2016; Manuel 2017).
16. Ironically, no professional association of academics has shown any interest in curriculum development in the discipline that defines its raison d'être.

References

Ashby, E. and M. Anderson. 1966. *Universities: British, Indian, and African*. London: Weidenfeld and Nicholson.

Basu, A. 2002. 'Indian Higher Education: Colonialism and Beyond', in P. G. Altbach and V. Selvaratnam (eds), *From Dependence to Autonomy: The Development of Asian Universities*, pp. 167–86. Chestnut Hill, MA: Center for International Higher Education, Boston College.

Bell, C. 2009 [1992]. *Ritual Theory, Ritual Practice*. Oxford: Oxford University Press.

Deccan Herald. 2017. 'Kasturirangan-Led Panel to Prepare Final Draft of Education Policy', Bengaluru, 27 June, pp. 1, 8.

Dube, S. C. 1988. 'Higher Education and Social Change', in A. Singh and G. D. Sharma (eds), *Higher Education in India: The Social Context*, pp. 46–53. Delhi: Konark.

Indiresan, J. 1993. 'Quest for Quality: Interventions versus Impact', in S. Chitnis and P. G. Altbach (eds), *Higher Education Reform in India: Experience and Perspectives*, pp. 157–69. New Delhi: Sage Publications.

Jayaram, N. 2003. 'The Fall of the Guru: The Decline of the Academic Profession in India', in P. G. Altbach (ed.), *The Decline of the Guru: The Academic Profession in Developing and Middle-Income Countries*, pp. 199–230. New York: Palgrave Macmillan.

———. 2006. 'India', in J. J. F. Forest and P. G. Altbach (eds), *International Handbook of Higher Education: Part Two: Regions and Countries*, pp. 747–67. Dordrecht: Springer.

———. 2007. 'Beyond Retailing Knowledge: Prospect of Research-Oriented Universities in India', in P. G. Altbach and J. Balán (eds), *World Class Worldwide: Transforming Research Universities in Asia and Latin America*, pp. 70–94. Baltimore: The Johns Hopkins University Press.

———. 2009. 'Higher Education in India: The Challenge of Change', in D. Palfreyman and T. Tapper (eds), *Structuring Mass Higher Education: The Role of Elite Institutions*, pp. 95–112. New York and London: Routledge.

———. 2015 [1990]. *Sociology of Education in India* (2nd edn). Jaipur: Rawat Publications.

Manuel, T. 2017. 'At Least 82 in UGC's List of "Preferred" Journals Can Be Classified as "Predatory"', *The Wire*, 25 January 2017. Available at https://thewire.in/102950/predatory-journals-ugc-research/, accessed on 5 July 2017.

Mascarenhas, A. 2017. 'Study Rings Alarm over Indian Work in "Predatory" Journals', *Indian Express*, 9 January. Available at http://indianexpress.com/article/india/study-rings-alarm-over-indian-work-in-predatory-journals-4465429/, accessed on 5 July 2016.

Ministry of Education (MoE), Government of India.1962 [1950]. *The Report of the University Education Commission (December 1948–August 1949)*. Delhi: The Manager of Publications, Government of India. Available at http://www.educationforallinindia.com/1949%20Report%20of%20the%20University%20Education%20Commission.pdf, accessed on 27 June 2017.

———. 1971 [1966]. *Education and National Development: Report of the Education Commission, 1964–66*. New Delhi: National Council of Educational Research and Training.

———. 1985. *Challenge of Education: A Policy Perspective*. Delhi: The Controller of Publications.

Ministry of Human Resource Development (MHRD), Government of India. 1986. *Programme of Action: National Policy on Education*. New Delhi: The Controller of Publications.

———. 1991. *Towards an Enlightened and Humane Society: Report of the Committee for Review of National Policy on Education 1986*. New Delhi: The Controller of Publications.

———. 2009. *Report of the Committee to Advise on the Renovation and Rejuvenation of Higher Education*. New Delhi: MHRD, Government of India. Available at http://www.aicte-india.org/downloads/Yashpal-committee-report.pdf#toolbar=0, accessed on 29 June 2017.

———. 2016. *National Policy on Education—2016: Report of the Committee for Evolution of the New Education Policy*. New Delhi: MHRD, Government of India. Available at http://www.nuepa.org/New/download/NEP2016/ReportNEP.pdf, accessed on 29 June 2017.

Naik, J. P. 1982. *The Education Commission and After*. New Delhi: Allied Publishers.

National Commission on Teachers (NCT). 1985. *Report of the National Commission on Teachers-II, 1983–85*. New Delhi: The Controller of Publications.

National Knowledge Commission (NKC). 2007. *Report to the Nation 2006*. New Delhi: NKC, Government of India.

Planning Commission, Government of India. 2012. *Committee on Corporate Participation in Higher Education: Report of N. R. Narayana Murthy Committee*. New Delhi: Planning Commission, Government of India.

Pinto, M. 1984. *Federalism and Higher Education: The Indian Experience*. Bombay: Orient Longman.

Pranjpe, M. R. 2005. 'Establishment of Indian Universities: Resolution of the Government of India, 12 December 1856', in S. K. Sharma and U. Sharma (eds), *Encyclopaedia of Higher Education: The Indian Perspective*, Vol. 1, pp. 95–110. New Delhi: Mittal Publications.

Pulla, P. 2016. 'Predatory Publishers Gain Foothold in Indian Academia's Upper Echelon', 16 December. Available at http://www.sciencemag.org/news/2016/12/predatory-publishers-gain-foothold-indian-academia-s-upper-echelon, accessed on 5 July 2017.

Raza, M., Y. P. Aggarwal and M. Hasan. 1985. 'Higher Education in India: An Assessment', in J. V. Raghavan (ed.), *Higher Education in the Eighties*, pp. 95–173. New Delhi: Lancer International.

Soanes, C. and A. Stevenson (eds). 2004. *Concise Oxford English Dictionary* (11th edn). Oxford: Oxford University Press.

Tickoo, C. 1980. *Indian Universities*. Madras: Orient Longman.

Times of India. 2007. 'UGC to Switch Over to Semester System', 16 September. Available at http://timesofindia.indiatimes.com/india/UGC-to-switch-over-to-semester-system/articleshow/2372989.cms, accessed on 10 July 2017.

Times of India. 2012. 'Induction Training Must of College Teachers: NAAC', 29 August 2012. Available at http://www.indiaeducationreview.com/news/induction-training-must-college-teachers-naac, accessed on 30 August 2012.

University Grants Commission (UGC). n.d.-a. *Model Curriculum*. Available at http://www.ugc.ac.in/page/Model-Curriculum.aspx, accessed on 10 July 2017.

———. n.d.-b. *UGC Model Curriculum: Sociology*. Available at http://www.ugc.ac.in/oldpdf/modelcurriculum/socio.pdf, accessed on 10 July 2017.

———. 2010. *UGC Regulations on Minimum Qualifications for Appointment of Teachers and Other Academic Staff in Universities and Colleges and Measures for the Maintenance of Standards in Higher Education*. New Delhi: UGC.

———. 2015. Notices @ UGC, published on 10 April 2015. Available at http://www.ugc.ac.in/ugc_notices.aspx?id=1077, accessed on 10 July 2017.

———. 2016. *Annual Report, 2015–16*. New Delhi: UGC. Available at http://www.ugc.ac.in/pdfnews/3710331_Annual-Report-2015-16.pdf, accessed on 4 July 2017.

Varghese, N. V., G. Malik and D. R. Gautam. 2015. *Teacher Recruitment in Higher Education in India: The Role of National Eligibility Test (NET)* (Research report submitted to University Grants Commission). New Delhi: Centre for Policy Research in Higher Education, National University of Educational Planning and Administration.

12 The Non-academic Uses of the Public University

An Optimistic Note*

SATISH DESHPANDE

What are universities for? In a book with exactly this title, Stefan Collini (2012), professor of intellectual history and English literature at Cambridge University, and a prominent warrior in the recent battles around higher education of the past decade in Britain and elsewhere, offers a useful definition of a modern university. As an absolute minimum, for Collini (ibid.: chapter 1, section II) the modern university might be said to possess at least the following four characteristics:

1. That it provides some form of post-secondary-school education, where 'education' signals something more than professional training.
2. That it furthers some form of advanced scholarship or research whose character is not wholly dictated by the need to solve immediate practical problems.
3. That these activities are pursued in more than just one single discipline or very tightly defined cluster of disciplines.

* This is a revised and expanded version of my presentation at the Plenary Symposium on 'Higher Education and Its Present Crisis' at the 42nd All India Sociological Conference held at Tezpur University, 27–29 December 2016. I am grateful to the managing committee of the Indian Sociological Society and its president, Sujata Patel, for this opportunity.

4. That it enjoys some form of institutional autonomy, as far as its intellectual activities are concerned.[1]

If this is what universities are for, and it is an 'absolute minimum', then Indian universities are in trouble. Over the past decade in particular, and arguably even earlier, our higher education has tended towards the expansion of 'professional training' rather than 'education', usually in a 'tightly defined cluster' of applied disciplines, accompanied by a marked shrinking of 'institutional autonomy'. However, we can take consolation in the fact that we are in good company, since broadly similar developments seem to be underway in higher education across the world.

But considered from a rational perspective, any such consolation would be short-lived because of the heavy odds facing Indian higher education. Perhaps the most potent justification for pessimism is the fact that the state's policy towards higher education has lost all semblance of coherence, and this is not a regime-specific phenomenon but a secular trend that has persisted with only minor shifts regardless of the party in power. Other things being equal, an incoherent but interventionist policy is certain to do far more damage than mere inaction or neglect, and this is precisely the type of policy we have had ever since Shri Kapil Sibal's appointment as the minister for human resource development in May 2009.[2] Given the state's continuing importance in a field like higher education where viable business models are hard to devise, there is ample room for pessimism.

This note tries to open a small window of hope in this otherwise bleak landscape by taking the perverse step of focusing not on what universities are 'for' but on some of the things that they end up doing. Not all of these 'doings' are unintended or unforeseen—some may actually be desired consequences, while others are more or less inevitable by-products. What I wish to consider is the eclectic set of actions and effects that remain after subtracting or setting aside the usual objectives of the university, which are broadly about the transmission and production of knowledge or skills.

As Collini (2012: chapter 3) notes, debates about the 'uses' of the modern university have been going on now for almost two centuries. So much so that those entering this area must not only 'cultivate a high tolerance for repetition' but also overcome the 'eye-glazing truisms' and the recurrent 'binary oppositions' that are found here. Since there seems to be continued scope for confusion in spite of all this repetition, let me try—at the risk of further repetition—to be as clear as possible.

Despite appearances, the longstanding conflict between 'liberal education' and 'practical education' is not a standoff between 'useless' and 'useful' knowledge, nor is it a battle between non-instrumental perspectives advocating liberal education 'for its own sake' and instrumental perspectives favouring pragmatic disciplines like STEM (science, technology, engineering, mathematics). The conflict is really one between different kinds of uses, or more accurately, it is about the hierarchy of uses: which uses are to be prioritised for the investment of public funds? Those who argue for a broad-based liberal education sometimes present their views as being 'non-instrumental', because they are arguing for education 'for its own sake'. But this does not mean that they are arguing for education to be without purpose or for it to be literally useless—they just have a specific sense of what is useful. However, what is common to both sides of the debate is that they focus on the intended consequences of particular types of academic enquiry or training. This chapter is not concerned with this debate—it does not deal with the academic or scholastic aims of the university. Instead, it explores some of the *non-academic aspects* of the public university and asks that these aspects also be taken into account when arguing (whether from an 'instrumental' or a 'non-instrumental' vantage point) about the pros and cons of Indian higher education today.

Thus, this note is about the non-academic uses or consequences of the university, which are not usually included in the arguments used to justify the institution. It is selective even within this general area. Some of the better-known non-academic uses of the university—like its role in nurturing sports or institutions like the National Cadet Corps (NCC) or the National Service Scheme (NSS)—are not considered here. Because of the lack of reliable data, I will also ignore the important role of higher education in recent times as an avenue of investment, i.e., as a profitable commercial venture. The three non-academic functions that are considered here envisage higher education as an avenue of employment, as a vehicle for promoting social mobility and as a unique enabling civic space. For some reasons that are obvious and some that will become clearer later in the discussion, these non-academic uses are more relevant and important for state or state-funded education rather than private higher education, so the latter sector is not considered here. Finally, I must emphasise that what follows is not a definitive analysis but speculative thoughts intended to provoke debate and more substantive research.

Higher Education as an Employer

In a drastically job-scarce environment like that of India in the current decade, how significant is the higher education sector as a provider of employment? According to the International Labour Organization (ILO), approximately 72.8 million persons are employed in regular waged or salaried jobs in India (ILO 2016).[3] And according to the latest edition of the *All India Survey of Higher Education 2015–16* (AISHE), the total number of teachers (including all kinds of institutions and all types of posts) is about 15.18 lakh (or 1.5 million) (MHRD 2016: T-69–70, Tables 21a and 21b), while the total number of non-teaching employees (from Group A through D) is about 11.25 lakh (or about 1.1 million) (ibid.: T-79–80, Table 23). The total number of jobs in higher education is thus about 26.43 lakh (or 2.6 million). This means that higher education is home to roughly 3.6 per cent of the workforce employed in the regular wage and salary segment. This is a small but not insignificant number; however, it needs to be qualified in several ways.

To begin with, there is one obvious reason why the AISHE estimate may be on the lower side—the survey is based on actual responses. Since institutions that did not respond to the survey are excluded and since coverage in all categories of institutions has been less than 100 per cent, particularly for 'stand-alone' institutions (that give diplomas and certificates rather than degrees), full coverage would obviously raise the employment figures. On the other hand, there are many issues about the quality of jobs in higher education as well as the extent to which posts remain vacant for long periods. As anyone with first-hand knowledge of an Indian university would know, a significant number of teaching posts remain unfilled for decades at a time. While there are no authoritative statistics on this, some estimates made by journalists (based on inputs from bureaucrats and teachers' unions) suggest that 'chronic' vacancies may be as high as one-third of the total strength.

A much more rampant problem is that of temporary appointments. It has been suggested that as many as 40 per cent of jobs in the higher education sector as a whole (and a much larger proportion in private institutions) are 'permanently temporary' (Varma 2013). However, the AISHE data itself shows only 7.4 per cent of the teaching staff is temporary, which is almost certain to be an underestimate. One also has to consider the structure of educational employment, which is very much like a pyramid, as shown in Table 12.1. Less than one-tenth of all jobs are at the professor level, while more than two-thirds are at the assistant professor level.

Table 12.1 Post-wise Composition of Teaching Jobs in Higher Education, 2015–16

Designation	*Number*	*% share*
Professors	1,46,021	9.61
Associate Professors	1,74,657	11.50
Assistant Professors	10,09,196	66.45
Demonstrator/Tutor	76,933	5.07
Temporary Staff	1,12,006	7.37
Total	15,18,813	100.00

Source: Based on MHRD (2016: T-71–73, Table 22).

But the real brunt of informalisation has been borne by the non-teaching staff. While AISHE does not provide data on temporary non-teaching staff, this fact is well known to anyone familiar with universities. A large proportion of non-teaching jobs have been converted into contract appointments or outsourced altogether. The AISHE data on non-teaching staff also shows a pyramid-like structure, with almost 70 per cent of jobs being in the Group C and Group D categories (MHRD 2016: T-79, Table 23).

Despite these serious qualifications, given that the employment situation is becoming grimmer by the day, there is still something to be said for the small contribution that higher education makes towards providing employment. Particularly for those paid at the University Grants Commission's (UGC) prescribed rates, teaching jobs are definitely 'decent jobs' that are otherwise so rare in the neoliberal economy. But we also need to place this in perspective. The Modi government had pledged to create 2 crore jobs every year. As against this goal, actual job creation in 2015 and 2016 has been at an all-time low with 1.6 and 2.3 lakh jobs respectively, compared to the 10.1 lakh jobs created in 2009 (see Roy Chowdhury 2017). While the informalisation drive has affected public universities as well, and large numbers of posts remain unfilled, there is still some solace in the employment aspect of higher education.

Higher Education as an Engine of Social Mobility

While higher education is only one source of employment among many, and not a very large one at that, it is unique in being almost the sole resource for significant social mobility. In a country like India with a large and very unequal population, which is at the same time globalised and media-saturated, aspirations can be a source of immense frustration. This may seem paradoxical but is in fact only to be expected. In a sluggish and isolated social context, there is nothing to stoke aspiration, no reference groups that are much better off and can thus spark envy or the desire to emulate. Where all these influences are present, tensions build up, which can only be alleviated by the hope of some form of self-improvement or mobility. But mobility requires resources, especially when we are speaking of it in societal rather than individual terms. Historically, large-scale social mobility has been due to sustained economic booms (like the three decades following the end of the Second World War) or triggered by programmes of massive redistribution.

In the globalised, neoliberal world of today, individual countries no longer have sufficient leeway to initiate or sustain broad-based growth. In the time of 'jobless growth', the illusory gross domestic product (GDP) statistics are meaningless for the vast majority of people. There seems to be no recipe available today for initiating broad-based mobility through the economy. At the same time, the prospects for significant redistribution towards the have-nots from the haves is simply not on the horizon—if anything, neoliberal policies have been responsible for redistributing in the reverse direction, with the super rich growing even richer at the cost of the poor and the merely affluent. In contexts like India, where we can no longer hope to redistribute land or capital, higher education holds out hope as the only resource that is in principle unlimited and that can help drive social mobility.

We must not forget that higher education has in fact being playing this role already. The early post-Independence investment in higher and especially technical education enabled generations of first-time entrants to make the transition from the rural to the urban world and from a pre-modern to a modern economy. This major transformation had a peculiar social dimension that remained largely unnoticed at the time. The vast majority of those who benefited from state-funded higher education in the decades between the 1950s and the 1970s were from the so-called upper castes. Ironically, therefore, higher education did function as the gateway to mobility, but because this gateway was utilised (or was available) only to those who were already at the topmost rungs of society, it did not change the social structure. Or rather, it did change things by cementing caste hierarchies and allowing the upper castes to convert their traditional caste capital into modern meritocratic capital.

Today higher education is in a very different situation. There has been massive expansion—on a scale not matched before in human history (other than the parallel case of China). Between 2000–01 and 2015–16, enrolment has quadrupled, and the number of universities has tripled.[4] This means that, on average, three new universities were set up *every month* during this period and 4,800 new students were enrolled *every day* for 15 years! This is a tremendous expansion, and although there are no precise estimates as yet, all indications are that a very significant proportion of those in higher education today are first-generation learners. Because of the extension of Other Backward Class (OBC) reservation, and the withdrawal of the exemption granted earlier to some elite institutes, most institutions are more inclusive today than they have ever been. The social composition of higher education, especially of its elite institutions, has changed dramatically over the past decade. This is nothing short of a revolution.

But there remain stiff challenges to be overcome. The enabling of access for hitherto excluded castes and communities has provoked stubborn resistance to full inclusion, most poignantly brought home by the tragic suicide of Rohith Vemula. Unlike access, which can be forcibly ensured, full acceptance and integration cannot be imposed from above—it must be fought for. Finally, there is also the fact that higher education can only enable mobility; it cannot ensure it. The economy has to generate jobs for the newly qualified to be employed and thus attain mobility. If this does not happen, higher education could well produce the opposite—frustration and social rage. Nevertheless, in the Indian context, the role of higher education in facilitating social mobility cannot be ignored.

Higher Education as an Enabling Civic Space

A little noticed non-academic feature of higher education is that it may be playing a very crucial and unique role as a relatively safe, inclusive and egalitarian space where young people from all social groups—and a wide stretch of the class spectrum—can interact. It is actually difficult to come up with alternative sites where this could be possible. Most spaces are neither inclusive nor egalitarian, like the world of work where hierarchy is not only the norm but also usually corresponds with the larger social hierarchy.[5] The most inclusive sphere is perhaps politics, but here too women are mostly absent. Despite the unevenness of their representation across disciplines, it is a fact that women are the group that has registered the biggest jump in enrolment. Taking higher education as a whole, women accounted for 46.2 per cent of the total enrolment in 2015–16, which shows that it may achieve gender parity before any other sector of Indian society.

According to AISHE 2015–16 (MHRD 2016), the total enrolment in Indian higher education is about 3.46 crore (or 34.6 million).[6] The social composition of this gigantic student body is given in Table 12.2.

Table 12.2 Social Composition of Students Enrolled in Higher Education, 2015–16

Category or Community	*% of Enrolment*	*Approx. % of Population*
Scheduled Castes (SCs)	13.9	16.6
Scheduled Tribes (STs)	4.9	8.6
Other Backward Classes (OBCs)	33.8	42.0
Persons with Disability (PWD)	0.2	2.2
Muslims	4.7	14.2
Other Minorities	2.0	4.5
Upper-Caste Hindus*	40.6	20.0
Total	100.0	

Note: * 'Upper-Caste Hindus' are estimated as a residual category in both columns since no official data is available.

Source: Based on MHRD (2016: T-49–50, Tables 14 & 15). Population data is taken from National Sample Survey Office (NSSO) estimates for OBCs and Census of India 2011 for the rest.

This is still far from an ideal mix. All groups other than upper-caste Hindus are under-represented, some of them—like Persons with Disability and Muslims—drastically so, but it is difficult to think of any other social site that is equally inclusive. Moreover, it is not merely a question of inclusion; the conditions of inclusion also matter, and here the higher educational institution stands out because it is probably the only civic space that is both inclusive and relatively egalitarian. Of course, there are strong and resilient hierarchies between disciplines, between institutions, and also between classes and castes, but it is nevertheless true that higher education offers a space where these may be negotiated and even challenged.[7]

Indeed, this may be what is really unique about the university space—not that it is egalitarian in fact, but that it is forced to be egalitarian in principle, and deviations or violations from this norm can at least sometimes be named explicitly, and efforts to challenge them can garner some support. While all such 'cases' or 'struggles' remain few, what is crucial is the larger social resonance that they have. It is very important for a deeply hierarchical society like India to have spaces of this sort where people can have access to experiences and relationships that are not available in the naturally segregated spaces of everyday life. With elite institutions too having had to become more inclusive, higher education today is genuinely a space that can transform lives by the sheer fact of its existence. This is a site that is in urgent need of ethnographic documentation.

Chilling proof of the power of the university space is found in instances of honour killing. For young women from the lower middle class and/or orthodox families, college is the first experience of any real freedom, even if it is carefully circumscribed. This can incite the urge to experiment and explore in ways that patriarchal families find unbearable. The case of Bhawna Yadav, a student at a well-known college of the University of Delhi, shows how exposure to this environment led her to change in ways that had tragic consequences when she was strangled by her own parents because she married a man of her choice whom she had met in college (see Jain 2014). However, the publicity and the protests and debates around this event would surely have had some effect on those in the social vicinity. One could think of other, less drastic, kinds of experiences that have a long-term liberating effect, like being able to relate to people of other castes or communities in ways that would never be possible 'at home'.

These are examples, not arguments. The point is that higher education offers a legitimate space for freedom from incessant surveillance and control of different sorts. Whatever their gender, caste or class, for young people from backgrounds where privacy or freedom are not taken for granted, the university or college can be an inspiring and fertile haven. By allowing for the fashioning of selves and the claiming of agency, often for the first time, the university plays an unintended, mostly unwitting, yet crucial role in hastening social change.

In this note, I have suggested that, while we will, and should, continue to debate the academic aspects of the university, perhaps we should also pay attention to its non-academic aspects. For these are as real as any of the more conventional aspects of the university in the sense that they too have real consequences. Attending to these apparently parenthetical facets of higher education could lead us to a fuller, more self-reflexive perspective on it.

Notes

1. I only have access to a digital version of this book in epub format, and so am unable to provide page numbers.
2. As is well known, the most recent policy document, the T. S. R. Subramanian Committee report, was effectively disowned by the very government that commissioned it. So there is currently no comprehensive statement of policy, though specific initiatives abound. For details, see the symposium in the *Economic and Political Weekly* on this report (*EPW* 2016b). For more general critiques of recent policies on higher education, see Academics for Creative Reforms (ACRE 2015); the symposia on 'The University Under Siege' (*EPW* 2016a); and the articles on higher education in the special issue of the *India International Centre Quarterly* on 'Education at the Crossroads' (*IICQ* 2016).
3. Table 1 of the 'India Labour Market Update' for July 2016 (ILO 2016) gives the total number of employed persons as 472.9 million for 2011–12, the latest year for which data is available. The same table estimates the share of regular wage and salaried employment for 2013–14 at 15.4 per

cent of total employment. Applying this proportion to the 2011–12 total employment figure gives us the estimate for the regular wage segment of the labour market as roughly 72.8 million persons (15.4 per cent of 472.9 million.)

4. In 2000–01, total enrolment was 86.3 lakh and total universities were 254 (MHRD 2011: Statements 1 and 2). In 2015–16, the respective figures were 346 lakh and 799 (MHRD 2016).
5. Moreover, women are severely under-represented in the world of paid work, with the female workforce participation rate in India declining recently (despite extremely low already) to around 14–18 per cent in urban areas. This is a much-discussed problem; for a recent analysis see Mehrotra and Sinha (2017).
6. This figure is obtained by adding together the all-India enrolment count for universities, including all types covered in the survey, i.e., public and private colleges and universities at both state and central levels as well as distance education institutions.
7. For a discussion of the problems that persist beyond formal entry into elite educational spaces by virtue of reservation, see the essays in Deshpande and Zachariah (2013), specially those by Anoop Singh and N. Sukumar.

References

Academics for Creative Reform (ACRE). 2015. 'What Is to Be Done about Indian Universities?' *Economic and Political Weekly*, 50 (24): 25–29.

Collini, S. 2012. *What Are Universities For?* London: Penguin.

Deshpande, S. and U. Zachariah. 2013. *Beyond Inclusion: The Practice of Equal Access in Indian Higher Education*. New Delhi: Routledge.

Economic and Political Weekly (*EPW*). 2016a. 'Symposium: The University under Siege', with contributions by U. Kumar, S. Deshpande and P. Chatterjee, *Economic and Political Weekly*, 51 (11).

———. 2016b. 'Symposium: Draft Policy on Education 2016', with contributions by T. S. R. Subramanian, A. Sadgopal, S. Deshpande, A. Kidwai, D. Nawani and L. N. Venkatraman, *Economic and Political Weekly*, 51 (35).

India International Centre Quarterly (*IICQ*) 2016. *Education at the Crossroads*, special double issue, edited by Apoorvanand and Omita Goyal, Winter 2015–Spring 2016.

International Labour Organization (ILO). 2016. 'India Labour Market Update', July, ILO Country Office for India.

Jain, A. 2014. 'Bhawna Yadav: Small Dreams of "Honour Killing" Victim', *BBC News*, 21 November 2014. Available at http://www.bbc.com/news/world-asia-india-30141719, accessed on 3 February 2019.

Mehrotra, S. and S. Sinha 2017. 'Explaining Falling Female Employment during a High Growth Period', *Economic and Political Weekly,* 52 (39): 54–62.

Ministry of Human Resource Development (MHRD) 2011. *Statistics of Higher and Technical Education, 2007–08*. New Delhi: Ministry of Human Resource Development, Bureau of Planning, Monitoring and Statistics, Government of India.

———. 2016. *All India Survey of Higher Education 2015–16*. New Delhi: Ministry of Human Resource Development, Department of Higher Education, Government of India.

Roy Chowdhury, J. 2017. 'No Jobs? Let Them Eat…', *The Telegraph*, 18 May. Available at https://www.telegraphindia.com/1170518/jsp/frontpage/story_152234.jsp, accessed on 3 February 2019.

Varma, S. 2013. 'Indian Higher Education: 40% of College Teachers Temporary, Quality of Learning Badly Hit', *Times of India*, 10 November. Available at https://timesofindia.indiatimes.com/india/Indian-higher-education-40-of-college-teachers-temporary-quality-of-learning-badly-hit/articleshow/25520250.cms, accessed on 3 February 2019.

Contributors

Satish Deshpande teaches sociology at the University of Delhi. His research interests include caste and class inequalities, contemporary higher education and language issues in Indian social science.

Kamala Ganesh is former Professor and Head at the Department of Sociology, University of Mumbai. She has worked on gender and kinship, culture and identity, and sociology of the Indian diaspora.

Farhana Ibrahim is an anthropologist whose research interests include the study of borders, policing, migration and ethnographic perspectives on the state. She teaches at the Department of Humanities and Social Sciences at the Indian Institute of Technology Delhi.

N. Jayaram is Visiting Professor at the Institute of Public Policy, National Law School of India University, Bengaluru. His research interests focus on the sociology of higher education, the study of Indian diaspora and research methodology.

Surinder S. Jodhka is Professor of Sociology at the School of Social Sciences, Jawaharlal Nehru University, New Delhi. His research interests include the study of rural society and agrarian change, social inequalities with a focus on caste and the political sociology of community identities.

Pushpesh Kumar teaches at the Department of Sociology, University of Hyderabad. His present academic concerns include queer movements, queer pedagogy, religion and queer issues, and Marxism and queer theory.

Nandini Paliyath is a doctoral research scholar in sociology at the Department of Humanities and Social Sciences, Indian Institute of Technology Bombay. She has a master's degree in social work and an MPhil in planning and development.

Rajni Palriwala is Professor in Sociology at the University of Delhi. Her research focuses on gender relations, covering care and emotion, citizenship and the welfare state, kinship, marriage and dowry, women and work, women's movements and feminist politics, cross-cultural and comparative studies, and methodology.

Sujata Patel is National Fellow, Indian Institute of Advanced Study. Her research interests are in the areas of social theory, history of sociology/social sciences, urbanisation and city-formation, social movements, gender construction, and caste and class formation in India.

Rowena Robinson is Professor of Sociology at the Department of Humanities and Social Sciences, Indian Institute of Technology Bombay. Her publications are in the areas of minority studies, ethnic conflict, Christianity, civil society and constitutional law.

Sudha Sitharaman is Professor in the Department of Sociology at Pondicherry University. Her research interests lie in the fields of sociology of religion and sociology of Muslim communities.

Suryakant Waghmore is Associate Professor of Sociology at the Department of Humanities and Social Sciences, Indian Institute of Technology Bombay. His research interests lie in sociology of social movements, development and identity politics, and changing caste and sociation in rural and urban India.

Virginius Xaxa, former Professor at Delhi School of Economics and Tata Institute of Social Sciences, is presently Visiting Professor at Institute for Human Development, Delhi. His research interests include issues of tribes and plantation labour.

Index